THE *Complete Guide* TO *Telemarketing Management*

THE Complete Guide TO Telemarketing Management

JOEL LINCHITZ

This publication is designed to provide accurate and authoritative information in regard to the subject matter covered. It is sold with the understanding that the publisher is not engaged in rendering legal, accounting, or other professional service. If legal advice or other expert assistance is required, the services of a competent professional person should be sought.

Linchitz, Joel.
The complete guide to telemarketing management / Joel Linchitz.
p. cm.
ISBN 0-9658925-0-6
previously
ISBN 0-8144-7863-8
1. Telemarketing—Management. I. Title

Library of Congress Catalog Card No.: 97-092214

First AMACOM paperback edition 1993.

Printing number

10 9 8 7 6 5 4

Contents

An Introductory Note From Tom Hopkins

I congratulate you readers of this book on investing wisely in your minds. I have enjoyed watching Joel work hard over the years to fill a void in the sales and marketing industry. The use of Joel's research, development and expertise in telephone techniques and strategies is something vital to many companies today. Having reviewed the material and analyzed the concepts, I salute Joel and know that anyone can improve his or her telephone effectiveness if he or she will apply the material within this volume. By gleaning at least one or two ideas that are applicable to your specific situation, you will tremendously increase your overall productivity, thus your income level. After all, that's what we're all looking for, isn't it?

Acknowledgments

I am greatly indebted to many people who contributed their valuable time and energy to help me make this book the most complete and authoritative work on telemarketing today.

Major thanks belong to Elise Healy without whose help this book could not have been completed.

Special thanks to Lucy Lasky who has shared my life for the last 15 years and has provided editorial advice, expertise and the necessary moral support to help me keep going. Additional moral support was provided by members of my family: Reuben and Pearl Linchitz and Marsha Moss.

Additional thanks belong to the following people for their contributions to specific chapters of this book: Stephen and Ira Belth of Belth Associates who supplied a major portion of the information on list development; Steve Rand of Dun's Marketing for his contribution on list development; Louis Taft and David Stahl of AT&T; Andrew Waite of *Inbound/Outbound* magazine; Bill Church, Joan Marks, and Amy Oksner for their contributions in the area of telecommunications technology and automation; Lucille Rhodes for her assistance on legislation and telecommunications; Joan Mullen for her help on legislative issues; and Richard Brock for his contribution to the chapter on automation.

Also helpful were Stan Livacz of Interactive Marketing for contributing to the direct mail chapter and Lynn Yost for her help with the illustrations.

Thanks also to Nona Aguilar and Frank Stetz for editorial assistance.

Lastly, I thank the following people for their support and encouragement: Roger Bell, Al Peaston, Mary Ellen Hickey-Gogel, Bruce Gogel, Dara and Nina Lasky, Marty and Linda Morris, Jill and Randy Moss, Carolyn Martino, Marc and Francette DeHove, Sylvia Figarsky, Carol Caprio, Chick Westover, and Jane Kinzler.

Introduction

ALL people in business today have phones they use every day—to listen, to obtain information, to persuade. I view those business phones as resources. And used pro-actively, every phone in your organization can be a profit-making resource. This book explains how.

Telemarketing is no longer new, and many fine books on the topic are available today. But most deal with telemarketing as if there were only one way to go about achieving success. *The Complete Guide to Telemarketing Management* is different; it shows that the design and implementation of your telemarketing program are determined by your *specific application.*

Although its main focus is on business-to-business telemarketing, the *Guide* also covers the full range of inbound and outbound telemarketing applications, including business to consumer. If the more complex and sophisticated requirements of high-ticket, business-to-business telemarketing are understood, then the same principles can easily be transferred and applied to low-ticket and consumer telemarketing programs.

There are tested, fundamental principles of telemarketing. Years of "trial and error" telephone selling have given way to controlled, systematic methods. Today, telemarketing means being in control—of your message, your market, your costs. This book is for business leaders, marketing and sales executives, and business owners who sense that they can use this type of telemarketing and want that kind of control.

Consider the following statistics:

- Nearly 265,000 U.S. companies will be using telemarketing in the near future.
- Yearly sales of goods and services by phone now total $224 billion.
- Annual growth of products sold over the telephone between now and the year 2000 is estimated at 15–20 percent.

Currently, over 57.8 billion a year is spent on telephone marketing, placing it firmly in the upper ranks of major marketing media. Two factors have primarily fueled this growth trend.

First, while costs of all other marketing media have risen dramatically, *telemarketing costs have actually gone down.* Second, new developments in telephone marketing have made it much more attractive than conventional marketing methods. This is particularly true when telemarketing is employed *in conjunction with* conventional methods, as part of your overall marketing plan.

The Complete Guide to Telemarketing Management provides fundamental telemarketing principles, using a step-by-step, "how-to" approach. It answers these key questions:

- How can I use the telephone to increase sales and profits?
- What information do I need to achieve that result?
- What are the tools my people need to achieve that result?

Part I of the book concentrates on the first question, providing basic concepts needed to understand how a successful telemarketing strategy achieves return on investment (ROI) of $20:1 (or better). It explains why telemarketing is *not* telephoning. To some readers, Part I may seem unnecessary or "too theoretical." Nothing prevents them from skipping ahead, of course, though the following fact should make them hesitate: *Fifty percent of all telemarketing programs fail within six months*—fail to produce projected sales, fail to support the marketing plan, fail to generate black ink. Knowing at least some of the theory and the psychology of telephone communication (and how to make it work for you) can make the difference in sales dollars, market share, and your bottom line.

Part II takes the fundamentals from Part I and shows how to use them to plan and develop a systematic telemarketing strategy. The focus is primarily on outbound, business-to-business telemarketing, for two reasons:

1. Outbound, business-to-business telemarketing presents the most complex challenge.
2. The other types of telemarketing (consumer sales, inbound sales, customer service), though less challenging to develop and manage, can be built on *the same basic principles.*

Case histories and examples culled from nearly fifteen years of telemarketing management and development experience are used throughout Part II. They demonstrate clearly how clients in a range of industries use these fundamental principles to increase sales, market share, and bottom-line income. Equally important, the case histories document the pitfalls the unwary can stumble into and show how to avoid them.

Part III is devoted to one of those pitfalls: the critical issue of *scripting*. More than any other factor, lack of a good script can kill an otherwise solid telemarketing program because your script is the key to controlling the medium. Most marketers—including many ad agency professionals—are not comfortable writing telemarketing scripts. Their scripts tend to be too wordy and end up being unbelievable. Anyone who has been on the receiving end of a telemarketing call—and by now most readers have—knows just how phony many scripts sound. So I devote four chapters to this topic and walk you through the process of developing scripts for both inbound and outbound calls.

Part IV concentrates on specific knowlege and skills telemarketing staff must have to carry out a telemarketing strategy and achieve its objectives. For managers, it offers detailed guidelines for making key decisions about hiring, training, compensating, and motivating telemarketing personnel. Examples of checklists, training exercises, forms, and procedures are provided so the new telemarketing manager can adapt them easily.

One of the key issues in telemarketing is *training*. This book emphasizes how to teach the important skills of *probing* and *paraphrasing* because without them, your telemarketers cannot control the call.

In addition, I address the problem of "fear of phoning"—particularly common in programs that involve getting outside salespeople on the phone to generate appointments. However, *every* telemarketing manager must confront and manage this fear or risk declining profits. How do you get telemarketers to handle fear of phoning, stay on the phone, and overcome it? My solution to this common problem is detailed in Part IV.

The focus in Part V is on key implementation issues, with practical advice on how to approach automation, telephone equipment, and long-distance services, and the major legal and ethical issues that telemarketing technology has raised.

Telemarketing isn't a cure-all for sagging sales or a quick fix for product quality that doesn't meet the competition's. But properly planned and executed, telemarketing does deliver your message—to people who are ready to buy—and convert them to customers effectively and predictably. *The Complete Guide to Telemarketing Management* distills what I've learned about this amazing medium and shows why it can work for you.

PART

I

Why the Telephone Works as a Major Marketing Medium

CHAPTER

1

Getting the Most Out of Every Phone You Own

I hear! I hear!

Dom Pedro II, Emperor of Brazil, upon first communicating by telephone, 1876 (Robert V. Bruce, *Alexander Graham Bell in Conquest of Solitude*)

TODAY most people smile at Dom Pedro's exclamation of amazement. With nearly 273 million telephones in the United States alone—including over 70 million business phones—most Americans now take instant telephone communication for granted.

"Everyone," it seems, has a phone these days. At home, at work, in the car, even on airliners anyone can punch a few buttons and call across town or across continents. But does "everyone" really know how to get the most out of this powerful means of communication? The answer is no. Using the phone the way most people do is like using a powerful computer to perform simple, one-time calculations. Used properly, computers increase productivity. Used properly, so can your telephones.

Start with the three essential characteristics of telephone communication that follow:

1. It summons a response.
2. It is audio only.
3. It is interactive.

These characteristics differentiate the telephone from every other communication medium. Knowing them, and their special advantages, is your first step toward getting the most out of every phone you own.

THE TELEPHONE IS A SUMMONS

Have you ever settled down after a long day to relax, maybe read the paper, only to have the phone ring? Many would be tempted to let it ring, but most people get up and answer it most of the time. Why is a ringing telephone so hard to ignore?

Clearly, it's the power of curiosity at work. (Think of the extreme case of the passerby who answers a ringing public phone—a call that can only be meant for someone else.) The *summons* of the phone is nearly irresistible because it raises questions:

- Who's calling?
- Why?
- What's in it for me?

In addition to arousing curiosity, the summons of the phone makes us stop what we're doing to answer it. It interrupts us. Though we may idly doodle while on the phone, it is close to impossible to do anything very substantial. At least initially, we give the phone our *undivided attention.*

Other media, such as radio or television, rarely make us focus on their message to the same extent. Perhaps only during "live" broadcasts in times of crisis or coverage of major sports events are we riveted to the television in quite the same way as we are during the first few seconds of a phone call.

No matter what your business purpose in dialing, this summoning property of the phone puts you in a supremely powerful position. If you have the means to satisfy the curiosity of the person you've summoned to the phone, you're closer to achieving the purpose of the call. If you know how to sustain the call recipient's attention after the first few seconds, you've begun to make your phone, and potentially every phone your business pays for, a revenue producer.

But the opposite also holds true. If you call people, you're interrupting them and grabbing their attention. If you're not prepared to satisfy the questions your call immediately raises and keep attention focused, then you're missing opportunities—for sales, leads, information, or whatever the purpose of the call is.

THE ENVIRONMENT OF THE TELEPHONE

Communicating on the telephone means conveying your message in a solely audio environment. You must shape your message to fit the requirements of this environment. If you compare the solely audio environment with other environments, you can see why different approaches are needed. In the movie theater, a hush falls over the audience at a movie theater when the lights go down. As images fill the immense screen and the sound track begins, the audience is swept into the film's reality.

Watch the same film on television and it doesn't have nearly the same effect. The space is much smaller, and the screen is, too. The quality and volume of the sound are much lower. Frequently, some segments of the film may be cut to meet network requirements. In total effect, the film is much less of an encompassing experience on television.

Movies combine both audio and visual media to convey time, place, characters, and their interactions. When a competent director makes a movie, he or she creates a "world" that envelops the audience.

Within this world the director can shape the audience's senses to achieve a specific emotional state. A fine movie will not only accomplish this, but will also affect the audience in some permanent way. Lower quality movies are more easily shrugged off—"It was just a movie." Their emotional effect—whether pity, fear, horror, or some other—is temporary.

Compared with films, television generally lacks this capacity to envelop the audience and produce a sustained emotional state except perhaps when it is conveying real events as they happen. Radio comes closest to the telephone in the environment it provides for conveying a message. It is an intimate, audio only environment. Just a few decades ago, leaders like Churchill and Roosevelt were identified largely by their distinctive voices, as transmitted by radio. Marshall McLuhan best described the impact of the isolated, amplified human voice:

> If we sit and talk in a dark room, words suddenly acquire new meanings and different textures. . . . All those gestural qualities that the printed page strips from language come back in the dark and on the radio. Given only the sound of a play, we have to fill in all of the senses, not just the sight of the action.[1]

The classic example of the power of the human voice in this environment—its power to arouse, excite, and inspire action—occurred one evening in 1938. That night, the great actor/director Orson Welles threw the entire New York metropolitan area into panic. Welles announced over his *Mercury Theater* radio program that an army of Martians had just invaded New Jersey. Using the device of the news flash, he created a graphic scenario of extraterrestrial attack. The response of his audience is history. Hundreds ran from their homes, seeking protection from the unseen army. Telephone lines were jammed with calls for help. Some even reported sighting the creatures. All of this resulted because of the human voice.

[1]Marshall McLuhan, *Understanding Media: The Extensions of Man* (New York: McGraw Hill, 1964), p. 303.

Like the radio, the telephone provides an environment for the human voice to create a scenario and convey a reality. In the vacuum created by this single focus, the importance of voice quality is enormously heightened.

When you listen to a voice on the telephone, you inevitably "see" with your ears. You are stimulated to supply the missing data the medium does not convey. The *sound* of the message you receive is as important as its *sense*.

Clearly, a key to communicating well in an audio only environment is the *voice quality* of the communicator. Tone, rate, and inflection can create an image in the listener's mind and inspire action. And though you don't need to be a Churchill or Roosevelt to communicate well, you do need to make a conscious effort. A good telephone voice differentiates professionals from amateurs.

The audio only environment of the phone also means you must choose your words carefully. You don't have eye contact and body language to help you convey your message. And you can't see your listener's expression. You may see this as a negative. What it really means, though, is that the medium imposes a special requirement on you—to script your calls.

Looked at another way, the nonvisual aspect of telephone communication works *for* you. Your appearance or taste in clothing can't detract from your message, and your aids, such as scripts, cannot be seen.

THE TELEPHONE IS INTERACTIVE

Like direct mail, the phone allows you to get a direct response from each individual you call. But unlike direct mail, the phone doesn't limit you to an initial response. Even when the response on the phone is negative, you can still interact and probe for the reasons behind it. You may even be able to turn the initial negative response into a positive one. At the least, you can get valuable information:

- Does this person have needs our company can meet, either now or in the near term?
- If so, when should we call again to receive a positive response?
- If not, let's remove this name from the "live" file so we can concentrate on more likely candidates.

The telephone allows you to have an individual **dialogue** on a mass scale. Think about the following:

- Five people on the phone (two four-hour shifts) can make an average of 200 presentations in a single business day.
  That's 1,000 a week and 4,500 each month.
- Five people on the phone calling consumers at home between 5:00 and 9:00 P.M. can make seventy-five presentations per hour.
  That's 300 per evening, 1,500 per week, 6,000 per month.

Clearly, the telephone can be used as a mass medium. Yet because it allows for individualized exchange, it is both less alienating and more flexible than other mass media.

How can you get the potential of this interactive mass medium to work for your business? How can you get the most out of every phone you own? There are two main points to remember.

First, whether you use the phone as a mass medium or not, every call you make should have at least two planned objectives. The key word is *planned.* Without planning your call objectives, you can't have a dialogue because you don't know what you're looking for. One objective is always primary: a sale, an appointment, an agreement of some kind. The secondary objective(s) may vary, but often they amount to *information*—about timing, needs, other useful contacts—that brings you closer to achieving your primary objective.

The second point to remember is this: A dialogue is a give-and-take *process.* You listen and respond. If you (or your callers) are not prepared for this process or don't know the techniques it requires, you won't be getting the most from every phone you own.

SUMMARY

Three characteristics make the phone a unique communication medium:

1. It is a summons.
2. It is audio only.
3. It is interactive.

Each of these characteristics imposes special requirements on you as a communicator. If your calls meet these requirements, you have begun to get the full return on your telephone investment.

The summons of the phone means it arouses curiosity and focuses attention. As a communicator, you must be able to quickly satisfy that curiosity and sustain that attention.

The audio-only characteristic of the phone means that the sound of your voice and the words you choose to convey your message are all you've got to create an impression. So telephone voice quality can and must be enhanced, and careful scripting is essential.

The interactive characteristic of the telephone means that you must be prepared for a dialogue process when you call. This means knowing in advance what your objectives are and knowing how to use dialogue techniques to achieve them.

CHAPTER

2

Psychological Dimensions of Telephone Communication

NOW that you know the unique characteristics and demands of the telephone medium, the rest should be easy, right? Think ahead for a moment and imagine this scenario:

You place a call to convince a key person to join you in a deal. Your call interrupts and summons this decision maker to the phone. You've made a strong claim on that person's undivided attention. Isn't it possible—in fact, likely—that your call has stirred up emotions or created tension? What about your feelings? Aren't they keyed up for the call? How can communication take place in this charged emotional atmosphere? Doesn't real communication require just the opposite? What can you do about it? Your first step is to recognize what's happening, both to you and to the person you're called.

TELEPHONE STATIC AND RAPPORT

By nature, the telephone encourages an emotionally charged atmosphere. After all, it interrupts, it arouses curiosity, it demands attention. Any factor that heightens this atmosphere is an obstacle to conveying your message. I call these factors "telephone static."

Factors that reduce the emotionally charged atmosphere build an atmosphere of "rapport." Rapport simply means you've connected on some level with the other person, and this person is receptive to your message. You (or your employees) can reduce static on every call if you recognize what's causing it and practice ways to build rapport.

Telephone static is usually caused by fear or anxiety—in your mind as well as in that of the person you've called. The following are the most typical fears in the caller's mind:

- *Rejection fear.* Will the person I've called say "no" or even hang up on me?
- *Qualification fear.* Am I talking to the person who has the authority to decide?
- *Time fear.* Do I have enough time to get the important points across?
- *Objections fear.* Am I getting this person's *real* objections?
- *Sales fear.* Can this sale be made? Can I make it? How much should I sell?
- *Closing fear.* Is it time to close?

But your fears and anxieties aren't the only source of telephone static. The person you've called may very well be experiencing, though not expressing, similar feelings, typically a series of questions running like a tape through his or her mind:

Why is this person calling me?
How long will it take?
Can I trust this person?
Do I need more information?
Should I make this decision alone?
How can I shortcut this process?
Can I afford to do this?
Can I change my decision later?

Feelings are facts. Throughout the call, you must be alert to these facts and be prepared to deal with them.

EMOTIONAL TONE

"Emotional tone" is an individual's unique way of viewing things. It is bound up with social, educational, and professional background and personal needs, fears, resistances, and desires. On the phone or in face-to-face communication, an individual's use of language provides clues to his or her emotional tone.

For example, a person trained as an engineer may use the word "economical" to describe a project or machine that pays for itself in the long run. But the financial officer may take an entirely different view. To someone trained in finance, an "economical" project includes such factors as the time value of money and opportunity costs.

Both individuals must sign off on your proposal. Knowing this, and recognizing that each has a different view of whether it's "economical," you adjust the phrasing and emphasis of your proposal accordingly. If you don't, one or the other will receive a distorted version of your message.

The following traditional Zen story illustrates the point:

Trading Dialogue for Lodging

Provided he makes and wins an argument about Buddhism with those who live there, any wandering monk can remain in a Zen temple. If he is defeated, he must move on.

In a temple in the northern part of Japan, two brother monks were dwelling together. The elder one was learned, but the younger one was stupid and had but one eye.

A wandering monk came and asked for lodging, properly challenging them to a debate about sublime teaching. The elder brother, tired that day from much study, told the young one to take his place. "Go and request the dialogue in silence," he cautioned.

So the young monk and the stranger went to the shrine and sat down. Shortly afterward, the traveler rose and went to the elder brother and said: "Your younger brother is a wonderful fellow. He defeated me."

"Relate the dialogue to me," said the elder one.

"Well," explained the traveler, "first I held up one finger, representing Buddha, the enlightened one. So he held up two fingers, signifying Buddha and his teaching. I held up three fingers, representing Buddha, his teaching, and his followers, living the harmonious life. Then he shook his clenched fist in my face, indicating that all three come from one realization. Thus he won, and I have no right to remain here." With this, the traveler left.

"Where is that fellow?" asked the younger one, running to his brother.

"I understand you won the debate."

"Won, nothing. I'm going to beat him up."

"Tell me the subject of the debate," asked the elder one.

"Why, the minute he saw me, he held up one finger, insulting me by insinuating I have only one eye. Since he was a stranger, I thought I would be polite to him, so I held up two fingers, congratulating him that he has two eyes. Then the impolite wretch held up three fingers, suggesting that between us we have only three eyes. So I got mad and started to punch him, and he ran out and that ended it."[1]

Clearly, emotional tone—whether the product of physical disability, intelligence, professional education, ambition, or social class—can distort your message. Successful telephone communication demands that you seek clues to the emotional tone of the person you call and adjust your message to accommodate it.

[1]*Zen Flesh, Zen Bones,* edited by Paul Reps (New York: Doubleday, 1961). Reprinted with permission of Charles E. Tuttle Company of Tokyo, Japan.

There are general rules to help you or your employees reduce the psychological barriers to telephone communication and build rapport on the phone. Most of this is done *before* a single call is ever made. You've already taken the first step: recognizing that psychological obstacles are going to be there—in the caller's mind and in the decision maker's mind. Here are your next steps:

1. *Limit carefully whom your calls must reach.* Use a rifle, not a shotgun approach, to define your market so you limit the kinds of individuals you must communicate with.
2. *Get a handle on what you can expect from each market segment.* Do this by making test calls before, not after, you get 500 people on the phone.
3. *Find out the "hot buttons" of the individuals you're calling.* Make sure they're in the scripts you develop for each segment your calls must reach.
4. *Be sure you can deal with the worst.* Practice and role play, particularly worst-case scenarios, to confront your fears during training.
5. *Make enough calls.* It's getting your message across *enough* times that matters, so be sure you know how much is enough.

Planning, researching, testing, training—everything you do *before* you call gives you the psychological edge *during* the call. Most of the rest of this book is devoted to showing you how.

SUMMARY

The key psychological factors that reduce rapport or distort the message you want to convey on the phone are

- Telephone static
- Emotional tone

Accommodating these psychological factors helps you develop rapport and build the basis of a business relationship. Most of what you can do to handle these factors should be done *before* you dial—through planning, research, testing, and training. You'll see the results both *during* your calls and later in your bottom line.

PART

II

Shaping a Telemarketing Strategy

CHAPTER

3

Getting Started: Determining Objectives and Costs

TELEMARKETING is used today in a staggering variety of ways, from interstate banking to software sales. This chapter presents a framework to help you decide on telemarketing objectives for your organization and gives you an idea of the cost *factors* involved in a telemarketing strategy. It is not meant to suggest what your costs will actually be because they vary tremendously, depending on the strategy you put together.

INBOUND TELEMARKETING

Inbound telemarketing can be divided into *sales/order entry* programs and *customer service* programs. These aren't necessarily mutually exclusive; many companies have both, as well as some type of outbound program. But here I discuss them separately.

Some typical sales/order entry programs, and common users of each, are as follows:

- Reservations sales (airlines, hotels, car rental firms)
- Catalog sales (specialty retailers, department stores)
- Service sales (package pickup and delivery, credit and other financial service accounts)

The customer service category includes programs such as:

- Order inquiry (retailers of all kinds, service firms)
- Consumer product information (manufacturers, banks, service firms of all kinds)
- Technical assistance/information (electronics, software development, pharmaceutical firms)
- Complaints (organizations of all types)
- Accounting/billing problems (organizations of all types)

As Figure 3-1 shows, these inbound programs form a sales potential hierarchy. To one degree or another, every one of them presents an opportunity to enhance the value of transactions conducted on inbound calls, *over and above* their primary purposes.

Rule one in planning any telemarketing program—inbound or outbound, sales or customer service—is this:

1: Look Within Your Own Organization First

If your company already operates one (or more) type of inbound program, review them to find ways to get more out of your investment. Here are some examples of how you can enhance the value of every inbound program:

Figure 3-1. Inbound sales potential hierarchy.

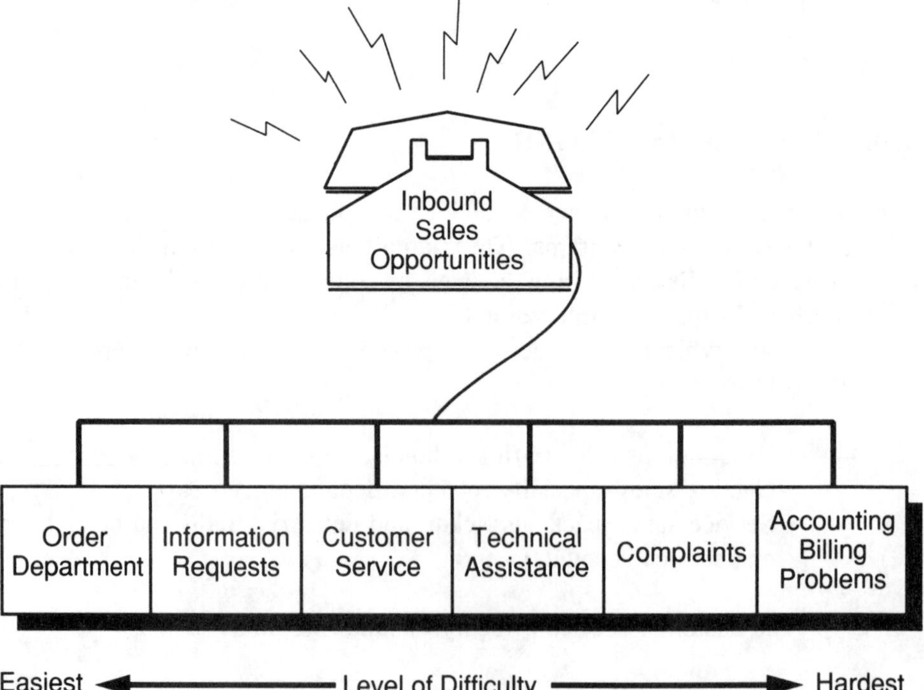

Program Type	*Opportunity*
Reservations sales	Order upgrades
Catalog sales	Up-sell and cross-sell tie-in items
Service sales	Build high-volume usage through multilevel pricing
Order inquiry	Suggest sales of related items
Consumer product information	Provide incentive to call local distributor today
Technical assistance/information	Suggest sales of related products
Complaints	Provide incentive to restart the relationship
Accounting/billing	Notify callers about special sales or promotions

Every inbound call isn't necessarily an opportunity to get an extra sale or incremental value, and every attempt won't be successful. The point is that by setting one of these opportunities as an objective for your inbound program (and by providing the other tools needed to achieve it), you can get the incremental sales *enough of the time* to make the program a success.

The most powerful factor in favor of achieving incremental sales or enhanced value from an inbound telemarketing program is simply that the callers already have a *strong relationship* with your organization. In most cases, they are already customers or have made the decision to buy. They know your organization and its products. This is the best possible atmosphere for add-on, upgrade, and suggested selling.

Chapter 4 provides details on the power of relationships and discusses the prospect hierarchy. For now, just remember rule two in planning your telemarketing program:

2: ALWAYS BUILD ON EXISTING RELATIONSHIPS

This rule also applies to both inbound and outbound programs, and I refer to it throughout this book.

OUTBOUND PROGRAMS

Outbound telemarketing can support your marketing plan in a number of ways. Figure 3-2 illustrates a hierarchy of six basic outbound program objectives, showing them from the easiest to achieve to the hardest. Again,

Figure 3-2. Outbound sales potential hierarchy.

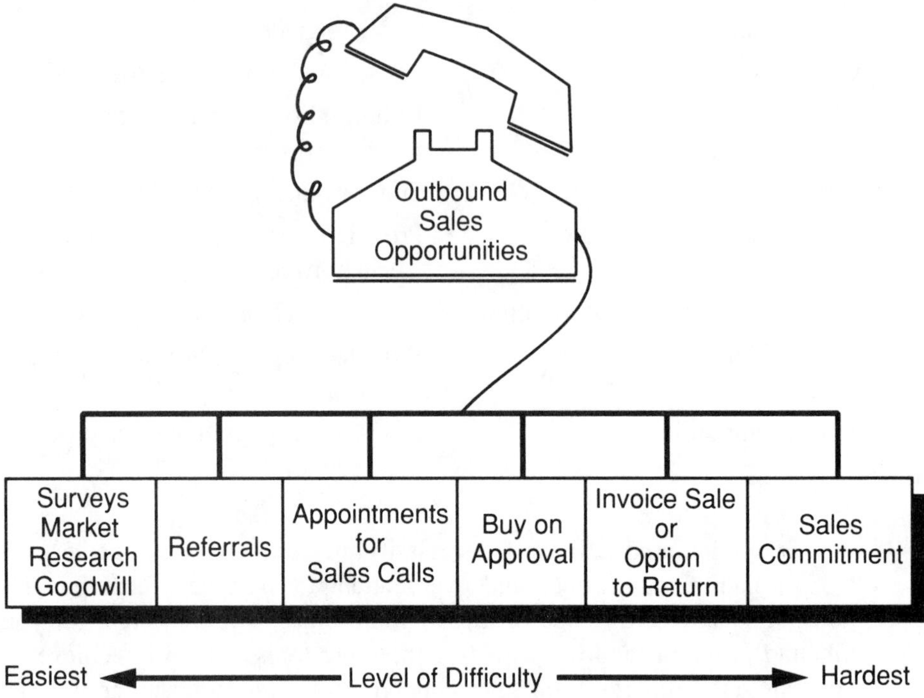

these programs are not mutually exclusive; many organizations use more than one type.

Market Research

Market research calls seek data rather than a sales commitment. Normally, they involve a presentation of your product or service, together with a scientifically designed questionnaire. The questions are carefully developed to allow statistical analysis of the responses and measurements of the market for your product or service.

Developing a formal market research questionnaire and selecting the market segments to be tested are specialized tasks, where quality counts. Because you use market research results to make key decisions, the project should be conducted at the highest level of professionalism. For this reason, most organizations rely on specialized market research firms to develop and conduct formal surveys.

However, it is possible to conduct less formal market research surveys internally. For example, you may want to simply "take a reading" among current customers about potential new features for an existing product or service. Two or three hundred calls can accurately tell you what you need to know, and at far lower costs than if you used a market research firm.

The basic point is that the call objective—data—is the least difficult outbound objective and requires the lowest investment in personnel. As we move up the scale of difficulty, personnel costs rise. Compensation is necessarily higher in order to attract personnel of the necessary caliber, and training and support costs rise as well.

Referrals

Referrals are a major source of business for organizations of all types, large and small. The name of a satisfied customer, known to your prospect, is one of your strongest tools for building rapport on an initial call.

In some respects, referral calls are similar to sales calls because they require a brief presentation and a close in which you ask for a name, not a sale. However, as a primary objective of outbound calls, obtaining referral names requires less skill and training than sales. Referral calls can be a part-time or temporary operation that feeds names to your full-time sales force.

Obtaining referrals may be a secondary objective on outbound sales calls because they salvage some value if the primary objective of the call is not achieved. This is particularly true when you are using telemarketing to sell high-ticket, low-volume items, such as specialized software products.

Appointments for Sales Calls

Next in order of difficulty is the objective of scheduling appointments for field sales personnel to meet with prospects. Appointment-setting programs separate the "suspects" from the prospects for a product or service and set a specific time and date when qualified prospects agree to see a field sales representative. Appointment-setting telemarketing programs are particularly useful for selling relatively high-ticket items (business services, telecommunications systems, data-processing equipment, and the like).

Appointment-setting calls begin to approach the true outbound sales call in terms of the sales skills, phone techniques, and product knowledge required. You can handle this type of program in two ways:

1. Develop a separate telemarketing group that specializes in scheduling appointments for assigned field sales representatives.
2. Train field sales staff in the telemarketing techniques required, and use appointment setting as a time and territory management tool. (See Chapter 16.)

Approval Sales

An approval sale commits the prospect to purchase merchandise after examining it for a specific period of time. Though it is a sale, it is less of a commitment to buy than an invoice sale. On the whole, approval sales are used for intermediate and higher priced products. The approval period gives the qualified prospect a way to reduce the risk of buying a product sight unseen.

Approval sales programs are certainly successful—the publishing industry is a prime example. Return rates of approval sales programs are the key numbers, and they can be kept within manageable limits. The critical requirements are the following:

- Carefully screened lists
- A professionally trained telemarketing staff
- Strong quality control through incentives, supervision, and monitoring

Invoice Sales

Invoice sales commit the prospect to pay for merchandise on the date specified on the invoice. This type of program is particularly successful for selling to large institutions (libraries, school, and hospitals) because the telemarketer can tailor the basic offer to meet these institutions' budget disbursement schedules. For example, a school administrator will commit to the purchase on the phone and accept the shipment with the understanding that the invoice enclosed with it will be postdated by thirty days, sixty days, ninety days, or more.

An invoice sales program has the same requirements as an approval sales program in terms of lists, staff training, and quality control. In addition, follow-up letters confirming the sale and the terms are essential.

Sales Commitment

At the highest level of difficulty is the outbound telemarketing program whose objective is a commitment to buy a high-ticket item. These programs are used to sell all types of products and services (computer hardware and software, office products, insurance, investment newsletters, and consulting services).

Sales commitment telemarketing is sometimes part of a two-tiered program. Typically, the first tier uses less skilled personnel to screen leads, make callback appointments, and obtain referrals. The second tier uses highly skilled telemarketers who are thoroughly trained to convey sophisticated or complex features to prospects. Their objective is to close the sale on the phone.

An alternative approach is to use direct mail to screen the market base. For example, you might mail to 100,000 prospects but telephone only the 2,000 who respond by mailing back a card or requesting a small premium. In this way, your telemarketers are talking only to people who are prequalified to buy.

TYPICAL START-UP AND OPERATING BUDGET

Clearly, the development and implementation budget for a sales commitment program will be greater than for other types of programs. In addition to obtaining tested lists, training qualified staff, and developing strong monitoring and control systems, you must be prepared for higher telephone costs and the costs of a direct mail program.

Yet the returns are there—as high as $20:1. It can be done, and you can make numbers like these happen for your organization, one step at a time.

The costs of any telemarketing program can run quite high and will vary with several factors corresponding to the prospect hierarchy:

- Your application—inbound or outbound
- Your product—its relative complexity
- The difficulty of the sale:
  - — Business-to-business high-ticket sales are the most expensive.
  - — Business-to-business low-ticket sales are less expensive.
  - — Business-to-consumer sales are even lower.
  - — Inbound sales, because the *cost per contact* is so much lower than outbound, is the lowest cost telemarketing program.

The key variable expenses that will affect your total costs are the following:

- Full-time staff, whose compensation is higher than part-time
- Professional telemarketers as opposed to "order takers"
- Training, which may be longer and more expensive for complex or sophisticated products and services
- Difficulty in reaching the decision maker (executives who are often in meetings) so that additional expenses for precall advertising and direct mail are required

Basically, the higher on the hierarchy your strategy is, the higher your costs. Most telemarketers consider three cost figures to be most significant:

1. Cost per hour
2. Cost per contact
3. Cost per lead or sale

Because costs per contact and per sale will vary tremendously, depending on how extensive your testing program and who, where, and when you call, I concentrate on cost per hour, which is somewhat more stable across different types of programs.

In outbound business-to-business telemarketing programs, costs per hour will generally range from $35 to $55 *or more* per hour; costs may be more than $55 per hour depending on your application and the expertise required. For example, it will cost more per hour to sell complex software requiring an engineering background than to generate leads for a demonstration/seminar on the same software because you can probably get away with using part-time people without a technical background.

Two of the key cost factors often overlooked in developing a telemarketing program are the costs of *product training* and *turnover*. The former involves the "hidden cost" of taking personnel who have the expertise off the job to conduct training. Turnover can involve significant costs because recruiting and training expenses must be incurred again when someone leaves.

Though the cost per hour is an important number, probably more important is its relation to your bottom line (your ROI). To illustrate, here is a hypothetical start-up and operational cost budget based on an actual client's experience. The assumptions this program was based on—which, of course, will differ from yours—are as follows:

- The client, an office equipment manufacturer, maintained a field sales staff of fifteen.
- An average close ratio of 25 percent (one out of four appointments) results in a sale.
- The telemarketing support program was designed to provide ten additional appointments a week.
- Testing determined that one appointment would be generated per calling hour.
- Hence, to generate 10 appointments a week (150 per week total), or 600 per month, would require 600 calling hours per month.
- A staff of five telemarketing reps (TMRs) and a telemarketing manager, calling 6 hours per day for a total of 30 calling hours per day would be required to maintain the 600 calling hour pace per month.
- Part-time secretarial support is needed.

In this hypothetical situation, I assume the manager will perform some calling to justify the compensation required to attract the necessary exper-

Table 3-1. Budget illustration, telemarketing start-up costs, 5 TMRs, 1 manager.

Item	*Cost*
Telephones	
Key equipment (7 lines)	$5,000
Installation	500
Line installation (Telco)	1,400
Workstations ($800)	4,800
Desks	
Chairs	
Acoustic dividers	
Other furniture	1,300
Secretary station	
File cabinet	
Recruitment	
Advertising	2,000
Head hunter (manager)	6,000
Productive time lost to training	
1 month's salary per person (6)	13,000
Direct mail (optional)	5,000
Office equipment	5,000
Copier	
Word processor	
FAX (optional)	
Total start-up costs	$44,000

tise. The reason is that the manager, who would be capable of managing a staff of ten to twelve, would be underutilized if managing a staff of only five TMRs.

Some important points to note in the following budget illustration are that costs for a telephone system and office furnishings have been included. Many start-up programs may already have telephones available and will not need to incur an installation expense. Likewise, many firms will have useable workstations and furniture available for telemarketing. In addition, computer hardware and software—which are usual components in an operating budget for a mature telemarketing program—have been excluded from the start-up budget. In other words, this budget assumes a manual information system. Finally, start-up costs have not been amortized into the operating budget because this might be done over varying terms (three years, five years, and so forth). In general, the figures in Tables 3-1 and 3-2 should not be viewed as "recommended" costs because salaries, benefits, and many other costs will vary tremendously.

Tables 3-1 and 3-2 show that what factors can be involved in telemarketing and how quickly your costs can approach $50—and more—per calling hour. An analysis of the illustration budget reveals the following:

Cost per hour	$50.00
Cost per contact	$8.30
Cost per appointment	$50.00
Cost per sale at 25 percent close ratio	$200.00

Does $200 per sale sound high to you? Frankly, it could be even higher. *This is why you must test every aspect of a telemarketing program prior to full-scale operation.* If, for example, testing showed that it took two hours instead of one to make one appointment, then your cost per appointment doubles to $100, and telemarketing may no longer be the most cost-effective route for marketing your product. For example, a major book wholesaler decided to use telemarketing to sell reference books to schools and libraries. The company knew that several publishing firms were doing quite well selling reference material by phone, so they put twenty-five people on the phone. Although the wholesaler sold units as

Table 3-2. Budget illustration, telemarketing operating costs.

Item	*Monthly Expense*
Salaries	
5 TMRs ($20,000/year)	$8,300
Benefits (20%)	1,700
Incentives ($9,600/year/TMR)	4,000
1 telemarketing manager ($35,000/year)	2,900
Benefits (20%)	600
Manager incentives ($12,000/year)	1,000
Secretarial (part-time)	800
Telephones	
600 hours ($.25/minute, 40 minutes actual talk time/calling hour = $10/hour)	6,000
Direct mail support	
3,000 pieces/month ($.50/piece)	1,500
Rent	
1,000 sq. ft., $10/sq. ft.	830
Utilities	300
Ongoing recruitment	150
Advertising (30% turnover)	
Supplies and miscellaneous	
List acquisition	
3,000 names/month, $75/thousand	225
Total monthly operating costs	$28,305
Operating costs/hour (600 hours/month)	$47.18/hour

successfully as the publishers, his margin could not stand the expense of telemarketing, and the program failed. Had he thought it out and tested first, the wholesaler might have concluded that telemarketing would be justifiable, but only for calling on large accounts, where revenue per contact would justify the cost.

Many telemarketing programs are actually successful even though their costs run high. For example, if field salespeople can spend 40 percent of their time selling, instead of the usual 20 percent, and therefore close more sales, then the cost of generating the additional appointments through telemarketing may be justified from an overall standpoint. If the field sales staff *doesn't* close more sales, then perhaps there's a problem with the sales staff, not the telemarketing costs.

SUMMARY

The two rules for planning any telemarketing program are:

1. Look within your own organization first.
2. Always build on existing relationships.

The hierarchy of six basic outbound program objectives, from least difficult to most difficult, is as follows:

1. Market research
2. Referrals
3. Appointments for sales calls
4. Approval sales
5. Invoice sales
6. Sales commitments

As you increase the level of difficulty of your program objective, your costs per calling hour can increase dramatically. Hence, advance testing is extremely important once you have decided on your objectives because costs can outrun profitability in some cases. Use the following checklist to organize costing for your strategy.

Start-Up Costs (Outbound)

☐ Telephones
- Equipment
- Installation
- Line installation
- Special equipment (headphones, monitoring)

- ☐ Office Space
  - Deposit
- ☐ Workstation furniture
  - Chairs
  - Acoustic dividers
  - Desks
  - Sound-absorbing wall and floor coverings
- ☐ Miscellaneous furniture
  - Files
  - Secretarial station
- ☐ Recruiting
  - Advertising
  - Agency fees (head hunter)
- ☐ Direct mail
- ☐ List acquisition
- ☐ Computer hardware, software, training (optional during start-up)
- ☐ Office equipment
  - Fax
  - Copier
  - Word processor

Operating Costs Checklist

- ☐ Long-distance usage
  - Day rates
  - Night rates
- ☐ Rent
- ☐ Salaries
  - Benefits
  - Incentives
  - Manager, supervisor, TMRs
- ☐ Utilities
- ☐ Training
- ☐ Recruitment (staff replacement)

- ☐ Other overhead expenses
  - Letterhead
  - Supplies
  - Postage
- ☐ Amortization
- ☐ Direct mail
- ☐ List rental

CHAPTER

4

Targeting Your Prospects

TELEMARKETING is targeted marketing. If you are not prepared to define who your telemarketing program is to reach, you are just telephoning. Your phone bill will be higher and your bottom line lower than if you target. Chapter 4 presents a prospect hierarchy to help you avoid the ''shotgun'' approach in developing your strategy. You can use it to focus your telemarketing strategy precisely—on individuals most likely to buy.

THE PROSPECT HIERARCHY

The prospect hierarchy shown in Figure 4-1 helps you get the telemarketing numbers on your side. It categorizes prospects according to the *strength of the relationship* they have with your organization. Is is another way you will apply the two telemarketing rules mentioned in Chapter 3:

1: Look Within Your Own Organization First

2: Always Build on Existing Relationships

We'll look at each prospect category in order, starting with current customers.

Current Customers

Your current customer file is the primary key to deciding who your telemarketing program will reach. Targeting your prospects must begin with an analysis of this file for two reasons:

Figure 4-1. Prospect hierarchy.

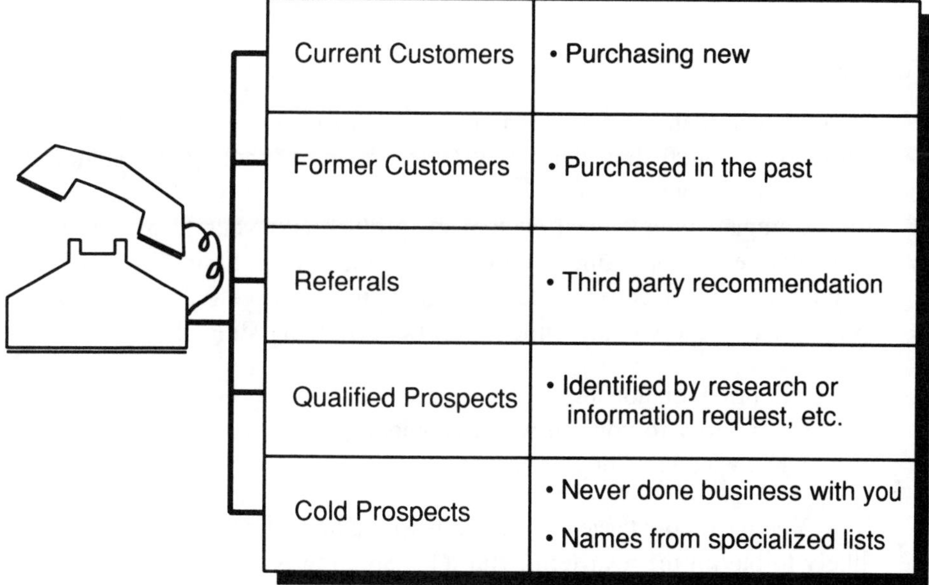

Current Customers
• Purchasing new
Former Customers
• Purchased in the past
Referrals
• Third party recommendation
Qualified Prospects
• Identified by research or information request, etc.
Cold Prospects
• Never done business with you
• Names from specialized lists

1. They have already established the strongest possible relationship with your organization.
2. They are the most likely source of additional sales in the near term.

Your analysis of your customer base should seek answers to these questions:

Who are my best customers now?
Why?
What do they buy now?
When do they buy it?
Who are the key decision makers?

Marketing professionals call the process of achieving the results of this analysis *data base marketing*. Data base marketing is the sophisticated method many marketers use today not only to create new customers but also to cross-sell and up-sell new products to the existing customer base. This process combines a computer (mainframe or PC), data base marketing software, and your targeted prospect data to produce a highly accurate customer profile and other state-of-the-art information. This information gives you maximum flexibility in segmenting and targeting your telemarketing program by prospect, product, offer, season, and so forth. Chapter

5 discusses this further. The basic point now is to start from your internal strengths—current customers—and build logically on that base.

Former Customers

Former customers are your next best source of leads for your telemarketing program. Though they don't buy from you now, their prior relationship gives you a strong reason to call.

Compare your "ideal customer" profile with your former customer file, and select the names of those who meet your basic criteria. Using telemarketing to reactivate old accounts is most successful if you handle it this way because you are building on the following strengths:

- A prior relationship
- Similarity to your current customers
- Knowledge of buying history

You have now targeted your calls to the hottest prospects—those most likely to buy in the near term. But telemarketing is a mass medium. It can reach thousands of individuals in a relatively short time. To get the most out of the medium, you will want to plan for the larger numbers of calls that make it cost-effective.

Your next step is to aggressively develop leads who are logical candidates for your product or service. But the remaining categories in the prospect hierarchy have progressively weaker relationships to your firm. To develop useful telemarketing leads from these categories, you need to make the relationship "warmer" in some way.

Referrals

Referrals are individuals suggested by a third party, usually a satisfied customer. The link to your customer gives you an opening to develop a relationship. Referral business can be an important part of your telemarketing strategy, but only if you go after it *systematically*. Plan the referral-generating piece of your telemarketing strategy using these tips:

- Make sure your customer service people are pro-active in asking for referrals on incoming customer calls.
- Set up a regular schedule of outbound service calls to all your current customers.
- Make every service call—whether inbound or outbound—a referral call as a secondary objective.
- Encourage referrals by sending a small premium to every customer who refers someone who converts to a customer.

Qualified Prospects

Qualified prospects are distinct from "suspects" for your product or service because they've *responded* in some way to your organization. Their response may be sending in a catalog request, returning a reply card or survey questionnaire, or calling a toll-free 800 number.

Their link to your organization is weak, but it is there, and your telemarketing program can strengthen it. Expanding your list of qualified prospects is basic to a cost-effective telemarketing strategy. It is the only way to get the numbers on your side.

Cold Prospects

At the bottom of the prospect hierarchy are cold prospects—individuals who have no current relationship to your organization. How do you start one? How do you "warm up" cold prospects? After all, they are the largest source of qualified prospects.

You've already taken the first step. By profiling your current ideal customer, you've defined a specific target market. Your next step is to select lists that meet the initial criteria you've defined (more about lists in Chapter 5). The key point is that you're building on what you already know about your strengths. It's another application of rule one:

LOOK WITHIN YOUR OWN ORGANIZATION FIRST

By using your customer profile criteria as the basis for selecting your initial list(s), you target your telemarketing to groups likely to be qualified. You are increasing the odds that the numbers will be on your side.

As your business develops, you may well target your market using new criteria, but essentially you will use the same process.

SUMMARY

The following steps will help you focus your telemarketing resources and program on individuals who are likely to buy:

1. Target your market—don't just telephone.
2. Start by profiling your "best customer."
3. Work through the prospect hierarchy:
   - Current customers
   - Former customers

  - Qualified prospects
  - Cold prospects
4. Consider investing in *data base marketing* software to speed up your analysis and give you greater sophistication and flexibility in focusing your telemarketing program.
5. After you've mined your internal lists and have the profile of your ideal customer, you are ready to acquire or assemble a list.

CHAPTER

5

Developing a Prospect List

JUST as telemarketing is not just telephoning, it isn't shotgun-style "prospecting" either. Telemarketing is targeted to specific individuals who are likely to buy. This brings up telemarketing rule three:

3: YOU'RE ONLY AS GOOD AS YOUR LIST

You've worked through the prospect hierarchy (Chapter 4) and developed criteria for your ideal customer based on your internal data base of customer files. Your next step is to develop a prospect list from external sources using your customer profile as your initial guide and other criteria you need to select new prospect sources.

For example, an insurance agency may find that its "ideal customer" is a married male with two children, thirty to forty years old, and owner of a small business. He is "ideal" because at his age and with his family responsibilities, his insurance needs are the greatest.

By taking this profile of the "ideal customer" and comparing it with current customers, the agency owner can select those who meet the basic criteria in terms of status and age. The goal of this part of the analysis is to find out which products could be sold to these selected customers to move them closer to the "ideal" customer profile.

This kind of analysis sounds like a lot of work, and it can be if done manually. But if your data base is computerized using the right software, you can segment your customer base and retrieve information based on the most minute factors, so your analysis becomes quite sophisticated. This effort is definitely worthwhile, for two reasons:

1. It gives you the best possible start for a telemarketing program because your initial calls are to individuals who already have a relationship.

2. It gives you a sound basis for selecting lists from external sources because you'll know who you're looking for.

VERTICAL MARKETING

Vertical marketing means focusing your telemarketing resources on carefully selected *groups* of "cold prospects." Because your organization has no prior relationship with these cold prospects, you need to "warm up" the relationship in some way. The selection process for vertical marketing is the key to doing this.

In a consumer-oriented marketing program, consumer groups are defined by "demographics." Age range, income, marital status, home ownership, and presence of children are key demographic factors, though there are many others. For business-to-business marketing, you first need to identify specific trades, professions, or industrial classifications to define the group(s) your list should focus on.

For example, when we developed an appointment-setting telemarketing program to support the field sales force at Automated Data Processing (ADP), we found that ten industries were represented by our "best customer" profile. We narrowed these ten down by selecting for size of annual sales. This process gave us five vertical markets we considered the "best of the best" to start with.

Your goal when targeting cold prospects is to identify as many vertical markets as possible. Use the following factors to organize your "best customer" analysis of your existing customer file:

- Buying patterns (what they buy, how often, and how much)
- Type of organization
- Size of organization
- Decision maker (title and/or department)

After you have identified the vertical markets your telemarketing strategy will target first, you are ready to obtain or assemble lists that meet your criteria. Start with your internal data base of current and former customers and previously qualified prospects who fit your "best customer" profile(s) (you can have more than one). Then move to outside sources of leads.

There are two basic types of external lists. *Response lists* are lists of consumers or businesses that have previously responded to a direct marketing offer. You can select these lists by type of direct marketing medium responded to, type of product, size of order, and so forth. The media you can choose from include the following:

- Direct mail—a single offer or catalog that an individual received through the mail

- Insert—an offer inserted into a package, magazine, or newspaper
- Card deck—a packet of offers from independent marketers on postage-paid cards that the responder mails back to each advertiser
- Space—an offer made through a display advertisement in any publication
- Inquiry—a response from an individual who independently requests information about a company or product
- Field sales lead—an individual identified by a field sales force as having an interest in a company or product

Compiled lists, the second type of external list, consist of names and addresses derived from individually supplied data, such as market surveys and questionnaires, or from secondary data, such as telephone directories, public records, retail sales slips, or trade show registrations.

The names and addresses on a compiled list appear there because they have some factor in common. This common factor may be quite vague, even misleading. For example, the common factor of a list compiled from a phone directory is not that the companies are from the same industry, but only that they have a listed phone number. You would need to enhance such a list with other data to select the names that meet your criteria.

Within both responder lists and compiled lists, you can request "hot" lists, meaning new or recently moved businesses, changes of business ownership or CEO, new phone numbers, and the like. Whether you use a response list, a compiled list, or both in your program, business-to-business telemarketing requires that you start by determining the *Standard Industrial Classification (SIC)* code for each of your vertical markets.

STANDARD INDUSTRIAL CLASSIFICATION

The U.S. government has developed the SIC code to categorize commercial enterprises. This is a four-digit number that corresponds to one of several hundred categories. The first two digits place an organization in one of thirteen major groupings, for example:

01 to **09**: Agriculture, Forestry, Fisheries
10 to **14**: Mining

The remaining two digits of the SIC code show the primary line of business and size. In addition, the Dun & Bradstreet Corporation of New York (D&B) has recently created a new SIC "2 + 2" enhancement system. This increases the number of classifications nearly fifteen times by further expansion of the SIC code to eight digits. This allows for a much finer selection of business list categories.

For example, if you were interested in targeting the promotion services category, you would normally select SIC code **7389:** Business Services. Using SIC "2+2," you can target more specifically by choosing any of the following subcategories of **7389:**

73890301:	Convention and show services
73890302:	Coupon redemption services
73890303:	Demonstration services
73890304:	Embroidery advertising

The D&B "2+2" system provides much greater ability to target specific industry lists. The drawback to this option is its potential cost, as some critics, list users, and suppliers have pointed out. Because compilers with small file universes may not benefit from "2+2" as much as the largest complier, this will severely limit the list user's supplier options. In addition, D&B's competitors have had to undertake much additional expense to recode and maintain the new enhancements, and these costs would necessarily be passed on to the list user. Keeping in mind that list enhancement raises list cost, you would need to decide whether your program could really justify the added expense. If you are trying to reach a broad-based audience, you may not need this enhancement.

The *Standard Industrial Classification Manual* is the directory of four-digit SIC codes. See Appendix 1 for the most recent update.

Why do you need SIC Codes for your markets? Here's an example of how they can be used to develop lists:

A client of ours in the air freight industry already had a solid customer base and wanted to expand. After profiling their "best customer," we decided to focus on companies that order or transport heavy equipment as part of doing business. By checking the SIC *Manual,* we isolated the SIC codes of organizations that fit this description.

Our call objective was to get "consignees"—people who order shipments—to specify our client for their shipments. Therefore, we needed to obtain the names of parts managers and purchasing managers for companies associated with the SIC codes we'd selected. We used a *list compiler* to obtain the list we needed. We mailed 50,000 pieces of direct mail to the list and received an excellent response of 7.5 percent. These "responders" formed the prospect list to start our telemarketing program. This strategy paid off in a substantial expansion of the company's business.

Think of this telemarketing strategy as a pyramid like the one shown in Figure 5-1. Careful research and analysis form the broad base. List selection using SIC codes is the next level. Then the pyramid narrows.

Figure 5-1. Vertical marketing pyramid.

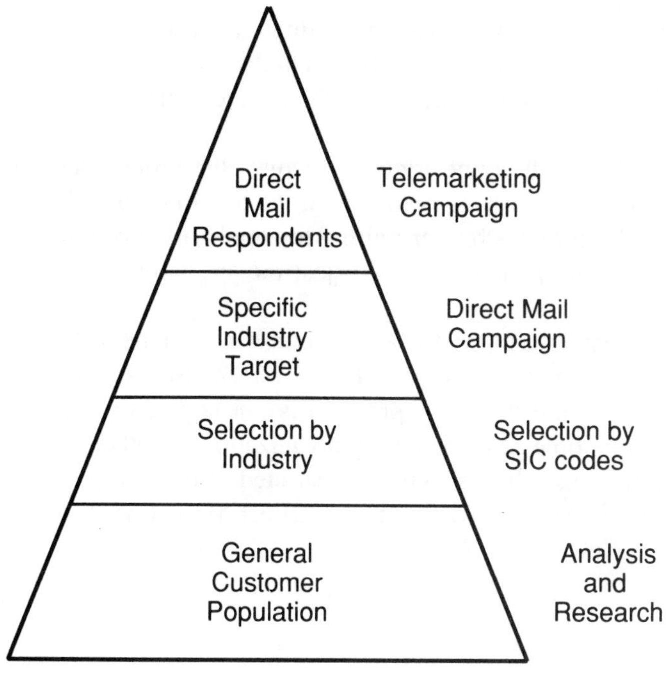

First, we used direct mail to sift out the most likely prospects on our list. At the top of the pyramid, our telemarketing program focused exclusively on these "warmed up" prospects—direct mail responders.

Chapter 8 discusses direct mail further. The key point now is that cost-effective telemarketing focuses on vertical markets. Using SIC codes and other segmentation criteria derived from your "best customer" profile to identify your initial "cold prospect" lists is an important way to achieve this focus.

OBTAINING PROSPECT LISTS

There are an incredible variety and number of mailing lists available today. Some have phone numbers as part of each record. Or you can assemble lists and tag them with phone numbers on your own. Or you can use list brokers, list compilers, and phone look-up services.

List Brokers

List brokers offer their services free of charge, like travel agents, because they rent their lists from the list owner or the owner's list manager at a 15 to 20 percent discount. (These are the same lists for which you would pay full price to an owner.)

List brokers started out servicing the direct mail industry. Many work with telemarketers and can supply phone numbers for specific lists on request, along with names and addresses, for an additional fee per thousand names.

Because of their discount pricing structure, list brokers tend to work with large organizations, whose needs run to the tens of thousands of names. You may be able to find a broker willing to supply a list of only 3,000 or 4,000 names, and they may even have just the specialized list your strategy requires.

If this list was developed for a competitor in your field, however, an honest broker will not rent it to you. If it is a response list, the list broker will have to make sure that your program is not targeted to the same audience at the same time as a competing organization. In other words, when and how you may use the list will be restricted. You can find the names of reputable list brokers by writing to the Direct Marketing Association, 6 East 43 Street, New York, N.Y. 10017.

List Compilers

List compilers are a major source that brokers tap for their lists. Compilers rent a particular product they created; brokers deal with the full range of available lists, regardless of the original source, and can be relied on to be somewhat more objective about any one of them. However, the compiler is sometimes the only one who can put together exactly the list you need. Compiled lists may cost more per thousand names, but they become your property and can be added to your internal data base with no limitations on the number of times you can use them. This factor, coupled with proven applicability to your needs, often makes the compiled list well worth the cost.

Dun and Bradstreet is currently the largest and one of the best known list compilers. For a price as high as $650 per thousand names, the D&B Market Identifier File (DMI) gives you the name, address, phone number, CEO or owner, and full identification profile for each company on file for the SIC you request. D&B's profiles are developed from credit research conducted by its own investigators and from responses to direct mail questionnaires.

American Business Lists (ABL) is another veteran list compiler. ABL derives its information from the Yellow Pages. Their file includes over seven million names, which they can select by company size, SIC, and whether the location is a headquarters or a branch. Other major list compilers are *Trinet, TRW, Ed Burnett,* and *Compilers Plus.*

Trade magazines and organizations are another source of specialized lists. Most will rent their subscriber lists, some on a regional basis.

A key point to consider in acquiring a list is format. Most professional list services will supply records in any of several formats, at your request. Some of the most common, and their advantages, follow:

- *Three-by-five index cards*—easily attached to prospect cards to make a complete record
- *Galley listing (computer printout)*—records can be checked off as calls are made
- *Pressure-sensitive labels*—useful when you plan a pre- or postcall mailing
- *Magnetic tape*—best for storing extremely large numbers of records
- *Diskettes*—for PC-based automated telemarketing management systems

In the consumer area, *R. H. Donnelly, Metromail,* and *R. L. Polk* are the major compilers. These companies develop their files from the phone book white pages and motor vehicle registration information. All their lists allow for selection according to various demographic factors, and most offer an indicator of direct mail responsiveness (such as recency of response, frequency of responses, or size of order).

Details for contacting these and other list compilers can be obtained from the Direct Marketing Association. However, after doing the research and comparing middlemen rates with your internal costs, you may decide to assemble your own list.

Whatever your motivation, the first place to begin is the *Standard Rate and Data Service (SRDS).* SRDS publishes standard guides that present detailed information on every individually owned mailing list in the country. The SRDS guides tell you the source and size of lists and where to write or call to order them. The basic volume is published annually and is updated through supplements twice a year. Many libraries subscribe to SRDS guides.

Another significant source for assembling your own list is the *Directory of Directories,* published by Gale Research and also found in public libraries. This directory briefly describes all trade association, professional society, and commercial organization member directories.

State and local chambers of commerce publish industrial directories for their membership areas, and these are often available at nominal charges. The Bell operating companies publish the phone book Yellow Pages, though they usually do not list owners' names.

For assembling your own consumer-oriented list, the *Criss-Cross Directories* published by Coles and R. L. Polk are indispensable. These organize the white pages of the phone book by ZIP code and street and are usually available in the public library.

In some localities, commercial services rent lists of new homeowners based on real estate transaction records. Or you can go to the source yourself—city or county records offices, where titles, deeds, and tax records are filed. Some credit bureaus, like TRW and Equifax, offer lists of credit card holders and other consumer credit users.

Telephone Look-up Services

If your list does not come with telephone numbers, as is often the case, you can use a look-up service to find the matching numbers. These services consist of computer matching from the company's telephone directory data base or a manual look-up from telephone books.

None of these options is 100 percent successful, however. There are always consumers with unlisted numbers, and some list owners (such as magazine publishers) will not supply numbers or allow them to be looked up. Among the outside look-up services, computer-based matching has a success rate of up to 55 percent on consumer numbers and over 60 percent on business numbers. A manual telephone look-up by a service can average 60 percent or better for consumer numbers and up to 90 percent for business numbers. A manual look-up done by your own staff, presumably more dedicated to the task, can achieve success rates as high as 80 percent for consumer numbers and 90 percent or better for business. (However, I don't advise using telemarketing personnel for this basically clerical task.)

Obtaining your list—whether from a middleman or through your own research—can be a big investment in both money and time. Here are a few tips to help make sure your investment pays off:

- If you are renting a list, get a sample (most companies have a minimum of 1,500 names), and make test calls in advance. Carefully record any erroneous information (wrong numbers, wrong ZIP code, duplicate records), and add up the errors. If more than 15 percent of the records in your sample contain bad information, don't rent the list. Go to another source. (See Chapter 18 for more on testing.)

- *Never* start a telemarketing program with a list that does not contain phone numbers. You can either pay a look-up service a fee per name or have your own personnel do the look-ups, but it is completely counterproductive for telemarketing staff to do this during a phone campaign.

- List development is an investment that requires maintenance. Considering the numbers of records involved over time, you will enhance the value of the investment if you automate your records management system once you get beyond the testing phase. Automation allows you to store large numbers of records, access them quickly, and cross-reference them; it is the basis for ''data base marketing.''

List management software is available for all types of computer hardware and should be investigated before implementing your telemarketing strategy. A good source of software information is the Direct Marketing Association's Directory of Computer Software Suppliers. See Appendix 2 for other software suppliers and resources. Chapter 19 of this book covers the important topic of automation in more detail.

SUMMARY

This chapter addressed the issue of how to obtain prospect lists for your telemarketing campaign. It began with a description of how to target those prospects who are in most likely to respond to your offer. This is accomplished by identifying those attributes that make up your current customer profile.

There are basically two types of lists that can be used for your telemarketing campaign: response and compiled lists. Response lists are made up of direct marketing buyers of products and services while compiled lists are of names of individuals with like characteristics.

To obtain lists of prospects you would go to one or more of the following sources: brokers, compilers, and trade organizations.

With rented lists of names, their format is very important to your telemarketing effort. Various formats are discussed along with their strengths and weaknesses.

For those new to renting prospect lists, this chapter offered descriptions of the various sources available: Standard Rate and Data Service, Directory of Directories, Chamber of Commerce lists, *Criss-Cross Directories,* and others.

For those lists that do not come with telephone numbers, there are look-up services available. The chapter ended with tips on how to get the most out of your lists once they are obtained.

CHAPTER

6

Organizing Your Telemarketing Approach

PROFITABLE telemarketing depends on research and planning. During this phase, you determine call objectives, define target markets, and develop your list. However, a telemarketing strategy takes shape not only by planning *whom* to call, but also *how* to call.

This chapter describes the two principal approaches you can use to organize how your telemarketing program will function:

- The ''total control'' approach
- The ''dialogue'' approach

Although I present these two approaches separately, they are in fact two extremes on a continuum. Any really successful telemarketing strategy contains elements of both. You should use your creativity to develop the right ''mix'' from both—for your objectives, your markets, and your organization's style.

TOTAL CONTROL TELEMARKETING

The total control approach to telemarketing can be compared to a manufacturing production line. Its objective is to produce the highest possible number of contacts at the lowest possible cost. As in a production line, total control telemarketing carefully regulates every input to the process and monitors every output.

A key element in this approach is the *verbatim script*. Prior to implementing the telemarketing program, the developer conducts a formal market research project to develop and test a script. This script incorporates responses to prospects' questions and objections. Telemarketing personnel are trained to use it verbatim. No variations are allowed.

At its most extreme, the total control approach can do away with human personnel entirely. A computer can be programmed to dial preselected (or even random) phone numbers in a given ZIP code. Then the phone system activates a taped sales message, often using the voice of a celebrity. At the conclusion of the taped message, prerecorded instructions allow the prospect to place an order, which is recorded on blank tape. (See Chapters 20 and 21.)

In another variation, a human caller may make the calls, request permission to play a tape, and then come back on the line to close the sale.

The total control approach offers a number of advantages and some disadvantages:

Advantages

- *Higher predictability.* The test phase establishes accurately how many contacts per hour are required to generate a given revenue stream.
- *Lower costs.* Operating costs per contact tend to be lower, for these reasons:
  - Training is short and limited.
  - Compensation is in the minimum wage range or slightly above.
  - Telephone service costs per contact are minimized by the short duration of each call.
- *Higher volume.* Very large numbers of hourly calls and contacts are achieved.

Disadvantages

- *Higher turnover.* "Burnout" occurs more quickly, so you must continually replace personnel.
- *Less flexibility.* Using the script verbatim means that some sales opportunities are lost.
- *Larger lists.* Outlays for lists of leads are higher because of the numbers involved.

Clearly, the total control approach to telemarketing has its place. For example, a cable television company set up this type of telemarketing program to reach tens of thousands of potential subscribers in its franchise area. But this particular program developed a problem that shows how critical the advance work is in telemarketing.

After the program had been in operation for several months, management noted that though production figures met targets, actual installations were skewed low in certain ZIP codes. They found that a large proportion of prospects in these ZIP codes were non-English speakers; so telemarketers had to talk through interpreters, often children, in the prospect's home. Subscribers had little or no idea what they were agreeing to on the phone and refused to allow service installers into their homes as scheduled. This problem could have been overcome by doing the following:

- Testing list samples from every ZIP code in advance
- Requiring validation calls on a sample of every hour's production
- Monitoring telemarketers on-line to discover potential problems early

DIALOGUE TELEMARKETING

The dialogue approach to telemarketing is at the opposite end of the spectrum from the total control approach. In general, this approach uses the two-way communication capability of the telephone much more and concentrates far less on its mass-marketing capability.

At its best, the dialogue approach can be used successfully to sell complex, sophisticated business or consumer products. To succeed, it requires highly skilled telemarketing personnel. They must be problem solvers—people who can quickly size up prospects on the phone and adapt a skeletal script to an individual situation. Strong training in listening skills and telemarketing techniques is essential.

The dialogue approach has both advantages and disadvantages:

Advantages

- *Lower turnover*. The higher caliber staff can better handle the stress involved in telemarketing.
- *Lasting business relationships*. Because it uses more of the natural advantages of the phone, the dialogue approach builds business relationships that generate additional revenue over time.
- *Greater flexibility*. Telemarketers using the dialogue approach can spot sales opportunities on the phone and act on them.

Disadvantages

- *Higher costs*. Though research and development costs are about the same as those for the total control approach, unit costs (per contact or per calling hour) are higher, for several reasons:
  - — Compensation costs to attract and retain personnel are higher.
  - — Training is more extensive.
  - — Telephone costs may be higher if a two-tiered approach is used.
  - — Mailing and support costs may also be higher.

- *Lower volume.* Generally, the longer presentation required by the dialogue approach means that fewer contacts per hour will be made.

The two approaches are not mutually exclusive. Most successful telemarketing strategies use elements of both. One of the best examples of this is the telemarketing program of a well-known financial service organization in New York.

This company had historically used space advertisements in the *Wall Street Journal* and other publications to generate inquiries about its very broad range of financial products. It would then mail out literature and prospectuses in response to inquiries. When the telemarketing project began, the company was getting a very respectable 3 percent conversion rate on its mail program, but it wanted to raise it.

The company developed an outbound telemarketing program to follow up leads generated by the space advertisement program. The strategy began with test calls to develop a script and see what the potential was. Having decided to weight the telemarketing program toward the dialogue approach, the company hired five individuals with a financial sales background—a Series 7 broker's license was required—and trained them as telemarketers.

The call objective was to provide the facts investors need in order to bring them to a decision about a specific financial investment. Training emphasized listening skills and probing techniques, so specific needs could be brought into the conversation. Strong industry knowledge and product fact sheets allowed the telemarketers to supply the facts credibly. In the resulting candid exchange of needs and information, the telemarketers successfully built trust and rapport—and it showed in the figures:

- Conversion of inquiries increased 500 percent (to 18 percent).
- The initial group of five telemarketers was expanded to thirty, and the company plans to double to sixty in the near future.

This is a case of a rather sophisticated product and, initially, at least, relatively low call volumes to prequalified prospects. Financial decisions are not usually impulsive; most investors consider them carefully and have many questions about them. The telephone, using a dialogue approach, was an ideal way to deal with these specific issues. Yet some elements of the total control approach were needed, too. Advance testing to develop the scripts and other support materials was thorough. Monitoring and supervision had to be extremely tight to avoid quality problems that would reflect poorly on the company's reputation. But the start-up program, which took four months to develop and implement, quickly paid for itself in a much higher conversion rate and commission income.

SUMMARY

This chapter discussed two basic approaches to telemarketing:

1. The total control approach
2. The dialogue approach

Though their advantages and disadvantages were discussed separately, each is really an extreme on a spectrum. Most successful telemarketing strategies use elements of both approaches. To decide which elements fit best with your product, your market, and your organization, you must know the advantages and disadvantages of each.

CHAPTER

7

Telemarketing Tactics

UNTIL now, I've dealt with broad strategic issues: whom to call, which list to use, how to organize. In every case, I've emphasized how to base these strategic decisions on the unique strengths of the telephone medium. Now you need to think more in terms of the tactics that will make your strategy succeed. Again, I show how these tactics follow from the telephone's qualities as a communication medium. I expand on some familiar concepts (alternative call objectives, capturing attention, and risk-relieving factors) to show how to structure an offer for the phone.

MERCHANDISING FOR THE PHONE

The telephone is an interactive medium, allowing the seller to exchange information with a prospect through a dialogue. As you plan the offer your telemarketers will present on the phone, never overlook this dialogue quality.

Alternative Objectives

In Chapter 3, I presented call objectives for both inbound and outbound telemarketing and identified additional sales opportunities that each type of call potentially represents. For example, the primary objective of inbound customer service calls is to deliver a service (take the order, answer the inquiry, resolve the complaint). Each type of call should also be designed to build sales or build the sales relationship—through order upgrading, cross-selling, incentives to increase service usage, etc. By designing one of these *alternative objectives* into the inbound script, you increase your sales opportunities, now and over the life of the relationship.

Likewise, in outbound telemarketing, the primary objective may be to obtain qualifying information, set an appointment, or make a sale. Alternative objectives should always be designed into your outbound script, too. They have several important advantages:

- They can pay for a call that otherwise would have produced no revenue or impact.
- They can set up the need for a follow-up call, so you can move the prospect closer to the primary objective.
- They can enhance your telemarketers' morale by giving them a second, less difficult call objective to achieve.

Here are some alternative objectives to use on outbound calls if the primary objective isn't achieved:

- On calls to set appointments, ask for a referral.
- On calls to sell a $100 item on approval, offer a $10 report or catalog as a "loss leader."

A large publishing company wanted to use outbound telemarketing to sell reference books to libraries across the United States. What worked for them was alternative "packages" to increase the margin each call could earn on average. Books were grouped in sets of three, giving the publishger a higher total margin, and the sets were offered at a discount to librarians. As an alternative, librarians could order individual titles.

Capturing Attention

The telephone is a "summons." Prospects must interrupt their routine to answer it and, initially, at least, are "all ears." They give their total attention to the phone because they want answers to the questions in their minds. The best telemarketing tactic is to have strong, reasonable answers to those questions.

Telemarketers should strive to capture attention in the first fifteen to twenty seconds of the call. You must provide an immediate reason for the prospect to stay on the line, or you've lost your opportunity. Follow these three simple guidelines:

1. Tell the prospect why you have called.
2. Let the prospect know you want only a limited amount of time now.
3. Let the prospect know a benefit of talking with you.

Here are some examples:

This is Bill Davis with City Insurance. I'm calling because Ron King suggested you may qualify for a new insurance plan we've developed specifically for commercial printers. I'd like to take a moment to talk to you about what we've been able to do for Ron.

Ms. Smith, I'm Liz Kendall with Vision Computers. We're one of the largest suppliers to General Motors, and we're conducting a special campaign to tell engineers in your area about our portable PC.

Mr. Jones, you've been ordering your office supplies from us for several years. Now we've developed a special reorder service, and I'd like to take a few minutes to tell you how it saves you time and money.

Once you've grabbed prospects' attention, you need to maintain it. Despite their initial interest, most people will be wondering when they can get back to their interrupted activity. As a result, you won't have time to present every aspect of your product or service line. To maintain prospects' attention, you must be selective:

- Select only products and services whose features and benefits can be conveyed within a few minutes.
- Present only those features and benefits that the prospect needs the most.

I say more about features and benefits in Chapters 10, 11, and 13.

Finally, your offer needs a strong incentive for the prospect to act *now*, on the phone. Here you can really make the "charged atmosphere" of the telephone work for you. The telephone call interrupts routine and captures attention long enough to provide the reasons to act. In essence, it creates the impulse to act. Your offer must take advantage of this impulse by providing an incentive to act now.

At a major air freight company, telemarketers offered a specially designed map as an incentive for prospects to use the company for their next shipment. This type of incentive works well when you are seeking to establish a relationship. Other types of incentives to act immediately are limited-time discounts or introductory prices.

Risk-Relieving Factors

The conventional wisdom is that complex or high-priced products and service can't be sold on the phone. Yet there are successful telemarketing programs for organizations of every type, selling $100,000 software packages, expensive office equipment, and many kinds of intangibles. A key tactic is the "risk-relieving factor." This is particularly important when your program is calling cold prospects (people who have no prior relationship with your organization).

A convinced prospect, sold on the benefits of unseen merchandise or services, will often want some form of recourse—some way out of the decision to buy. Perhaps the prospect feels the decision may be overruled by someone who reviews purchasing decisions. Or perhaps the prospect is concerned that the product or service will turn out to be unsatisfactory. In designing your offer for the phone, you must evaluate how much of a risk the commitment entails and how far you can reasonably go to relieve that sense of risk.

Plan this part of your offer carefully. Who will be the decision maker: a line manager, senior executive, husband and wife, committee? When a single individual lacks sole buying power, you need to balance the cost of making multiple calls to other decision makers against the cost of providing a risk-relieving factor.

Approval sales and invoice sales are two of the most commonly used risk-relieving factors in telemarketing. Remember the following tips if you decide your offer will incorporate one of them.

Approval Sale. An approval sale relieves prospects' risk by providing a limited time to examine a product before paying for it. Approval periods of five, ten, twenty-one, or thirty days are the most common. Advance test calls will tell you the approval period needed to meet your sales targets; select the shortest one possible.

Some prospects have the misimpression that an item shipped "on approval" is an inspection copy; they expect to return it and order a "new one" after the purchase is approved. This is obviously undesirable, so you must carefully communicate the terms of the approval sale on the phone. In addition, you must plan to monitor the frequency of returns and damaged goods. In this way, you will spot problems early and can take action.

Two "preemptive" actions you can take are the following:

1. Pay commissions on receipt of payment, not on orders shipped.
2. Verify orders on a random basis. Have a checker call customers to announce shipment date and details, verify the address, and restate the approval terms. If the prospect has been sold on the approval factor and *not* on the product itself, this becomes an opportunity to cancel the order.

Because materials such as recordings and tapes are easily copied and returned, it is more sensible to play a brief demonstration tape on the phone and use the invoice sale method rather than the approval method.

Invoice Sales. An invoice sale relieves risk by emphasizing that the seller stands behind the product or service sold. Within a specified period of time, the seller will accept returns of items that do not perform as expected because of miscommunication at the time of sale. Payment is due when the shipment arrives or when service is initiated. Ownership is assumed to rest with the purchaser, not the seller.

Invoice sales are one of the more difficult call objectives. They require highly trained telemarketers, careful management, and valid advance testing. The invoice sales method has been used successfully by book and record clubs, publishers, office products manufacturers, and many others.

To use the invoice sales method effectively, it is also essential to develop a *confirmation letter,* which is mailed to the customer immediately after the sale and should include the following:

- Description of the product or service ordered
- Price
- Shipping date
- Payment terms agreed to by the purchaser
- Notation that if a purchase order is required by the buyer's organization, it should be marked "Confirmation Only"
- Telephone number for customers to call in case of questions or problems with the order
- Signature of telemarketer who sold the order

Many invoice sales telemarketing programs include payment-facilitating terms as part of the offer. Some typical examples are the following:

- Acceptance of credit cards
- Use of installment payments
- Extension of payment period by thirty, sixty, or ninety days from shipment date, depending on known credit rating of the market you are selling to
- Postdating the invoice to coincide with budget disbursement schedules (for institutional purchasers)
- Payment of a 25 percent deposit on receipt of shipment, with balance due at a future date agreed to on the phone

If you decide to use one of these payment-facilitating methods, be sure to include the specific terms agreed upon in your confirmation letter.

SUMMARY

This chapter introduced the idea of merchandising your offer for the specific requirements of the phone. It presented three tactics you can use to achieve the goals of your telemarketing strategy:

- Alternative objectives
- Capturing attention
- Risk-relieving factors

CHAPTER

8

Direct Mail and Telemarketing

DIRECT mail and telemarketing are natural partners in marketing both business and consumer products or services. A combination of direct mail and a coordinated telemarketing follow-up can generate anywhere from four to eight times the business expected from the mail program alone. Likewise, a well-orchestrated postcall mailing can significantly increase sales revenues.

Of course, not every marketing objective requires the additional expense of direct mail. This chapter presents guidelines for integrating direct mail with a telemarketing strategy. Specifically, it covers the following issues:

- Which situations require direct mail?
- How do you design and coordinate direct mail that gives maximum support to a telemarketing program?

DIRECT MAIL: DO YOU NEED IT?

To decide whether you need direct mail support for your telemarketing strategy, start by looking at two primary factors:

1. The strength of the existing relationship
2. The difficulty of the primary call objective (Figure 8-1)

If the existing relationship is strong (current or former customers, for example), you may well be able to avoid the cost of direct mail. And if your call objective is low on the scale of difficulty (setting appointments, for example), you almost certainly can depend on telemarketing alone. Gen-

Figure 8-1. Degree of difficulty of call based on relationship to customer, cost of product, and prospect type.

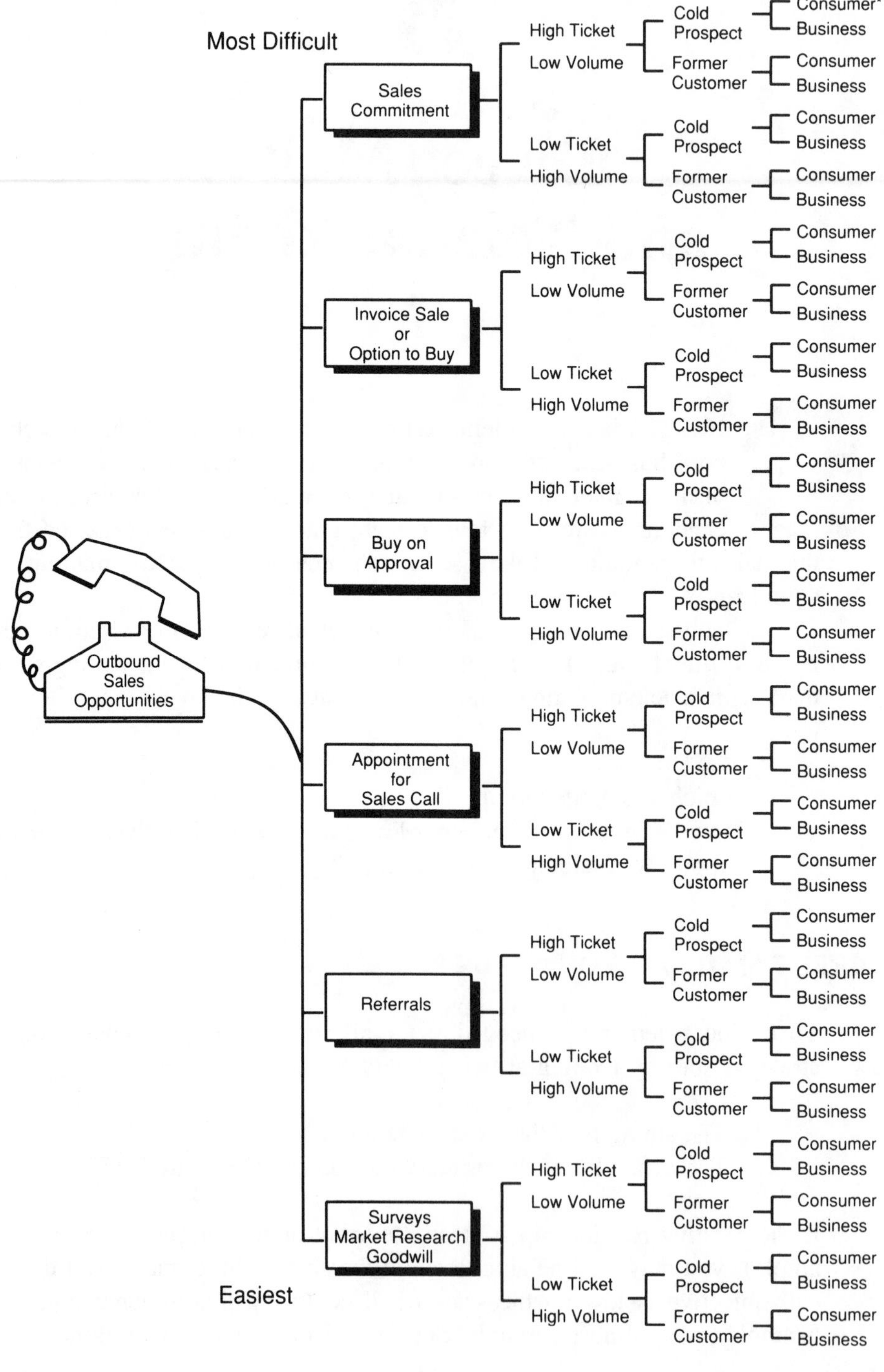

* Hardest call to make

erally, the more difficult the primary call objective and the weaker the relationship, the more likely you are to need direct mail support. The following case histories and discussion show how some companies have resolved the question of using direct mail.

1: Cold Calling to a New Market

A business-oriented software development firm, purchased proprietary rights to a software application for home PC users. Although the company had a strong position in the business market, it had little recognition in the home user market—no strong relationship.

The company planned to use the new software package to build recognition and share in the consumer market. Its telemarketing strategy was to obtain invoice sales of the package, priced initially at $209.95, with an optional package costing $49.95.

The company obtained a list of 10,000 names—prospects who had purchased compatible hardware and who were professionals in the upper-income range. Initial test calls showed what the company had suspected: the company's reputation had very little carryover effect in the consumer market, and prospect resistance was strong.

2: Cross-Selling to Current Customers

A manufacturer of plastic films used in food packaging bought an industrial coatings company to complement its own line. Many current customers were considered to be good prospects to be cross-sold the coatings line. The firm developed a telemarketing strategy concentrating on purchasing managers and offering an initial price reduction. During the test calls, the company found that its customers were reluctant to place orders without a full review of the coatings' technical specifications and without the approval of all senior department personnel who would be affected by the decision.

In both cases, direct mail support is indicated, though for different reasons. In case 1, the business relationship is weak, and the call objective is at the upper end on the scale of difficulty. Compu-Sys's solution was to develop a "warm-up" letter and mail it prior to full-scale telemarketing. Figure 8-2 is a direct mail letter that illustrates these key elements:

- It explains who will be calling and when.
- It introduces the company and stimulates curiosity about the product and the call.

Figure 8-2. Sample warm-up letter.

[*Your Company Name*]

[*Date*]

Name
Title
Company
Address
City-State-Zip

Dear ________:

If you're in the ____________ business today, you know that there are some insurance coverages you've got to have, and some you'd like to have but can't get or can't afford.

Primo Insurance, one of the oldest and most respected insurance companies in the world, knows the needs of ____________businesses, and is introducing the Executive series to meet them.

Primo challenges you to find a more comprehensive, flexible policy for your specific needs as a ____________, at a price you can afford.

I've enclosed an Executive series brochure, and will be calling next week to answer your questions; if you'd like, we'll schedule a free review of your current business insurance plan.

I'm looking forward to talking with you.

Sincerely,

TMR/Sales Agent
____________, Account Specialist

Another possibility is using a larger list, enclosing a business reply card, and calling only prospects who qualified themselves by returning it.

Mailing a properly designed warm-up letter will accomplish the following objectives:

- *It makes it easier for telemarketers to get through to decision makers.* Though only a fraction of the letters may be read, the telemarketer can tell a screen, "I'm calling in reference to the letter I sent Mr. Jones last week."
- *It saves telephone calling time.* If a prospect has no interest in the product, the telemarketer can quickly disqualify him or her and move on to other prospects.
- *It achieves sales faster.* The mailing gives advance information about your product. Interested prospects will more likely be ready with questions when the scheduled call is made.
- *It provides name recognition.* This gives your TMRs a slight "edge" when they call and increases the chance of developing a positive response.

In case 2, there was a solid customer relationship, but the product in question was technically complex. Prospects were reluctant to order—even with an introductory price break—without reading the technical specifications and consulting others.

We changed the primary objective of the initial call from getting an order to obtaining qualifying information to set an appointment for a telephone meeting—with all decision makers on the line. Between calls, we mailed a follow-up informational letter providing full technical specifications.

The follow-up mailing, including requested documentation or brochures, should be considered under the following circumstances:

- When your product or service is too complex for a brief explanation or its benefits are supported best through diagrams, tables, or other visuals
- When the price of your product or service requires approval at several levels of targeted organizations

You should almost certainly use a follow-up mailing when one of these two conditions is combined with any of the following:

- Your product is new and competing in a field dominated by a better-known product.
- Your organization has a weak relationship with prospects.

A correctly designed and properly timed follow-up mailing will accomplish the following goals:

- *It eliminates confusion.* The follow-up letter answers questions that were not covered in prior contacts.

• *It provides essential ordering information to multiple decision makers.* This is especially important, because there may be decision makers who remain unknown to telemarketing personnel. The letter, together with the recommendation of the primary contact, provides convincing support for approving the transaction.

• *It makes closing on the second call more likely.* On the second call, the prospect is presumably much more receptive to placing an order because technical or organizational issues have already been dealt with.

DESIGNING AND TIMING DIRECT MAIL SUPPORT

Precall (Warm-up) Mailings

Precall mailings are most effective when you are working with lists of specific names, not simply titles and company addresses. In designing your direct mail support, avoid large-scale bulk mailings to unnamed prospects for these two reasons:

1. These mailings lack the high personal impact a telemarketing strategy needs to build on.
2. Telephone follow-up is difficult to achieve in a timely fashion, so impact is reduced further.

Certainly, in some situations, it isn't possible to obtain individual names. But even in those situations, your telemarketing program will benefit to some extent. The fact that a brochure was mailed gives your staff a legitimate reason to call and follow up and enhances their chances of reaching decision makers.

In those situations, be aware that the support delivered by such direct mail is significantly lower quality, and your telemarketing results will reflect this. The cost:benefit ratio may still be acceptable, however, and your test calls should give you these numbers. (See Chapter 18.) In any situation, always observe the following basic design and timing rules for precall mailings:

• *Design.* Leave some important information out of the mailing piece.

The major function of the mailing is to prepare the prospect for the subsequent telephone call. Hold back something crucial—something the telephone call alone can supply, such as the following:

— Special discount information available only on the phone
— Rebate offers for phone customers only
— Special prices on related products available to phone customers only

• *Timing*. Divide your mailing, and stagger the drop dates.

Your telemarketing staff must be able to follow up every letter *within forty-eight hours* of the day prospects receive them. You can divide the mailing by sales territory, ZIP codes, time zone, or some other way.

You can stagger the mailing into monthly, bi-monthly, or quarterly segments, depending on the total size of the mailing and the capacity of your telemarketing staff.

Because gauging the forty-eight-hour limit can be difficult, telemarketers should make one or two hours of test calls to see if the mailing piece has been received. This is usually enough to judge whether full-scale telephone follow-up should be started.

How to design and develop a direct mailing is beyond the scope of this book. However, there are certain essentials every precall letter should contain. Whether you are writing your own letters or using a direct mail agency, be sure that your precall letter does the following:

- Reminds prospects of any prior relationship they have had with your organization
- Uses short paragraphs to describe the primary features and benefits of the product or service you will be calling about
- Provides the day, date, and approximate time ("after 2:30 P.M.") you will be calling
- Suggests items prospects can think about prior to your call (for example, a cost comparison or additional features they may be looking for)
- Avoids sales-related titles in the signature (instead, choose titles that suggest expertise in a specific area—for example, "Manager, Software Development")
- Looks as personalized as possible:
  - — Uses first class mail and postage stamps rather than bulk mail and the company meter
  - — Uses company letterhead and high-quality paper stock
  - — Uses word processing and laser printing
  - — Uses wide margins and generous amounts of white space for easier reading
  - — Includes a personal signature in contrasting ink
  - — Contains a handwritten postscript alluding to the upcoming call

You may not be able to take all these steps to personalize your letter, but the more you take, the more impact your letter will have.

A final element you may want to consider as part of your precall mailing is the use of *reply cards*. Some of the most effective telemarketing strategies rely on direct mail to generate qualified leads through reply cards.

Developing this type of program usually requires professional counsel, which is well worth the expense. Here are some guidelines to evaluate reply cards used for telemarketing:

- *Always* include a line for area code and phone number. This seems obvious, but expensive mail programs have failed because telephone follow-up calls were delayed.
- *Never* use a card that says, "Please send additional information" or "Please have a representative call me."
- *Always* use a card that says, "I would like some additional information." This allows you to provide the information in the manner you see fit and avoids any negative connotation that sales calls may have.
- *Always* use a card that allows the prospect to identify specific needs or interests:

  I want to know how I can qualify for a thirty-day trial of. . . .
  My office/department/firm now has ____ copiers.
  Our monthly copying volume is
  ☐ *50–100 copies*
  ☐ *100–500 copies*
  ☐ *500+ copies*

The timing requirement for responding to reply cards is particularly important. Your program should be fully staffed so that follow-up calls can be made within forty-eight hours of receipt of reply cards. The longer the time lag, the lower the return you can expect on your investment in this type of mailing.

Follow-up Mailings

In some situations, it is advisable to use the telephone first, to qualify prospects and identify their specific needs and interests. This effort is followed up by mailing a letter or supporting literature providing the needed information and setting up the second call.

The objective of the second call is to obtain a commitment. This approach is highly successful when you are selling high-ticket items or complex, sophisticated products and services. The following rules apply to developing materials for follow-up mailings:

• *Develop a range of materials.* Each product or service you sell on the phone should have a distinctive mailing piece. This way, prospects can select according to their individual needs or interests. Simultaneously, you identify their needs precisely and can target the objective of your second call.

If your organization offers only one product or service, develop a series of information kits, each targeted to different account sizes or levels of need. You can determine this in the first call, which you can use as a survey call. The kits may vary in length or type of graphics used, but all provide basically the same information—and a good basis for a second call.

• *Always indicate when the second call will be made.* This may be as simple as clipping a business card to the literature with the date and time of the call handwritten on it. Or you can use a formal, typewritten note requesting that prospects put the date and time in their office calendars.

The following case history will show you how well direct mail can work along with telemarketing.

3: Targeting an Inactive Customer Base

A major cruise line wished to develop a telemarketing program that would target a market that historically produced little business for the company. Its research showed this market had potential, but conventional space advertising plus field sales efforts were not reaching it effectively.

Its direct mail/telemarketing program brought in $250,000 in additional business the first month. In the second month, that business doubled.

Prior to the telephone effort, the company mailed 2,500 information kits about its cruise services, cooperative advertising plan, and so forth. A precall letter was attached to the information kit and personalized as follows:

- The letter was individually addressed.
- The letter was signed by an individual "cruise specialist."
- The cruise specialist's photograph was reproduced on the letter, in color.

The letter was a conversation piece. Its message was simple: "We're interested in doing business with you and will pay special attention to you." It also prepared the recipient for the follow-up call and provided an 800 number as a free hotline.

The staff for this outbound program was carefully selected and trained. The calls were made within forty-eight hours after the mailing was received.

A high percentage of the prospects had actually read and retained the mailed materials. Most welcomed the opportunity to discuss the company's cruise packages. They responded strongly to the idea that they now had a specific individual to call to make reservations and get updated information. And their response showed in the additional business they gave the company. It has since targeted other "dormant" markets and repeated the program.

USING TELEMARKETING AND DIRECT MAIL FOR LAUNCHING A NEW PRODUCT

One of the most challenging marketing objectives is to introduce and direct market a product that has never been available before.

One technique that I found to be very successful is used by Stan Livacz, a direct-marketing specialist. It is a two-step process that uses a survey technique and combines direct mail with telemarketing.

The first step is to mail a personalized letter and questionnaire to the prospect audience, asking for their assistance in evaluating the new product or service. The questionnaire consists of a list of the benefits and features with an explanation of each. It asks each prospect for feedback on the importance of each feature and benefit to them. Typically, the respondents are asked to circle a number corresponding to the perceived level of importance each feature and benefit has for them.

In this way, the marketer can involve the prospect audience in the process of learning about a new product and how it might help them. Because a survey mailing of this type requires a commitment of several minutes of time on the part of the prospect, a low-cost premium, such as a solar calculator or other useful item, is offered (not enclosed with the questionnaire) as a "thank you" for taking the time to participate in the survey.

Among the questions in the survey are qualifiers to determine whether the prospect would consider purchasing the product or service and in what time frame. Typically, these questions are placed at the end of the questionnaire.

This direct mail technique usually produces a high response rate. In the case of a new marketing data base product, for example, the response rate was 8.6 percent. In the case of a regional bank offering a new financial services club tailored to the needs of specific businesses, the response of a combination of current bank customers and non-customers was 23 percent.

In the case of the regional bank, over 80 percent of the respondents indicated that they would be interested in joining the financial services club. This group formed a tremendously valuable target audience for a return telephone call to sign them up for membership.

In the case of the marketing data base company, sales executives who were targeted on the original mailing were called. Those who responded to the mailing signed up for the product at a ratio of about six to one compared with those who did not respond.

Using the telephone to follow up survey leads gives the marketer of a new product or service the opportunity to overcome objections and answer questions in a way that is not possible with direct mail. At the same time, the combined cost of the direct mail and telemarketing programs tends to be much less than that of sending a salesperson to visit personally with each prospect. In most cases, direct salespeople are not available or the profit from the sale is too small to justify the cost.

When a marketer has funds and time to invest in media advertising in vertical and general business media in advance of direct mail and telemarketing efforts, the results can be enhanced significantly. The bottom line is that to obtain commitment from prospects for a new product, extensive explanation is often required.

A good rule is to test the water for a new product or service by sending out a very low-cost mailing to a limited number of prospects, and following up with professional telemarketing to determine the success rate and the cost of obtaining customers.

In direct marketing a new product or service, testing price levels can be the difference between failure and success. In the case of the marketing database company mentioned above, the president wanted to offer the product at a cost of $100. The direct response agency recommended that a price test be instituted at $99, $149, and $249, to find the perceived value of the product to its audience of sales executives. Not surprisingly, the company found that the $149 price was just as acceptable as the $99. The increased price was the major factor in making it profitable to direct market the product. The combination of direct mail and follow-up telemarketing were natural partners in evaluating potential for a new product or service.

Another inexpensive idea that can be implemented quickly is to send a letter to prospects with a media advertisement folded in. The letter tells the prospect that ''we wanted to be sure you personally had a chance to review this advertisement that will be appearing in [list of publications].'' This simple approach tells prospects that they are important and their feedback is valued. A business-reply letter with a postage-paid envelope or business-reply card asking the prospect several qualifying questions is included. This method is a very good alternative to a much most costly and time-consuming direct mail message and is just as effective in setting up a return telephone call. Figure 8-3 is a sample market survey letter and questionnaire produced by a professional direct response agency, Interactive Marketing Inc.

SUMMARY

The basic facts and guidelines on using direct mail to support a telemarketing strategy were covered in this chapter, which looked at typical situations in which direct mail support is especially useful:

(Text continues on page 66.)

Figure 8-3. Market survey letter and questionnaire.

Dear Friend,

Will you do us a favor?

We are conducting a marketing survey to determine the potential for a unique new membership organization, the **Select Business Leaders Club (SBLC)**, that will offer selected small business leaders a comprehensive package of financial services that includes no-fee reserve checking and corporate Gold Visa.

The SBLC is described on the attached survey along with a listing of the services it will include and their potential benefits. We would like you to evaluate each of the statements and indicate how important you think each service would be to you.

Since this survey is being sent to a limited number of small businesses, your individual reply is very important. Your answers can be provided in a few minutes by simply circling a number after each statement.

Because we appreciate your taking the time to complete the survey, we will mail to you a free, no obligation gift of the credit card size solar calculator/calendar shown below. It will fit neatly into your billfold or purse to help you keep track of your business commitments.

Thank you for your assistance.

Sincerely,

Senior Vice-President and Secretary
Commercial Banking Division

PS: This handy, attractive solar powered calculator/calendar will be mailed to you free and without obligation for completing the attached questionnaire.

Your opinions are requested on a potential new package of financial services.

Please correct any inaccuracies in your mailing label:

Name ______________________________

Company ______________________________

Street ______________________________

City ______________ State __________ Zip __________

Phone ( ) ______________________________

Answering the questions below places you under no obligation and the information you provide will be held in strict confidence.

A Brief Description of the Select Business Leader's Club

Recognizing that small businesses with above average track records require a broad range of corporate services, we have developed a "package" that delivers a comprehensive array of corporate financial services that will be available to firms who join SBLC. Members will receive, for a low annual fee, substantially more interest on time deposits and money management accounts. They will also pay lower interest on loans and receive many fee-paid services absolutely free. SBLC members will receive a membership card entitling them to many corporate banking services at no fee and for use in obtaining travel and entertainment discounts. In addition, members will be entitled to highly personalized financial counselling, enrollment in a worldwide networking club and national automobile club, and will enjoy special discounts on purchases of products and services.

(*continued*)

Figure 8-3. *Continued.*

With this brief description in mind, please evaluate the following services based on their importance to you. Using a scale of 1 to 4 (**1** = Not Important, **2** = Somewhat Important, **3** = Important, **4** = Very Important), please circle the appropriate number for each statement.

1. Free Financial Planning and Counselling

a. **Annual Financial Profile**—Members will receive an annual financial plan based on a meeting with a financial planner at the Bank, free of charge. The plan will take into consideration your business's total finanical picture along with your short- and long-term objectives.

Importance Rating **1** **2** **3** **4**

b. **Financial Counselling**—A Financial Services Executive will arrange for members to obtain free corporate financial counselling and may make appointments to discuss loans, pension planning, investments and other financial services.

Importance Rating **1** **2** **3** **4**

c. **Insurance Counselling**—Through the Financial Services Executive, members will be provided corporate insurance counselling by a licensed expert in the field of corporate benefits.

Importance Rating **1** **2** **3** **4**

- When your organization has a weak relationship with prospects
- When the primary call objective is relatively difficult
- When your product is new and has no history or perceived value

Direct mail can be used before calling (precall "warm-up" letters). Postcall follow-up mailings should follow specific design and timing guidelines to achieve maximum benefits.

CHAPTER

9

Telemarketing Strategies for Complex Products

THIS final chapter on shaping your telemarketing strategy takes a detailed look at two strategies that support high-ticket, low-volume sales. These products and services typically have a select, though dispersed market (for example, computer hardware and software, telecommunications systems and services, and investment products). You may consider such complex, sophisticated products and services as "inappropriate" for marketing over the phone, but they can be (and are) sold successfully over the phone every day. This chapter shows how to do it using two-tier telemarketing and teleconferencing.

TWO-TIER TELEMARKETING

Two-tier telemarketing uses the total control approach and the dialogue approach on two distinct levels or tiers to market complex products.

On the first tier, the *total control approach* is used to make a large number of calls to prospects. These calls are made by relatively inexperienced telemarketers, using a verbatim-type script. Their objective is to qualify prospects as to interest in and need for the product and income required for purchase. Strict adherence to the script is essential at this level, and close monitoring is required to ensure it.

Usually, first-tier telemarketers are part-time, paid the minimum wage or slightly more, plus a small bonus for meeting their call (not their lead) quota. The point of this type of compensation plan is to make sure that enough calls are made and that the leads developed really are qualified. Paying significantly more for high production of leads can cause problems in terms of quality (see Chapter 17). It is wiser to accept the cost of staff turnover than to pay more for poorly qualified leads.

Following this "prospecting" tier are the second-level calls, made by experienced, highly trained telemarketing professionals. They are usually full-time and work on a high commission basis. The objective of these calls is to close a sale to a qualified prospect. A mailing is often sent—to qualified leads only—between the two tiers. This mailing accomplishes three objectives:

1. It helps cement the relationship between the prospect and the organization.
2. It gives the second-tier telemarketer a strong reason to call.
3. It ensures the prospect has all the facts about the product or service.

Another variation on the two-tier approach is to use the first call to establish a foothold relationship by obtaining a small order. The second-tier call then seeks a major order. Both types of two-tier telemarketing require strict adherence to the script on the first-tier calls. This ensures that second-tier telemarketers call only leads who meet strict criteria for ability to purchase and need for the product or service.

Here's a case history of a variation on two-tier telemarketing.

1: Multi-tier Telemarketing

A major money-center bank had developed a new on-line information service, making world news and financial reports available via PC. This institution had multiple goals for its telemarketing program:

- To identify the key decision maker in the buying decision for this relatively high priced business service
- To explain to prospects how the service differs from the competition
- To organize the many features and benefits of the service into segments having strong appeal to specific classes of decision makers

A multi-tier program was needed to reach these goals. First, detailed, branching scripts were developed to identify the key decision maker in each market segment and to learn which features and benefits appealed most strongly to each segment.

The research (test) script revealed that the concept of "user-friendly" needed to be demonstrated over the phone. This is where a multi-tier telemarketing program began to take shape. The first call accomplished the following objectives:

- Introduced the product.
- Identified the decision maker and, if he or she was a qualified lead, prompted mailing of

a follow-up demonstration disk.

The second, follow-up phone call was informational—used to answer any questions the prospect had and to set up a third call for a demonstration over the phone. It also helped build the relationship so the third call could be used to confidently seek an appointment for a field salesman who would close the sale in person. The program is currently exceeding targets for first-year market share.

TELECONFERENCING

Teleconferencing is a truly unique way to sell or promote relatively sophisticated, expensive products and services to groups of decision makers. You have probably already used teleconferencing for communicating to business (or personal) associates in groups. You can set up a conference call through the local phone company conference operator or—for smaller conferences—by using your own bridging equipment to connect participants. Teleconferences for sales or promotional purposes differ from this type of conference call in some important ways: topic, agenda, moderator, and setting.

Topic

At one level, sales teleconferences are an organized discussion around a specific topic related to the product or service being promoted. For example, a pharmaceutical company that wanted to introduce its newest drug for the treatment of depression organized a series of teleconferences for doctors on the topic of advances in antidepressants. A collision estimating company, seeking to influence insurance companies to use its automated collision estimating service more often and more effectively, organized a series of teleconferences on speeding up claims processing.

The topic for a sales teleconference must be carefully selected for its appeal to decision makers, as well as its relation to the product sold. In developing a sales teleconference, it's important both to present the facts about your product or service and to plan for a lively exchange of views regarding the topic. So the topic needs to be timely and raise substantive issues in the minds of decision makers.

Agenda

It's common to circulate an agenda prior to any business meeting, including conference calls. For a sales teleconference, an agenda is imperative.

It provides a reminder of the date, time, and length of the conference. In addition, it shows the structure of the conference and reemphasizes its importance.

Here is an example of a teleconference agenda sent to participants about ten days before the call:

> We look forward to your joining us for a nationwide teleconference on "Computers in the Classroom." The teleconference will be on [*date*] at [*time*]. The agenda will include the following:
>
> I. Conference begins (9:15 P.M.)
> II. Introduction of participants
> III. Introduction of [*name*], guest speaker
> IV. "[*Topic*]" presentation by guest speaker
> V. Q&A and discussion
> VI. Poll of conference participants
> VII. Wrap-up and conclusion (10:00 P.M.)

Specific preparation instructions are often included with the teleconference agenda. For example, travel agents invited to a teleconference on new tours in China may be asked to note problems they've had making arrangements for customers traveling to China.

Moderator

As the sample agenda indicates, a moderator leads a sales teleconference. This is an experienced telemarketing professional as well as a confident group discussion leader. He or she should know how to manage group dynamics on the telephone and should be familiar with the industry from which conference participants are selected. Finally, the moderator needs to be well versed in the product or service the conference is designed to sell.

Setting

Most business teleconferences are scheduled to take place during regular business hours. But sales teleconferences are often best scheduled for the evening hours for the following reasons:

- *Higher impact.* Because participants are not in the midst of their usual daily business schedules, they are more open to hearing about the product or service.
- *Easier scheduling.* Influential decision makers are easier to schedule for after-hours teleconferences.

- *Lower costs.* Conference call rates drop dramatically after businesss hours.

The teleconference's setting is the key to its success and impact in selling high-priced or complex goods and services. During a professionally planned and conducted sales teleconference, three elements are at work: group dynamics, peer pressure, and the bandwagon effect.

Group Dynamics. In developing a teleconference—or series of teleconferences—you have taken the initiative to gather a group of decision makers. You have carefully selected them for their common background and interest in the conference topic. This tends to dispose the participants in favor of your organization and product or service. Group dynamics works for the seller.

Peer Pressure. In addition, you have prepared the participants to consider some type of commitment or take an action. You accomplish this through the invitation process and the advance circulation of the agenda. Therefore, when the moderator polls the participants at the end of the conference, peer pressure tends to operate in your favor.

Bandwagon Effect. During the teleconference, participants have the opportunity to express their viewpoints, ask questions, and listen to others do the same. By the end of the conference, enthusiasm is high, and a "bandwagon effect" has usually formed. It seems natural to try the product or service or place an order.

The actual commitment to try a product or place an order is nearly always formalized during a follow-up telephone call, visit, or mail contact. But the key is that the decision is made during the teleconference. There is also often a "ripple effect" from teleconferences. Participants are so affected by the conference that they spread the impact through their network of associates. One teleconference of eight participants will often affect four or five times that many.

How to Organize a Sales Teleconference

Your sales teleconference topic should meet these criteria:

- It should be strongly related to the product or service you are selling or promoting.
- It should be general enough to interest all participants.
- It must indicate that valuable information will be available to participants.

A book and media distribution service conducted a series of teleconferences designed to sell a $375 audio cassette program to high school and college teachers and librarians. The conference topic was "How To Use Audio Programs in the Classroom." This caught the attention of prospects and let them know they would get some specific ideas from the conference—ideas they could put to work right away in their own classrooms. Like any other sales method, teleconferencing must supply an answer to the question, "What's in it for me?"

The second step in developing sales teleconferences is to write an "invitation script," which trained telemarketers use to obtain conference participants. It contains the following elements:

- *Introduction and reason for call.* The telemarketer gives his or her name, organization, and an attention-grabbing statement about the teleconference.
- *Presentation.* The presentation explains what a teleconference is, how easy it is to attend, and how it benefits the participants:
  — A chance to talk with colleagues around the state, region, or nation
  — An opportunity to discuss a topic of professional interest to all
  — An opportunity to hear a leading figure in the profession or industry make a short presentation (this is optional and may be taped)
  — An opportunity to learn something new
- *Qualification of prospect.* This is usually a series of questions that determine the prospect's interest in the topic and need for the related product.
- *Closure.* The close is a request for participation at one of the scheduled teleconferences.
- *Wrap-up.* The telemarketer wraps up the call by obtaining the prospect's name and the address to which the formal invitation and agenda should be mailed.

It usually takes about thirty calls to produce fifteen participants. Of these, eight to ten will actually take part in the teleconference. Inviting should start about two to three weeks before the teleconference to allow time for mailed materials to arrive. The follow-up mailing should restate the conference time and date, provide a number to call for cancellations, and enclose an agenda.

Teleconferences usually should last about forty-five minutes. At the outset, the moderator should announce each participant's name and location and explain that only one person can talk at a time. These introductory matters should be handled in an upbeat, enthusiastic style because the moderator is setting the tone for the teleconference.

If the agenda includes a taped presentation by a guest speaker, the moderator introduces him or her immediately following the general introduction. After the presentation, the moderator opens up the conference for questions or opinions from the participants. The moderator should have a prepared list of questions to help get the ball rolling. It's important also to track who has had a chance to speak and who has not so that everyone's views are solicited during this phase.

After the discussion period, the moderator polls the group, asking each participant to indicate his or her interest in the product or service presented. Beginning the poll with the person who has been most enthusiastic in the discussion helps build a strong bandwagon effect. In a professionally run teleconference, eight out of ten participants will often commit to strong interest in the product presented.

The conference concludes with a wrap-up in which the moderator describes how subsequent contacts will be made (a phone call the following day is the most effective) and thanks the participants for attending.

The following day, telemarketers call each participant who responded positively during the poll and close the sale or commitment the teleconference is seeking. The conversion rate on these follow-up calls is usually about 80 percent.

Clearly, teleconferencing is not the right approach for every product or service. It makes sense for organizations that sell to specific professions or segments of industries. It is more expensive than the usual types of telemarketing in both planning and implementation. However, for higher-priced goods and services, it is a unique and enormously successful way to sell.

SUMMARY

This chapter presented two telemarketing approaches for selling high-ticket, low-volume products and services. The first one, two-tier telemarketing, uses a large number of calls up front to qualify prospects. At the second call, it uses the dialogue approach to close the sale. Often a mailing precedes the second call as a means to cement the relationship and build interest in the follow-up call.

The second approach, teleconferencing, requires carefully qualified prospects, usually from the same profession or industry segment. A professional moderator leads the conference in a discussion of a topic related to the product or service to be sold. During the teleconference, group dynamics and peer pressure build a bandwagon effect in favor of the product or service. Because of the high impact and excitement the teleconference generates, follow-up calls to teleconference participants result in a high percentage of sales.

Both approaches require extensive planning and advanced telemarketing knowledge. However, properly designed, both can be used successfully to sell a range of upper-end products to business executives and professionals.

PART

III

Scripting: The Key to Control

CHAPTER

10

Scripting Every Stage of the Call

THE single most important advance in telemarketing in recent years has been in the area of scripting. The reason is that telemarketers have three basic communication tools: a well-trained voice, a strong message, and the ability to draw the prospect into dialogue. The script supports all three. In addition, by controlling the key factors of whom to call, when to call, and what to say on the phone, you will accurately predict your results and ultimately control how much business you do on the phone. Very simply, the script is one of your major tools for controlling your telemarketing program.

REASONS TO SCRIPT

Most professional communicators use some type of prepared script to guide their presentations. Lawyers use notes to summarize a client's case for the jury; newscasters read the teleprompter word for word. Telemarketing scripts give telemarketers an ''edge'' because they *guide* every stage of each call in a logical and compelling order, enabling telemarketers to *anticipate* what will happen during the call and providing ammunition for handling any contingency. They also make sure every minute of the call really counts. Most telemarketing calls are short—often five minutes, rarely more than fifteen to twenty minutes. The script ensures that the telemarketer uses this brief time productively and consistently gets across the information that will convince the prospects to act now.

The phone is a *dialogue* medium; prospects want to ''talk back,'' and the phone lets them do it. By using a script, a telemarketer can get this two-way process going so that 50 percent of every call is listening to the prospect—yet the telemarketer can still stay in control of the call. This capability for building rapport through two-way communication is one of the major advantages telemarketing has over other marketing media, and scripting allows the telemarketer to maximize it.

TYPES OF SCRIPTS

There are three basic types of scripts. The *key point* or *outline script* is basically a checklist giving the skilled telemarketer the essential topics to cover during the call. Key point scripts are most often used when there is a strong relationship between your organization and the prospect. They may be used to accomplish any type of objective.

The *dialogue guide* is more "fleshed out" than the key point script and tracks each stage of the call. Dialogue guides often provide alternative *branches*—depending on the specific needs the prospect expresses—to guide the telemarketer through each stage toward the desired objective, whether it is a sale, an appointment, gathering information, or customer service. The dialogue guide takes maximum advantage of the two-way communication possible on the phone. It is particularly useful when specific needs must be established before an objective can be met.

Verbatim scripts are much more mechanical and one-sided. They are used when an unvarying, word-for-word presentation by less skilled telemarketers is required. Generally, this type is used for low-ticket, high-volume calls, where the audience is previously targeted for the product or service.

CHOOSING THE BEST TYPE OF SCRIPT

There are five interrelated factors to consider when deciding which type of script best meets your needs. The **first factor** is *the difficulty of the call objective.* I previously ranked call objectives in descending order of difficulty:

- Sale
- Appointment
- Up-sell/cross-sell
- Information gathering/surveys
- Customer service

But the *actual* difficulty level of the call also depends on the **second factor:** the *relationship status* of the prospect:

- Cold call
- Response to injury
- Current customer

The **third factor** to consider is the *product or service* itself (whether it is a high-ticket, low-volume situation, such as office equipment or computers, or a low-ticket, high-volume product, like computer supplies or subscription services). Generally, the more your product or service tends toward the upper price range, the more likely you are to need the more sophisticated approach of the dialogue guide.

The **fourth factor** to consider is your *prospect audience.* Should you establish needs in order to meet your call objective, or have you already identified an audience known to have a specific need? For example, if you are selling computer supplies to known purchasers of minicomputers, you have already targeted a specific need, and a verbatim script would probably work well. If you are making appointments for field sales representatives to sell electronic workstations, then your calls will need to establish the presence of specific needs, and the dialogue guide approach would be more advisable.

The **fifth factor** to consider when determining the type of script to use is the skill level of your telemarketing staff. What type of person will you have on the phone? A highly skilled sales professional working full-time to sell a sophisticated, high-ticket product is not going to need a verbatim script. A part-time telemarketer making survey calls will definitely need a verbatim script because you'll want to ensure consistency on every call. Figure 10-1 summarizes these five factors.

Figure 10-1. Factors to consider when planning your script.

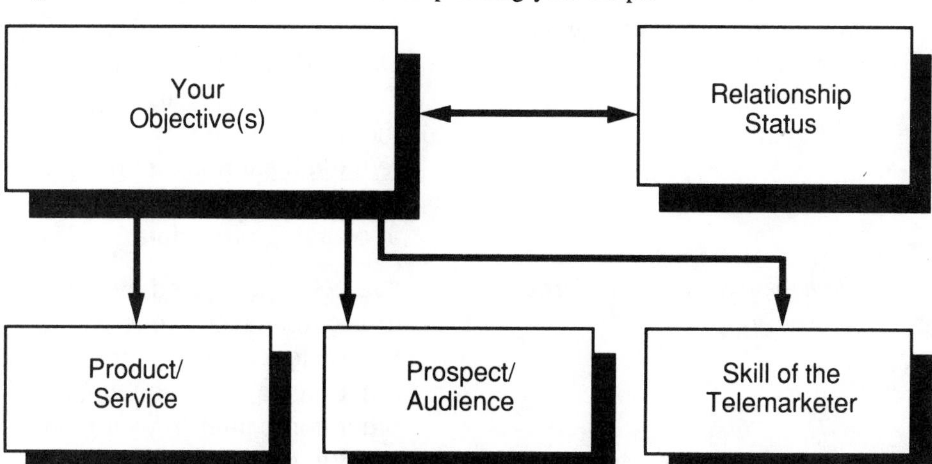

TEN TIPS FOR BETTER SCRIPTS

All good scripts have ten characteristics in common. They use *language and phrasing* to do the following:

1. Capture attention in the first fifteen seconds of the call
2. Press emotional "hot buttons"
3. Compress the message into direct, concise dialogue
4. Reflect the prospect's cultural level
5. Sound conversational
6. Build a logical case

And they are *structured* as follows:

7. To provide for interaction
8. To build a pattern of "yeses"
9. To have more than one objective
10. To enable the telemarketer to move easily from one stage or branch of the call to another

The following sample appointment-setting dialogue guide illustrates the kind of language and phrasing necessary for an effective script. It was originally printed on a single $8\frac{1}{2}''$-by-$11''$ page, using both sides. The sheet was then laminated to withstand constant handling.

DIALOGUE GUIDE

[Use prospect's name. Repeat name. Insert name of prospect's industry.]	Hello, Mr./Ms. ________. This is ________ calling for DataCo. Mr./Ms. ________, DataCo has <u>saved</u> its <u>clients</u> in the ________ industry a <u>remarkable</u> amount of <u>money</u> in the way they handle their accounting procedures.
[To hook interest, be enthusiastic and sincere!]	I've been <u>authorized</u> by our district manager to offer you a <u>free review</u> of your accounting functions to show you what other companies in your field are doing to <u>save money.</u>

CLOSE

[Get to the point. Ask for appointment early and often! If yes, record date and bridge to Probes. If no, go to Objection Guide. If still no, seek referral or send literature.]

Our district manager will be in your area next week. What day would be convenient for him to stop by? Would Thursday afternoon or Friday morning be convenient for you?

First, this script *captures attention in the first fifteen seconds* of the call by making a strong statement up front: DataCo saved money for other clients in your industry, and it is offering a free review. This gives the prospect a reason to stay on the phone and listen. In those first fifteen seconds of the call, your script must help the telemarketer pull the prospect away from every other concern and *listen.*

Second, the language is conversational in style, but not clichéd. It strongly presses *emotional "hot buttons"*—twice using the prospect's name, twice expressing the idea of saving money, and mentioning other clients in the prospect's industry. Also, it is *direct and concise,* getting to the point of the call without wasted words.

Finally, the language is on the *same cultural level* as that of the prospects, who were owners or officers of small to medium-sized businesses. Note words like "accounting procedures," "review of accounting functions," and "authorized." Before analyzing the rest of this script, let's look at some additional tips on scripting language.

Scripting for Visual and Emotional Impact

Because the phone is audio-only, you won't be able to use eye-catching photo layouts or graphics to support your case. But that doesn't mean you don't provide visual support. Instead of physical images, your script must incorporate strong *word images* and *power words* that create and hold attention. In the previous example, the words "district manager" conducting a "review of accounting procedures" might be considered a word image. By using just a short phrase, it conveys the benefit but allows the prospect to visualize the details.

A word image paints a picture for the prospect in a short phrase. For example, the words "black tie affair" immediately create in the hearer's mind the image of a sophisticated gala, with the men wearing tuxedos, the women in formal evening dresses. Every good script uses word image phrasing like this so the prospect can "see" the product or quickly visualize its benefits.

A second way to make the audio-only aspect of the phone work for you is to use emotionally charged ''power words'' in your scripts. Every industry has its own ''hot buttons'' that anyone involved in the field is aware of, and your scripts should certainly include these when appropriate. You've got a story to tell about your product or service and very little time in which to tell it, so your script must build emotional involvement from the start by using carefully selected power words.

One basic rule is to use the prospect's name and then repeat it. It's a single truth: People respond positively to the sound of their own name. Incorporating certain words and avoiding others are also important to achieve emotional impact. The following is a list of useful power words:

Power Words

affordable	*exclusive*	*scientific*
classic	*far-sighted*	*sensible*
clean	*fashionable*	*smooth*
compatible	*first*	*sophisticated*
crucial	*guaranteed*	*standard*
customized	*impeccable*	*substantial*
distinctive	*inexpensive*	*superior*
diversified	*innovative*	*tested*
durable	*new*	*timely*
efficient	*optimum*	*time-saving*
elegant	*personalized*	*unsurpassed*
exciting	*risk-free*	*value*

Sales trainer Tom Hopkins recommends avoiding legalistic terms like ''contract.'' He suggests ''agreement'' as an alternative. Likewise, find substitutes for words like ''buy'' and ''sell,'' which, though direct may raise negative connotations on the phone, where the buyer cannot see the seller. For example, you can substitute ''start service'' for ''buy'' in many types of scripts.

Logic

Logic is more convincing on the phone than in person because the communicator can't be seen, so that body language and other visual distractions don't interfere with the message. Therefore, on the phone, the power of logic is harder to resist. Use this to your advantage by building your script around the most convincing facts. Give the prospect sound ''reasons why'':

- Why the prospect should listen to you
- Why the prospect benefits from your product or service
- Why the prospect should act now

If you can anticipate these questions and develop strong, logical responses to them, you're on the way to a successful script.

Structuring a Script

In addition to using language carefully to fit the audio medium and incorporating strong logic, every good script must be properly *structured.* Basically, this means it must support both the interactive dialogue and alternatives that dialogue creates on the phone. Recall that the DataCo script provided an early opportunity for dialogue because the close (a request for an appointment) followed immediately after the attention getter. Scripts don't always structure the close so early in the call. But good ones draw the prospect into dialogue quickly—remember, it's a fifty-fifty exchange.

The second point to notice about the DataCo script is that it anticipates the prospect's possible responses to the request for an appointment *and gives the telemarketer a way to deal with either alternative.* Let's look at the remainder of the DataCo script to see this structure.

DIALOGUE GUIDE

CLOSE

[Get to the point. Ask for appointment early and often! If yes, record date and bridge to Probes. If no, go to Objection Guide. If still no, seek referral or send literature.]	Our district manager will be in your area next week. What day would be convenient for him to stop by? Would Thursday afternoon or Friday morning be convenient for you?
BRIDGE TO PROBES	So that our district manager knows what materials to bring with him, I'd like to ask you a few questions.

GENERAL PROBES

[Use Industry Probes if available; otherwise use General Probes.]	How do you process your accounting functions? Internally or externally?
[Make notes on Telemarketing Report as to method used.]	How do you process payroll? Manually or on a computer? What type of computer do you have? How do you process your payables and receivables?

What about invoicing, inventory, order entry?
Are you planning to change your method of processing any of these in the next twelve months?

CONFIRM APPOINTMENT

[Repeat prospect's name; give day, date, and time.]

Fine, Mr./Ms. ________, our district manager will come by on [*day*], the [*date*] of [*month*], at [*time*]. I'll just reconfirm your address. I have. . . .

[Read address from the prospect card.]

[Repeat date of appointment.]

Thank you very much for your time, Mr./Ms. ________. Our district manager will look forward to meeting you on the [*date*].

WHEN PROSPECT REFUSES TO MAKE AN APPOINTMENT, SEND BROCHURE!

[If yes, bridge to Probes.]

Would you be interested in receiving a brochure on DataCo's services?

[Use Industry Probes, if available, or General Probes.]

[Record responses on Telemarketing Report.]

So that we send only the information you'd be interested in, I'd like to ask you a few questions to pinpoint your needs.

Thank you very much for your time Mr./Ms. ________. We'll mail that information out today. Have a pleasant day!

SEEK A REFERRAL

[Asking for a referral will depend on the prospect's reaction to your presentation. It never hurts to ask!]

Do you know any colleagues who might be interested in learning how to save money on their accounting procedures?

[If no, thank prospect. If yes, note contact name and number, and go to Close.]	Thank you very much, Mr./Ms. ________. We'll contact him/her right away.

Notice that the script supports three possible prospect responses:

Prospect Response	*Script*
Appointment made	Probe for information
No appointment	Send brochure/referral
No interest at all	Get a referral

The two-column format supports this branching well because it allows the entire script to fit on one laminated page printed on both sides. Such a script could easily be ''embedded'' in software so that it would appear on a computer screen, along with prospect data from a computerized data base. Other script formats, such as bottom and side tabs, are also useful. Sample scripts using alternate formats are included in Chapter 11.

CONSTRUCTING A SCRIPT

The ''classical approach'' to script development starts by identifying your *call objectives*. This is the most important part of script development and the most often overlooked. It really involves two decisions:

1. What is the primary goal—the action you want the prospect to take during the call?
2. If you don't achieve the primary goal—and 90 percent of the time you won't—what is the next most important objective you will be satisfied with?

In other words, you need to decide what minimally will make the call productive. In business-to-business telemarketing, you will nearly always want to determine at least two call objectives in advance, and sometimes three.

In addition to assuring better productivity, secondary objectives give the telemarketer another way to make a call successful in some form. From the standpoint of a telemarketer who makes upwards of 100 calls a day and gets a negative response on 90 percent or more, this is absolutely essential. Otherwise it would be impossible to maintain the kind of positive attitude that telemarketing requires. More important, it is a way to make most of the calls productive because secondary objectives allow the TMR to collect valuable information for your data base. The following list of typical primary and secondary call objectives may help you think of others that relate to your specific situation. List your own primary and secondary call objectives on the worksheet.

Primary Goals

- Get a sale.
- Make an appointment.
- Qualify prospect for subsequent telephone contact for the sale.

Secondary Goals

- Get a referral.
- Get information necessary for a future sale (for example, the names of decision makers).
- Build rapport by sending a brochure.
- Find out when to call back in the future.

Worksheet
Identify Your Objectives

The primary action I want the prospect to take as a result of this call is:

____

____

____

Secondary objectives for each call are:

____

____

____

____

Determining your objectives is key to developing an effective script, but it's only concerned with *your side* of the call. Really good scripts are good because they give the telemarketer ammunition for handling all the initial questions on the *other side*—in the prospect's mind:

Who's calling?
Can I trust this person?
Why am I being called?
How long will this take?
Why should I listen?
What's in it for me?

These questions are present in everyone's mind when they answer the phone just because of the nature of the medium. The ringing phone is an interruption by an unseen caller who may or may not be worthy of time and trust.

A good script focuses attention on the call in the first fifteen seconds. Those first seconds are crucial for establishing that the call is worth the prospect's time, that it will take only a specific amount of time, and that the caller—even though unseen—has something that makes listening worthwhile. In other words, the first few seconds of the call can be scripted to answer the prospect's key questions and start *building a relationship*. During a properly scripted call, whether outbound or inbound, this process begins with the introduction and continues through every stage of the call.

THE STAGES OF THE CALL

Telemarketing calls involve the eight stages shown in Figure 10-2. If you're familiar with face-to-face selling, you'll recognize them. Though these fundamentals of the selling process are well known, I define them in a fairly elementary way so every reader has a common information base in adapting "classical" selling to a telephone context.

Introduction

The first impression and rapport building during the first fifteen seconds of a call not only give the telemarketer initial control of the call, but also help reduce objections during later stages. The following *introduction checklist* will help you make sure the introduction covers all the bases:

Identification:	Your name and the prospect's name Your company's name
Attention getter:	Why prospect should interrupt his or her activity for this call

Figure 10-2. Parts of a call/dialogue guide.

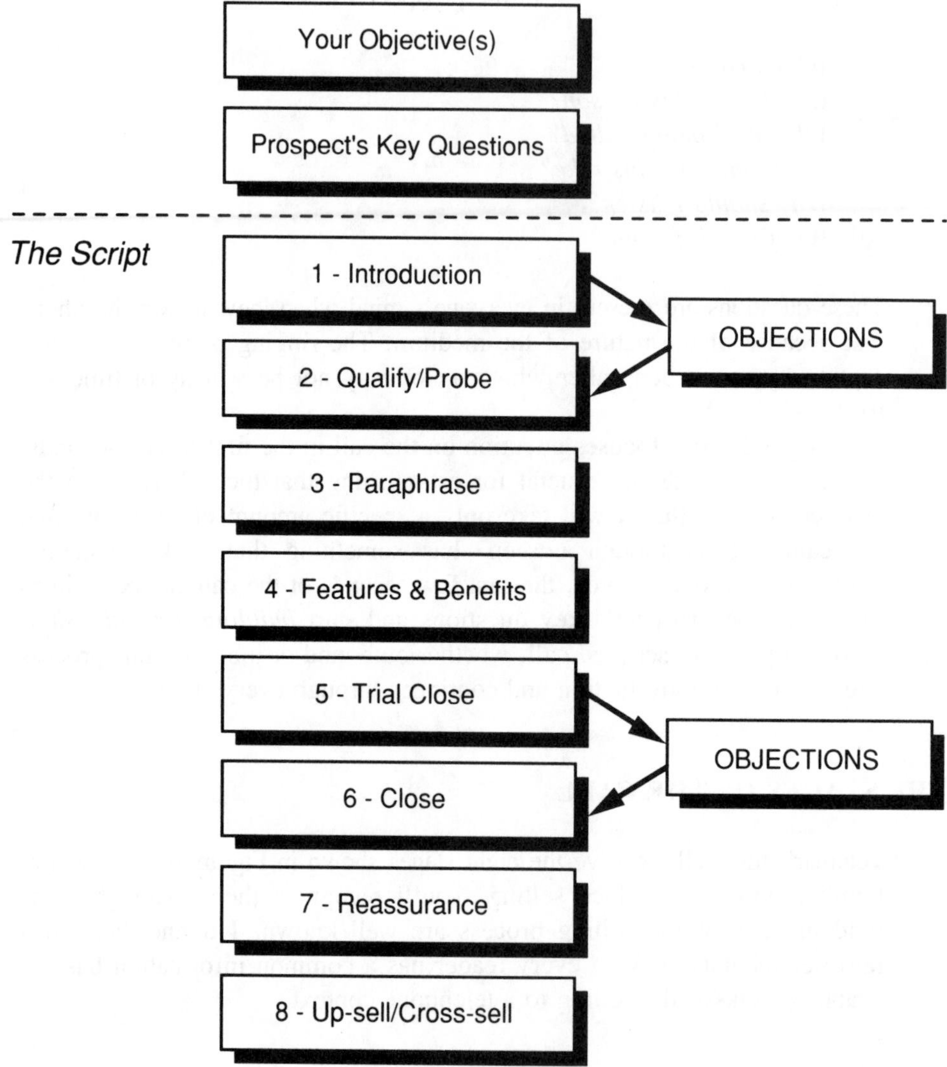

Source: Phone for Success(TM) training program, Joel Linchitz Consulting Services, New York, N.Y.

Reason for call:	Why prospect is being called
Initial benefit statement:	What's in it for the prospect
Request for time:	How long the call will take

The *identification* answers the question, "Who's calling me?" It should use the prospect's name, your name, and your company name.

The *attention getter* cuts through the "static" raised by the prospect's mental questions. It should briefly hold the prospect's attention so you can complete your opening statement.

In the DataCo script, the actual company name was an attention getter because it is a nationally known data-processing services firm. In addition to name recognition, the offer of a "free review" or any other appropriate premium can function as an attention getter. And there are many other types of attention-getting devices. Here are some common ones with examples:

• *Personal referral.* Short of calling your own customers, the personal referral is the strongest type of introduction you can use. It grabs attention and generates trust.

Hello, Mr./Ms. ________. This is ________ with ________ Corp. I'm calling at the suggestion of one of your colleagues, Bill Smith.

• *Industry reference.* The industry reference means using the name of a current customer who is in the same business as the prospect. An industry reference gets the prospect's attention because there is common ground between your company and the prospect's.

Hello Mr./Ms. ________. This is ________ calling from American Marketing. I'm calling because many banks in your area, such as Pacific Trust and Goldstar, are currently using our services.

• *Specific competition.* Similar to an industry reference, this is an even more pointed attention-getting device.

We provide low-cost accounting services to Alberts Bank and Trust right across the street.

• *Brand name identification.* Using a well-known organization that is already a customer—when true, of course—is an effective attention getter because it puts the prospect's company in the same category as such well-known companies.

I'm calling because General Motors, IBM, and Digital Equipment use our services.

• *Affinity group.* Creating affinity groups means recognizing the prospect as a member of a definable group by developing a customized program or discount especially for them.

We have a special program for members of the chamber of commerce such as yourself.

• *Major event.* An "event" may be a price rise, the passage of a new law, or even a natural disaster.

I'm calling because 30 percent of all homeowners who suffered damage in Hurricane Alice were not fully reimbursed by their insurance company.

• *Name Recognition.* Some organizations grab attention by virtue of their name alone.

I'm calling from the IRS!

• *Established relationship.* By far the strongest attention getter is a reference to a current relationship between the prospect and your organization.

Good evening Mr./Ms. ________. As one of our valued Goldstar Bank customers. . . .

Linking Attention Getters to Initial Benefit Statements

Typically, your introduction should link the Attention Getter to the Initial Benefits Statement. Once you've grabbed the prospect's attention, you want to quickly answer the questions "Why should I listen?" and "What's in it for me?"

In scripting this key part of your introduction, keep in mind that telemarketing works best when calls are organized on a "campaign" basis. In this way, the linkage of attention getter and initial benefits statement will create a natural sense of urgency on the phone. Also, once you've answered the questions in the prospect's mind, the Request for Time is a reasonable one because you've satisfied the prospect's curiosity. (The request for time may also be implied—for example, "I'd like to take a moment to tell you. . . ." If prospects don't want to hear it, they will say so.) The following examples will help you focus on this important tie-in:

• *Major event + initial benefits statement.*

Mr. ________, 30 percent of all people who suffered damage during Hurricane Alice were not fully reimbursed for their loss by their insurance company. I'm calling about a new homeowner's policy that many of your neighbors are getting to protect themselves against that kind of loss.

• *Brand name identification + initial benefits statement.*

Ms. ________, I'm calling because General Motors, IBM, and Digital Equipment are using our service to save time and money in processing their payroll checks.

• *Affinity group + initial benefits statement.*

I'm calling about a special program we developed exclusively for printers like you that will cut your equipment downtime by as much as 30 percent.

• *Personal referral + initial benefits statement.*

I'm calling because Bill Jones from ABC Company is using our telephone service, and he thought you might be interested in hearing about how much money we've been able to save him by lowering his long-distance telephone costs.

• *Established relationship + initial benefits statement.*

Good Evening Mr. ________. This is ________ from Goldstar Bank. Mr. ________, as a valued Goldstar customer, you have been invited to open a credit account that entitles you to a $5,000 preapproved line of credit.

Use the following worksheet to write an introduction for a call objective related to your product or service.

Worksheet
Script Introduction Checklist

☐ Identification
☐ Attention getter
☐ Reason for call
☐ Initial benefits statement
☐ Request for time

Using the checklist, write out a call objective and an introduction appropriate to it.

Primary call objective:

____

____

____

Introduction:

____

____

____

____

____

____

____

Probing Questions

Typically, in the next stage of the call, you want prospects to open up and tell you about their specific needs. To accomplish this, your script must provide probing questions, which serve three purposes:

1. They *elicit relevant information,* such as needs your product can fulfill, when the prospect will be ready to buy, other decision makers involved in the purchase, and so forth.
2. They *involve the prospect* in the communication process, which builds rapport and lets you hear—in the prospect's voice quality—many clues to how to direct the rest of the call.
3. They *qualify the prospect,* so if this isn't the right person to be talking with or the prospect has no need for what you have to offer, you can quickly move on to the real decision maker or terminate the call.

In summary, scripting probes in advance helps the telemarketer control the call.

Probing questions are of two types: open and closed ended. Open-ended probes are the "who, what, when, how" questions that get the prospect talking about business needs and other relevant data you need to tailor the presentation of your service or product on the phone. Closed-ended probes are yes/no questions; they help you focus on specific points of information that the open-ended probes reveal. You will usually want a careful mix of both types of probing questions in your script. In regard to a good mix of probing questions, recall the General Probes section of the DataCo sample script earlier in this chapter:

How do you process your accounting functions? Internally or externally?
How do you process payroll?
What type of computer do you have?
How do you process your payables and receivables?
What about invoicing, inventory, order entry?
Are you planning to change your method of processing any of these in the next twelve months?

Open-ended questions are particularly important because they get the prospect thinking and talking about his or her business needs. As important, they give the telemarketer the opportunity to *listen*. The information gained is useful for focusing the rest of the call on the prospect's needs. Even if they aren't helpful as information, the prospect's tone and choice of words are always critical. Is the prospect in a hurry, enthusiastic, tired, curious? All this and more are revealed in responses to open-ended probes. The key to developing good open-ended questions is to first identify a need your product and service can fill, then to think of ways to get prospects to talk about their needs. The following examples use several techniques to uncover needs:

- *Multiple choice:*

How would you describe your current investment objectives?—short-term income, quick profits, long-term savings?

- *Key features:*

If you could design the perfect copier for your business, what are the three most important features it would have to have?

- *Scale of one to ten:*

On a scale of one to ten, how important is *[Name a major feature of your product]* in your decision to purchase?

- *General:*

What is it you like best about your current banking relationship?

Closed-ended probes can be used to help you build the pattern of "yeses" that helps make a script, and the call, a success. The old rule that says "Never ask a question unless you know the answer" applies here. In scripting closed-ended questions, phrase them to get specific information that pins down the prospect ("On the basis of what you have told me, can I assume that you own your copiers?") while keeping the prospect involved in the call. Because the best way to learn is to try it yourself, use the following worksheet to write some probing questions related to your product or service.

Worksheet
Probing Question Checklist

1. Probe to elicit relevant information.
2. Probe to involve the prospect.
3. Probe to qualify the prospect.

Identify these specific business needs your product or service can fill. Then write probing questions to uncover those needs.

Need:________________________________

Open-ended question:________________________________

____

Closed-ended question:________________________________

Need:________________________________

Open-ended question:________________________________

____

Closed-ended question:________________________________

____

Need:________________________________

Open-ended question:________________________________

____

Closed-ended question:________________________________

____

Paraphrase of the Prospect's Relevant Needs

Paraphrasing or summarizing the prospect's responses to probing questions is an essential part of selling a complex business product or service because in a very subtle way, the repetition of needs allows the telemarketer to do the following:

- Clarify the most relevant needs.
- Bridge smoothly to features and benefits that meet only primary needs.
- Build a pattern of "yeses" that makes it more difficult for the prospect to resist making the commitment you want. If the prospect must compromise, it will not be on a primary need, but on a secondary issue where compromise matters less.

Paraphrasing is one of the most difficult skills to teach to TMRs because it requires them to take what the prospect has said and put it in their own words. Paraphrases usually begin with one of the following:

In other words
What I understand you to be saying is
If I can show you a way to get more ________ at a better price, would you at least consider an offer?

The DataCo sample script used an "up-front" trial close that did not require a paraphrasing stage. Another appointment-setting script developed for the office automation division of a major electronics manufacturer illustrates this stage. Here are the probing questions and features/benefits sections of that script. The objective is to set an appointment for a copier demonstration, not to sell the copier:

PROBING QUESTIONS

[*Use a mixture of open- and closed-ended probes to involve the prospect.*]	Can you tell me the make and model number of your present copier(s)? About how old is/are your copier(s)?
[*If leased, find out type and term of lease.*]	Do you own, lease, or rent your present copier?
[*Record whether applications are halftones, transparencies, artwork, invoices, computer output.*]	What kind of applications do you have?

[*Record number/month.*]

How many copies per month do you make?

[*Listen for features our copier has and paraphrase.*]

If you could get a new copier tomorrow, what kind of features would you like it to have?

PARAPHRASE

[*Summarize prospect's statements in your own words.*]

If I could show you a new copier that could do ________, would you be interested in a ten-minute demonstration?

FEATURES/BENEFITS

[*Present only the features elicited through probing. Remember you are selling the appointment, not the copier. So one feature/benefit ought to be enough to entice the prospect.*]

You mentioned you would like a copier that could do ________. Because our copier has ________, that means you can do ________.

Use the following worksheet to write paraphrases of perceived or expressed needs that allow you to talk about specific features and benefits your product or service offers. Remember, *relevant* needs are those needs that your product or service can fulfill. Although your script may not ultimately use every paraphrase of needs you develop, it is essential to prepare as many as possible in advance so your telemarketers can select those that fit best on any call.

Worksheet
Paraphrase of the Prospect's Relevant Needs

Expressed or perceived need:____

____

Paraphrase:____

____

____

Expressed or perceived need:____________________

Paraphrase:____________________

Expressed or perceived need:____________________

Paraphrase:____________________

Expressed or perceived need:____________________

Paraphrase:____________________

Presentation of Features/Benefits

A *feature* is an inherent aspect of a product or service. A *benefit* answers the all-important question: "What's in it for me?" Benefits, in other words, are what features *do* for a prospect. So it is benefits, not features, that sell.

Your task in developing the features/benefits section of your script is to *define the benefits of your product in terms of how they answer a specific need.* You've already begun this process by developing statements of anticipated needs that your product or service fulfills. Now you will need to tie those needs to specific features and corresponding benefits. This is where it is especially important to remember the guidelines on scripting *language*. To the extent possible, use word images to paint a picture of how your product's benefits meet needs. Work in some of the "power words" previously discussed, and get to the point concisely. Here is an example from a script developed for an airfreight company. The objective was to convince prospects to specify the company on their next shipment.

Probing Questions

Mr./Ms. ________, because we customize our program to suit your individual needs, before I describe it to you, I'd like to get some information about your company and your present airfreight program.

How often does your company receive airfreight shipments?
What do you do when you are expecting an air shipment and it doesn't arrive?
What steps do you take to locate your shipments?
How many calls do you make?

[*Wait for answer; then paraphrase their answers into a question.*]

1. *If you could have easier access to information on your air shipments, would that be of help to you?*
2. *In other words, what you are saying is that you do not have the control you need or would like on your shipments?*

Fly-By-Nite's program for [parts managers/purchasing agents/ad agencies] has several features that solve the problems you mentioned.

Feature

When you specify Fly-By-Nite, we assign someone to personally monitor your incoming shipments. He has total responsibility for seeing that your shipment was picked up on time and delivered to your door as quickly as possible.

Benefit

The advantage to you is that when you need information on your incoming shipment, all you have to do is call our special number, speak to your personal expeditor, and get advance arrival information on any of your shipments. You won't have to make special calls and waste your valuable time. Or if you prefer not to call, we can alert you by phone at no extra cost and give advance arrival information for each and every one of your shipments.

Because most telemarketing calls are brief, you will ordinarily not present every feature and benefit of your product or service. But it is important to fully analyze and script all the features and benefits your product offers because you cannot predict which will be useful on any given call. For example, the complete features/benefits analysis of Fly-By-Nite Airfreight might look like this:

Feature	*Benefit*
Personal expeditor	Monitors location of your package throughout shipment
Special telephone number	Advance information One call saves time
Telephone alert	No extra cost Saves time
Next-day delivery before noon regardless of size or weight	Fastest source for all shipment needs
Eight-hour delivery	Meets your deadline in an emergency situation

Many scripts are far too wordy because every feature and benefit is discussed. On any given call, only one or two of the features and benefits ordinarily will be relevant. You will usually put your strongest feature/benefit up front, as an attention getter. On the following worksheet, list all the features and benefits of your product or service in order of their importance. In this way, when you put your script together, a telemarketer can select the statements that best match expressed or perceived needs.

Worksheet
Presentation of Features and Benefits

For the key features of your product, list a corresponding benefit in order of importance:

Features	Benefits
____________________	____________________
____________________	____________________
____________________	____________________

________________________	________________________
________________________	________________________
________________________	________________________
________________________	________________________
________________________	________________________

Trial Close

The trial close is often in the form of a probing question, like the following:

How does what I've said sound so far?
Does it sound as if our product would fit your needs?

For example, the trial close section of the Fly-By-Nite Airfreight script runs as follows:

Would having this kind of personalized service, at no extra cost, be of value to you?

[If prospect objects, use one of the following paragraphs. If prospect says yes, go directly to Close.]

1. Mr./Ms. ________, one of the most important reasons you use an airfreight company is because you have an emergency and you need the fastest possible service. In addition to our personalized services I mentioned, we pride ourselves on our speed of delivery. All packages regardless of size and weight are delivered before noon of the next day. If you have an extreme emergency, we can get your package to you within eight hours. *How does what I've said sound so far?*

[Go to Close.]

2. You mentioned that you receive from *[competitor's name]*. If we pick up your shipment before 5 P.M., it will ride on *[airline]* flight and you will receive delivery in the morning. *Would having this kind of delivery fit your needs?*

[If prospect mentions competitor, make him aware of other services he is not getting, and proceed to Close.]

At this stage, you need to find out whether the prospect is with you, or if objections have formed in his or her mind. If you get a positive response to your trial close, this lets you smoothly make the transition to a close. The trial close gives you another "yes" statement and therefore builds momentum to the close.

If you get a negative response to the trial close—and you will more often than not—you must be prepared to respond to it and turn the conversation back to the close, as shown in the previous example. It is good to develop a separate objection response guide for each script and put it in flip chart form so that the telemarketer can easily handle common objections. Objection response guides are discussed fully in Chapter 12.

The Close

The heart of any company is selling, and the heart of selling is closing. As in face-to-face selling, the close in telephone selling can be direct or assumed. The direct close is just that—it asks for the sale directly. For example, the Fly-By-Nite Airfreight script uses a direct close:

On your next air shipment, what I would like you to do is to specify Fly-By-Nite Airfreight, and give us an opportunity to show you how our service can really benefit you. Would this be all right with you? When do you think your next shipment would be—within the next week, two weeks, month? I would like to call you back, after you have had the opportunity to use our services, to discuss our performance in terms of your needs.

[Optional]

I'm going to fill out a profile card for your account so that when you do call, your personal expeditor will have all the information he needs about your personal requirements.

Would you like a telephone alert?
Would next day before noon delivery be all right?
What is the frequency with which you ship?
What are the weights that you normally receive?

The DataCo sample script at the beginning of this chapter provided an example of a "forced choice" assumed close:

CLOSE

[*Get to the point; ask for appointment early and often! If yes, record date and bridge to probes. If no, go to objection guide. If still no, seek referral or send literature.*]	Our district manager will be in your area next week. What day would be convenient for him to stop by? Would Thursday afternoon or Friday morning be convenient for you?

Another type of assumed close assumes the sale is agreeable and asks a question to get the ball rolling (for example, "Can I have your address so we can get you started right away?" or "Based on what you told me, it seems that our investment fund would meet your needs. Let me explain some of the options you have in opening an account.").

If your call objective is higher on the scale of difficulty (see Chapter 3), it is best to prepare both types of closing statements for your script. For less difficult call objectives, such as asking for referrals or setting appointments, a direct close is often sufficient. Use the following worksheet to develop a close for your script based on your own call objective(s).

Worksheet
The Close

Using your own call objective, write a closing statement. Try to write it in both the assumed and direct close format.

Call objective:____

____

____

Closing statement:______________________________________

____

____

____

____

____

____

____

____

Reassurance

Your objective in scripting this stage of the call is to end the call on a supportive note and prevent "buyer's remorse." Reassurances can take different forms, depending on the type of commitment you obtained:

- *Thank the customer.*

We appreciate your business today Mr. Jones, and you can count on us to be there when you need us.

- *Verify customer information.*

Let's just verify the address for your order, and we'll ship it today.

- *Cement the customer's decision.*

You've made an excellent choice.

- *Provide customer service information.*

If you have any questions, use our toll-free 800 number, twenty-four hours a day, seven days a week.

Scripting for Secondary Objectives

On a successful call where you've achieved your primary objective, you may sense an opening for an extra sale. But no matter how good you become at controlling your calls, you won't meet your primary call objective every time or even most of the time. These are the reasons to always script one or more secondary objectives, especially for outbound calls having more difficult objectives. This way you can maximize every selling opportunity on these calls, and on inbound calls as well.

On successful outbound calls and on many inbound calls, some of your best opportunities are for up-selling and cross-selling.

- *Up-selling* means asking for an additional order, a longer subscription period, a higher-priced item, and so forth. In some situations, it can mean making an appointment instead of simply getting survey information or a referral name.
- *Cross-selling* means asking for an order for a related item or service, in addition to the one agreed upon.

Here are some examples:

Since you are buying safety goggles, I should make you aware of the price breaks we have available for volume purchases.

As long as you're purchasing the respirators, Mr. Jones, we have a special on the filters that go with them this week.

On outbound calls where you haven't achieved the primary objectives, your script should support a lesser, secondary objective. Very often, when prospects haven't agreed to the action you sought, they will agree to a lesser commitment. You'll get it only if you ask for it, though, so write it into your script.

- If you don't get an appointment, ask to send a catalog or other information.
- If you don't get a sale, ask for a referral.

Use the following worksheet to write out some possible up-selling, cross-selling, and secondary commitments that relate to your offer.

Worksheet
Secondary Commitments

Imagine you've closed on your primary commitment. Now write an appropriate up-selling or cross-selling statement:________________

____

____

____

____

Imagine the prospect hasn't agreed to your primary objective. Now write some possible secondary commitments that will give you a reason to call back:

____

____

____

____

SUMMARY

Scripting every stage of the call is recommended because a script supports the three main tools available to telemarketers: voice, message, and drawing the prospect into a dialogue. Scripting is also recommended because it summarizes what the telemarketer must accomplish with the call, it helps reinforce the two-way process of communication involved, and it helps build rapport.

The three types of scripts available were discussed: outline, dialogue guide, and verbatim. The chapter also provided guidelines to help decide which type of script is best for your particular purposes. A sample script was shown early in the chapter and was used throughout to provide examples of certain important aspects of scripting.

The eight stages of every call were discussed along with the specifics of constructing a script, use of word images and power words, logic and structure, and ten tips for better scripts. Worksheets were provided for developing your own objectives for each of the eight stages of scripting.

CHAPTER

11

Developing Your Own Script

AT this point, you should be ready to put your own script together. How do you start? The answer is to put down your pencil and forget about writing for now. Turn on your tape recorder, and pretend you are calling a prospect. Use your worksheets to guide you through each stage of the call. Try out the wording you've written for each stage. (Assume for the moment that the prospect does not object to your call or your presentation.)

When you've finished recording, transcribe the tape. You can use the worksheet that follows. Make notes for where you need to add instructions. This is especially true for the transitional points—from the introduction to the probing stage and from the presentation to the trial close. At this point, you should have a good first draft. You'll still need to write an objection response guide to accompany your script (Chapter 12). Before using it in full-scale calling, you'll need to test your script (Chapter 18). When you've completed both chapters, you will have a polished, professional script, ready to support your telemarketing strategy.

To enhance your script development efforts, including wording at every stage, transitions, and instructions, I have included several full-length sample scripts. Various types of business products, services, and call objectives are covered. You may want to adapt them for your own use or simply use them as a starting point for your script.

Worksheet
Dialogue Guide Outline

Your objective(s)—What action do I want prospects to take?

1. *Introduction*—Who's calling? Can I trust this person? Why am I being called? How long will this take? Why should I listen? What's in it for me?

2. *Qualify/probe*—Open-ended and closed-ended probes

3. *Paraphrase prospect's needs*

4. *Features/benefits corresponding to needs*—Sales message

5. *Trial close*

6. *Close*—Direct, assumptive, alternate choice

____

____

7. *Reassurance*—You can count on us.

____

____

8. Up-sell/cross-sell/secondary objective

____

____

SAMPLE SCRIPT A

The following script was developed for an insurance brokerage, which used it for a telemarketing campaign to set appointments for field sales representatives to sell commercial accounts. Note that alternatives are provided at the introductory, probing, and closing stages.

INTRODUCTION 1

[Speak in a friendly, confident, and businesslike tone.]

Mr./Ms.________, good morning/afternoon. This is ________ from US Insurance Brokerage. The reason for my call is that we've had remarkable success in helping organizations like yours get greater control over the cost of their insurance.

I'd like to take a moment to tell you a little more about USIB and how we might be able to help you manage the skyrocketing costs of business insurance.

[Make a smooth transaction to Probing Questions.]

Before I do that, I'd like to ask you a few short questions regarding your present insurance needs.

[Go to Probing Questions.]

Introduction 2

[Speak in a friendly, confident, and businesslike tone.]

Mr./Mrs. ________, good morning/afternoon. This is ________ from US Insurance Brokerage. The reason for my call is that we have provided creative insurance solutions for many organizations in the public and private sector.

We'd like the opportunity to introduce ourselves to you by giving you a review of your insurance program to make sure you're getting maximum value for what you're currently spending on premiums.

[Go to Close.]

Close

One of the senior partners of our firm is planning to be in your area next week. I have Tuesday morning or *[time]* on Thursday afternoon available. Which would be better for you? Great!

[If prospect does not agree, go on to answer his objections. If he does agree, go to Probing Questions.]

Before ________ stops by, I'd like to ask you a few quick questions that will help save time and make the meeting more productive.

Probing Questions

[Making appointments with prospects who have policy expiration dates from 90 to 120 days is ideal, 60–75 days is acceptable, and all others will be filed for later callbacks.]

Essential Questions

I understand you're in the ________ business. Could you tell me a little bit about what your firm does?

What do you consider to be your greatest insurance problem or need (low limits, difficulties in getting special coverage)?

After ________, what do you consider most important? When does your present insurance expire? What approximately do you now spend on insurance? Who is currently handling your insurance program?

[We are looking for premiums over $100,000. Try to get a breakdown on individual policies.]

Supplementary Questions

[Verify the number of employees and sales volume. Learn whether it's a public or private company. Learn the name of the company's accounting firm.]

Features/Benefits

Because we're one of the largest insurance brokerage organizations in the country, we have access to a range of insurance markets not normally available to other brokers, utilizing a network of professionals with expertise in many fields. USIB is able to resolve the most complex insurance problems and come up with alternatives that give our clients the most cost-effective business solutions.

Transition and Close

Because one of our senior partners is going to be in your area in the next two weeks, I'd like to have him drop by, say hello, and briefly review your insurance needs. I have ________ open and ________. Which would be more convenient for you?

Alternate Close

Based on what you've told me, I'd like to set up a meeting with one of the senior partners of our firm, who will give you a review of your current program to make sure your needs and goals are being met. Would Tuesday morning or Wednesday be better for you? Great! You'll be meeting with ________. Let me have your complete address.

SAMPLE SCRIPT B

The following sample shows how you can handle the problem of "penetrating screens" (such as secretaries and receptionists) to get through to the decision maker. Also notice that it provides three separate branches, depending on the prospect's responses to a survey.

Getting Through to the Decision Maker

Good morning/afternoon. May I speak with [*name on lead sheet*]?

[When decision maker comes on the line, go to Introduction. If the decision maker does not come on the line, use the following phrases to penetrate the screen.]

Receptionist: He/she is not in right now [or on vacation, away from his desk, on the phone, etc.].

Caller: When would be a good time to reach Mr./Ms. ________? *[Record time.]* Thank you. Bye.

Receptionist: Who is calling?

Caller: This is ________ from International Computer Corporation. Is he/she in?

[When decision maker comes on the line, go to Introduction.]

Receptionist: What is this about?

Caller: He/she *[or name of prospect company]* recently contacted us, and I'm calling back to answer some questions. Can you connect me please?

[When decision maker comes on the line, go to Introduction.]

Receptionist: Please leave your name and number. If he is interested, he will call you.

Caller: I'm going to be difficult to reach today. What's a good time to reach him today? Thank you. *[Terminate.]*

Introduction

Mr./Ms. ________, this is ________ calling for International Computer Corporation. We are a Fortune 500 company that has been processing returns for tax professionals for over twenty years. Mr./Mrs. ________, we'd like to thank you for having recently completed a survey that will help us determine the current and future needs of tax professionals like yourself. Based on the information we have, are you still using

- A service bureau *[Track A]*
- An in-house system *[Track B]*
- A manual system *[Track C]*

to process your returns?

Track A Script—Service Bureau

So far the results of our survey indicate that most professionals who use a service bureau are concerned about

- The speed of processing their returns
- The accuracy and quality of their tax returns
- And, of course, the price

[Optional]

To what extent does your current service bureau address those concerns?

[Wait for prospect's answer and reply.]

At ICC, we take pride in our ability to satisfy the needs and concerns of our clients by processing their tax returns quickly, accurately, and by providing the support they need to help them through the busy tax season. We do all this at a very competitive price.

[The following is optional if the prospect uses AAATax, Quiktax, or Lesstax.]

In fact, we can probably save you over 50 percent of your current cost for processing your tax returns.

Mr./Mrs. ________, our district manager ________ is in your area this week, and I'd like him/her to stop by and introduce himself/herself and give you a free cost:benefit comparison.

[Go to Close.]

Track B Script—In-house System

So far the results of our survey indicate that most professionals who have an in-house system are concerned about

- Having software updates to cover recent tax law changes
- Technical support to answer questions regarding their inputs
- Not being able to process all their different tax returns

To what extent does your system address these issues? At ICC, we've addressed these needs by providing our clients with a system they can access with their own computers. Our mainframe software gives our clients the ability to have the most up-to-date information available for preparing their tax returns. In addition, they get a full range of technical support and customer service support while freeing up their own computers for more pressing jobs.

Mr./Ms. ________, our district manager, ________ , is in your area this week, and I'd like him/her to stop by and introduce himself/herself and show you how some of our tax professional clients are using our system.

[Go to Close.]

Track C Script—Manual System

So far, the results of our survey indicate that most professionals who process their tax returns manually are concerned about

- The time it takes to perform the number crunching of preparing tax returns
- The accuracy of the numbers they input
- Their ever-increasing work load

At ICC, over 5,000 tax professionals have placed their trust in our ability to accurately process their returns and do it so easily that they have much more time to spend handling more accounts.

Mr./Ms. ________, our district manager, ________ , is in your area this week, and I'd like him/her to stop by and introduce himself/herself and show you why so many tax professionals who formerly processed their tax returns themselves have switched to using us.

[Go to Close.]

Close

Mr./Ms. ________, would [*day*] or [*day*] be better for you?

[If prospect answers with preferred day, go to Alternate Close.]

Alternate Close

Our representative has openings at ________, ________, and ________. Which time is best for you? *[Record time.]*

OK, Mr./Ms. ________. Let me make sure I have the correct address. Are you at *[street address and city*]? And what floor are you on? Is there a room or suite number? And we have your title as ____. Is that correct? *[Record correct data.]*

Confirmation

Thank you, Mr./Ms. ________. Our district manager, ________ , will be there on *[day]* at *[time]*. I think you are going to be very pleased. Bye.

SAMPLE SCRIPT C

The next sample script was developed for the telemarketing campaign of a large bank interested in increasing subscribers for its on-line financial information service. Because the service is fairly complex, the script provides more detail than the previous samples. Note that the presentation of features and benefits is variable, so the telemarketer discusses only features and benefits tailored to prospects' individual interests.

INTRODUCTION

Good morning/afternoon, Mr./Ms. ________. This is ________ from Bigbank International Report. We recently sent you information with an offer to try a unique on-line information service called International Report (IR). Did you have an opportunity to review it?

[If yes, ask prospect his opinion of IR. If no, add the following dialogue]

That's why we called. We realize that so much information comes across the desk of an executive that it becomes an impossible task to keep up. I'd like to take a moment to tell you about International Report, a powerful, easy-to-use, on-line tool that gives you more information in eight minutes affecting your business than you can get spending hours sifting through newspapers, periodicals, and other standard sources.

GENERAL PROBING QUESTIONS

[There is no need to ask the prospect all the following questions. Your goal is to find two or three important needs that IR can fill.]

Because our service has numerous features, I'd like to ask you a few brief questions so that I describe only what would be of particular interest to you in your situation.

1. How do you currently get the day-to-day financial information you need? *[If asked what is meant, examples to give are newspapers, periodicals, research library, on-line service.]*

[If prospect is currently using an on-line service, go directly to specific probes for on-line subscribers. It is not necessary to ask all these questions.]

2. Mr./Ms. ________, in your position, what kind of information do you track on a regular basis? Do you follow the markets, stocks, bonds, money markets, foreign exchange, futures options, etc?
3. Are you involved with managing your company's short- and long-term investment strategies?
4. How important is it to have authoritative information concerning developments in other countries? Do you have any international operations or conduct any trade overseas?
5. How closely do you monitor developments concerning your industry and your competitors? Would it be valuable to have in-depth company profiles and up-to-the-minute industry information any time you need it?
6. Do you have a PC and modem available for your use?

Probing Questions for Prospects Who Use Another On-Line Service

[Add the following questions if prospect is currently using another on-line service.]

- What do you like about the service you have now?
- If you could design the perfect service, what features would it have?
- Is it easy to access the information you want? (How difficult is it to move from one data base to another?)
- If our service could give you all the information your current service gives you, but in addition
  - — Gave you information at a lower price
  - — Made it far easier to access the information you need
  - — Gave you better coverage in your area of specialization

would you be interested in considering our service?

[Summarize needs, and go to appropriate Features and Benefits.]

Features/Benefits—Three Major Reasons to Use IR

Mr./Mrs. ________, there are three major reasons why International Report is such a powerful decision-making tool. First, International Report gives you a complete portrait of what's happening anywhere in the world that can impact your business. It's the only service that combines news, market rates, advice, analysis, and forecasts from fourteen of the most respected sources around the world.

Second, it's a snap to use. International Report is so friendly [easy to use] that new users can begin accessing it immediately, even without a manual. [All you need is a PC and a modem.]

Third, it's not expensive. With International Report you pay only for what you use. There are no hidden charges [no start-up fees], no extra data bases to pay for.

Would having this type of information available for immediate access the moment you need it be of value to you?

[If positive, go to Close.]

Features/Benefits—General Description of International Report

[The following should be used only *when you need to give a brief yet complete overview to the prospect. Otherwise, refer to the special sections of the Dialogue Guide that best meet the prospect's needs.]*

International Report is so comprehensive in scope that it covers virtually every area that might affect your business and investments. When you subscribe to IR, you have

- Immediate access to real-time market information from exchanges in the United States and around the world
- In-depth information that can affect your doing business in 150 countries
- Access to detailed information on 15,000 U.S. companies, including profiles and competitive information, plus up-to-the-minute developments in world and financial news.

But what makes International Report so valuable, Mr./Ms. _________, is that it doesn't just report facts. You get commentary, advice, analysis, and consensus forecasts from major sources around the world, allowing you to compare and contrast views and help you make better decisions.

Features/Benefits—Money Markets

Mr./Ms. ________, you mentioned that you need to keep track of the ________ markets. International Report provides you with comprehensive real-time rates for a full range of instruments, including [*choose prospect's area of interest*]:

- Certificates of deposit
- Dealer commercial paper
- Banker's acceptances

- Treasuries
- Federal funds

In addition to providing a full range of information about ________, what makes International Report so valuable is that it's the only service that combines rates, market news, commentary analysis, and forecasting, giving you the most authoritative up-to-the-minute information for making investment decisions.

ADDITIONAL FEATURES AND BENEFITS

Benefit	*Feature*
Saves time	It's easy to get the information you need. All information is organized by topic from one main menu.
Saves money	Pay as you go. There's one low per minute charge.
Available when you need it	Access it from your home, office, anywhere in the world twenty-four hours a day, seven days a week.

[Go to Close.]

CLOSE

Right now we're offering a trial subscription for only $20. This includes everything you need to get started and help you get maximum benefit from the service to enhance your business decisions. To speed up delivery, we can put this on your company credit card or bill your company directly. Which would you prefer?

[Get credit card information. Make sure prospect has right equipment (IBM-compatible, modem, etc.). If prospect declines offer, ask whether he would like some information, including a free demonstration disk. Ask for referral if appropriate.]

SAMPLE SCRIPT D

The following dialogue guide was developed for a major bank's telemarketing campaign to increase its consumer credit business. It's an excellent example of a script that is flexible and concise.

INTRODUCTION

Option 1

[Use a friendly, businesslike tone. Do not read word for word.]

Good evening, Mr./Ms. ________. This is ________ from Newbank. Mr./Ms. ________, as a select customer, you have been invited to open a credit now account, which entitles you to a $2,000 preapproved line of credit.

[Assess if this is a good time for the prospect to talk with you.]

Did you have an opportunity to review the information we sent to you?

Option 2

Good evening, Mr./Ms. ________. This is ________ from Newbank. Mr./Ms. ________, you have been preapproved for a credit now account, which entitles you to a $2,000 unsecured line of credit, available whenever you need it. Did you have a chance to review the information we sent you?

[Use a transition to Questions.]

[*If no*]
That's fine. I'd like to take a moment to give you some information on how the program can benefit you. Before I go over the program, I'd like to ask you a couple of brief questions to see if our credit now account could be helpful to you.

[*If yes*]
What do you think of this program?

[Ask prospect what he/she thinks of the program. Answer objections, if any, or go to close.]

PROBING QUESTIONS

[Don't make this sound like an interrogation. Omit most of this if you feel the prospect does not have much time or is busy.]

How would you characterize your credit card usage—frequent, moderate, rare?

[Ask any additional questions, if necessary, concerning the following.]

Interest rate
Access availability
Checks
Cash advance/amount
Repayment schedule
Acceptance

Are you currently paying any annual fees for your credit cards? What is the current rate of interest on your present credit card?

FEATURES AND BENEFITS

[Describe only features and benefits that interest the prospect.]

Now let me tell you how our program works. Mr./Ms. ______, when you open a credit now account, you have an unsecured line of credit available for up to $2,000, which is conveniently accessed through your Newbank cash machine or by simply writing a personal check.

Because interest rates are competitive (prime + 6 percent), you can use your credit line for various purposes (paying off higher interest rate loans, such as credit cards; emergency situations when you need immediate access to extra funds; or any other worthwhile purpose). And there are no maintenance or annual fees.

Does this sound like a program that would be of interest to you?

[Improvise your response as appropriate]

Features	Benefits
No annual fee	Savings
Cash advance to $2,000	Security, flexible
Standard repay plan	Lower monthly payment
Prime + 8 percent	Lower rate
No maintenance fee	Savings
No minimum check amounts	Flexible
ATM access	Convenient
Personalized checks	Prestige

CLOSE

[Make sure the prospect knows how to fill out the coupon.]

Mr./Ms. ________, this privilege is being offered only until *[date]*. You have an option of either completing the coupon we sent you and mailing it back to us or dropping it off at any Newbank location.
Which would you prefer to do? Stop by or mail it in?
That's great.

CROSS-SELL

[Mention additional credit lines available and other products the customer may be interested in.]

By the way, as long as I have you on the phone, do you currently have a credit card with Newbank?

SAMPLE SCRIPT E

One of the most common ways to develop new customers for services is to conduct seminars presenting specific areas of expertise. Telemarketing campaigns to qualify prospects and invite them to these seminars are extremely effective. The following sample script was developed for that purpose. Note the use of paraphrasing in this script to get the prospect to say "yes."

INTRODUCTION

Good morning/afternoon. This is ________ from Eagle Management Consultants in New York City.

OPENING STATEMENT

I'm calling this morning/afternoon because our current research indicates that a single hiring mistake can cost a company like yours a minimum of $18,000. Dr. Tom Eagle is conducting a workshop on "How To Find the Right People" in your area on *[date]* and *[date]*. If you have a few minutes, I'd like to give you some information on how the seminar works and tell you about a special offer we're making in connection with this telephone call.

[*Ask for time.*]

[Pause. If prospect agrees to listen, go to Transition. If prospect objects, answer per Q&A sheet, and ask for time again. If prospect objects again, terminate call.]

OPENING STATEMENT

Variant 1

I'm calling about a workshop to be given in your area on "How To Find the Right People." This seminar has been acclaimed for its immediate impact on improving the selection process, reducing costly turnover, and attracting top candidates. I'd like a few minutes of your time to explain some of the areas it covers and see if it fits your needs.

[Ask for time.]

[Pause. If prospect agrees to listen, go to Transition. If prospect objects, answer per Q&A sheet, and ask for time again. If prospect objects again, terminate call.]

Variant 2

The reason I'm calling this morning/afternoon is to invite you to attend a workshop that gives you a proven way to reduce costly turnover and attract top candidates to your department/organization. Eagle Consultants is so certain you will find this seminar a valuable learning experience and profitable in terms of saving money and time that they will unconditionally refund your seminar fee if you're not completely satisfied. I'd like to take a moment of your time to give you some information about the workshop and see if it fits your needs.

[Ask for time.]

[Pause. If prospect agrees to listen, go to Transition. If prospect objects, answer per Q&A sheet, and ask for time again. If prospect objects again, terminate call.]

TRANSITION

Before going into the topics covered by the seminar, can I get some background on your needs so I can be sure to cover the correct areas?

PROBES	Can you describe the kind of program you use to train line managers to select new hires?
	Have you purchased or created a program, or do you use an informal process where each department head uses his or her own methods?
	Do you first screen candidates and then send them on to department heads for a second interview?
	How many people are involved in the interviewing process?
	How would you characterize turnover in the company—low or high?
	Is there a particular department where turnover seems to be more of a problem?

PARAPHRASE OF PROSPECT'S RESPONSES

Variant 1	So to summarize, Mr./Ms. _____, you have no formal training in interviewing techniques; turnover is generally acceptable, but there are exceptions, such as in EDP and secretarial positions.
Variant 2	You mentioned, Mr./Ms. ______, that the company uses a two-step process, where you screen candidates in Personnel and then send them on to department heads. Turnover is more of a problem than it used to be, and you feel that certain department heads could improve their interviewing skills.
TRANSITION	Now let me tell you about how our program can meet your needs.

FEATURES/BENEFITS	Mr. ________, our workshop is specifically designed for companies like yours that do not rely on a formal program for screening and interviewing personnel. On entering the program, your managers go through an intensive two-day seminar, which includes role plays and extensive use of videotape for practice and feedback. The seminar covers every conceivable situation your managers encounter in screening and interviewing candidates. Managers leave the workshop with a clear, step-by-step set of procedures and guidelines that will greatly reduce time spent interviewing and almost guarantee they hire the right person for the job every time. And because they have hired the right person, you can ensure that your turnover costs will be much lower.
TRIAL CLOSE	
Variant 1	Does this sound like a program that would be of interest to you?
Variant 2	If our program actually does this, would it be worth sending a few of your top people to the seminar?
[If yes, go to Close.]	
CLOSE	
[Discuss price reduction for two or more attendees.]	Fine, we'll be giving the seminar on *[date]* and *[date]*. Which would be better for you?
[If no, go to Secondary Objective.]	

SECONDARY OBJECTIVE	Fine, Mr. ________. In that case, we do offer a free "miniseminar" where your managers would experience a quick overview of the full-scale workshop and get an idea as to whether it would help in your situation. There is no charge, and we've scheduled a miniseminar for *[date]* and *[date]*. Which would be better for you?
[If yes, discuss registration and location. If no, terminate call.]	

SUMMARY

This chapter continued the discussion of scripting. There were worksheets to help you practice writing various parts of a script.

The chapter concentrated on four actual scripts that address different situations common to most telemarketing environments:

1. Setting an appointment.
2. Penetrating a screen.
3. Selling a complex service.
4. Maintaining a flexible script.

CHAPTER

12

Developing an Objection Response Guide

OBJECTIONS, resistance, questions, negative responses—whatever you want to call them, every telemarketer, every sales professional experiences them every working day. The best of them welcome objections because they know they are *opportunities*—to engage in dialogue, to find out what's really going on in the prospect's mind, to sell, and, above all, to *close*.

Figure 10-2 diagrammed the eight basic stages of every telemarketing call. It showed that objections occur at basically two points in the call: after the introduction, when the prospect is trying to determine whether to stay on the line and listen, and again at the trial close. It's important to understand that prospects may interrupt and object at any point during the call; they do not always follow neat diagrams. But no matter when it occurs, an objection should be welcomed, recognized, and answered. This chapter helps you develop an objection response guide so the focus of the call can return to the goal you've set.

WHAT AN OBJECTION REALLY TELLS YOU

As a consumer, whenever you are faced with making a purchasing decision, you base your decision on how much you know about the product and what it is going to do for you. This knowledge consists of the product's features and benefits, especially the latter. When you don't have enough information, or you have the wrong information, your concerns may take the form of an "objection." This leads to a basic rule: *Before telemarketers can achieve the goal of any call, they must satisfactorily answer any and all objections or questions that prospects feel are important.*

FORMS OF OBJECTIONS

In order to handle objections, you must first recognize them. When you're dealing with someone face-to-face, there are all sorts of visual signs of an objection. Recognizing objections on the phone is different because there are no visual clues. Telemarketers must train their ears to listen for clues in the prospect's voice. Even a "yes" in a certain tone may be an objection.

Here are some forms objections may take:

Question: *Why is it so expensive?*
Statement: *It just costs too much.*
Vague: *I'm not interested.*
Silence or hesitation: *Uh huh . . . um.*

Once you recognize the resistance, you must uncover the actual objection. First you must make sure that the objection is stated clearly and is agreed upon by both the prospect and the telemarketer. Telemarketers truly need to understand objections completely so they can answer them effectively and move toward the close.

FOUR RULES FOR RESPONDING TO OBJECTIONS

An effective response to an objection always follows four simple rules:

1. Express understanding.
2. Agree or appreciate the prospect's viewpoint—*never* argue.
3. Cite proof or offer alternatives.
4. Get agreement and close.

The following example is taken from an objection response guide developed for a major telecommunications company. This is a strong objection and a strong response. The numbers in brackets refer to the four rules so you can see the process:

OBJECTION: You're the sixth person who called me this week.

RESPONSES:

[**1**] I can understand your frustration, Mr. ________.

[**2**] I'll bet each person claimed to have the best service at the lowest price. And frankly, in a way, they are not lying to you. Each company that has called you has the lowest rates to certain cities.

[**3**] What makes our service different is that ______ combines six of the largest telephone companies (including the ones I mentioned) all with the cheapest rates somewhere, and our computer automatically switches your call to the least expensive service based on where you are calling.

[**4**] In other words, with one company, you get the cost benefits of all six major services combined. How does what I said sound so far? [*Go to probing questions to get the information you need to close.*]

You can see from the instructions in this example that your goal is to get the conversation back on track toward a close. This is a good reason to keep your objection response guide physically separate from your script. That way, you can easily move back to the probes in the script and then to the close.

Additional Techniques for Handling Objections

• *Third-party "testimonial."* This technique expresses empathy with the prospect's point of view and refers to a third party's experience to add credence to the answer.

TMR: I understand how you *feel*, Mr. ______. Many of our subscribers have *felt* that our service was expensive, until they *found* that it not only gave them access to more information, but also helped them make better decisions.

• *Agree and explain.* Many objections can be handled by agreeing that the prospect has a valid question, then showing him or her proof in the form of features and benefits.

PROSPECT: It sounds a lot like the service I have now.

TMR: I agree that it does sound that way, but you'll be glad to know that our service provides such additional data bases as company information and foreign exchange, along with analysis and commentary to help you interpret market movements.

• *Agree and redirect.* Prospects will sometimes object because they don't see that what you've presented is any better than what they have now. Using this technique, the telemarketer agrees with prospects and directs them to a feature and benefit that sets the product apart.

PROSPECT: It sounds more expensive than my current policy.

TMR: Yes, I can understand your concern with cost, but if you can get both the special coverages you need and faster claim service, wouldn't that be valuable to you?

• *Agree and offer an alternative.* On occasion, prospects will focus on only one part of your offer. By agreeing and reminding them that it's only one part of your total offer and you are offering a wider range of choices, you can often overcome this type of objection.

PROSPECT: I have been to that type of interviewing workshop before, and it didn't seem worth it.

TMR: I can appreciate that, Mr. ________, but our two-day seminar is far more than just a workshop. It's a complete approach to the problem of personnel selection and turnover, using the latest human resource development techniques. And we guarantee that if you are not satisfied, the fee is refunded.

• *Agree and rephrase into a question; then answer the question.* Often it is helpful to rephrase a prospect's statement into a question that you can easily answer.

PROSPECT: We use another service.

TMR: So what you're saying is "Why should I change to DataCo?" Well, one major reason is that DataCo has developed a program specifically for medium-sized businesses in your industry, and it will save you money on your processing costs, just as it does for ________ and ________. Our district manager can show you how when he gives you a free review of our current procedures. What day next week would be good for you?

No matter which of these techniques you use to handle objections, remember these basic rules:

1. *Recognize* objections for what they are—questions that must be answered before the telemarketer can close.
2. *Never argue or show hostility*—arguing, discourtesy, or intimidation of prospects doesn't work.
3. Every time an objection is successfully answered, your prospect's interest increases.

BUILDING A COMMON OBJECTION FILE

Figure 12-1 reproduces an objection response guide developed for the outbound telemarketing program of a large insurance company. It shows the full range of the most common objections that may occur over the course of an outbound call. Of course, some may not apply to your product or business, but basically most will and can be adapted to almost any field.

The bottom-tabbed flip chart format provides easy access. The objection phrase is printed on both the tab and the page containing the strongest answer. Read through this sample; then try working out your own response to objections on the worksheet that follows.

Friend in the Business

It's nice to be able to have a special relationship. Lots of people have friends and relatives in the insurance field. But because insurance is a very competitive industry, there can be a wide range of coverages and

Figure 12-1. Bottom-tabbed objection response guide.

FRIEND IN THE BUSINESS

TOO EXPENSIVE

SEND LITERATURE

I'M SATISFIED

NOT READY TO MAKE A CHANGE

HOW DID YOU GET MY NAME?

WHO IS ________ AGENCY?

I HAVE ENOUGH INSURANCE

YOU'RE THE SIXTH PERSON WHO'S CALLED

NOT INTERESTED

TOO BUSY

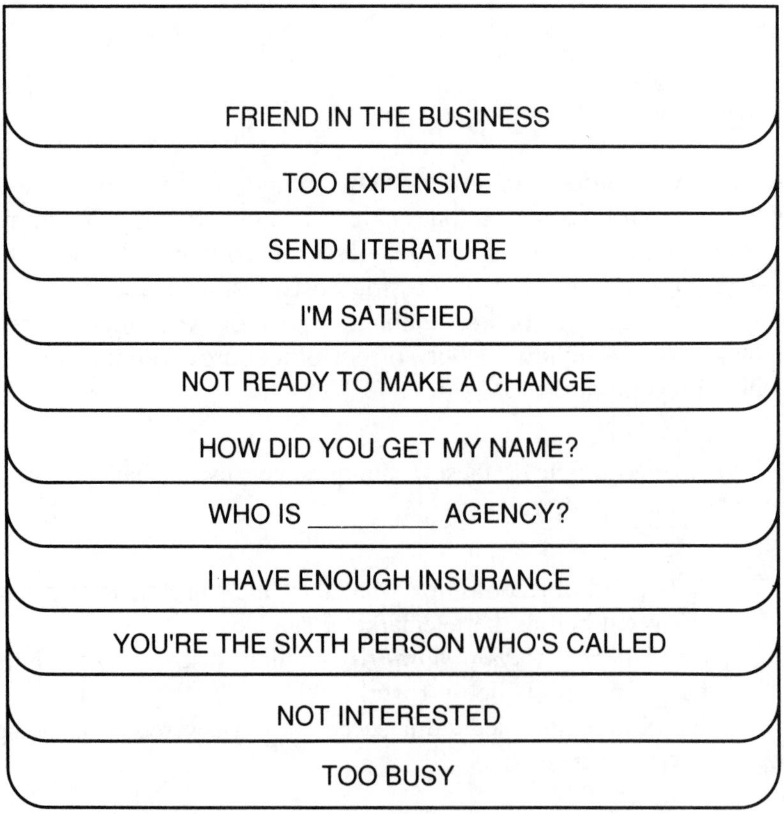

prices. Why don't I give you a free comparison so you can be certain you're getting the right coverage at the right price?

[Go to Close.]

Too Expensive

I can certainly appreciate your point of view. To be honest, it's quite possible our program might cost you a little more, but we've seen many cases where people have spent considerable money on insurance only to discover later, when they had a loss, that their policy wasn't adequate. At our agency, we believe it's our responsibility to make sure you have the right program. I'd like to have *[agent name]*, one of the principals of our firm, come down and give you a free comparison. Then if you still feel that you're better off with what you now have, you haven't lost anything. Isn't it worth a few minutes of your time to make sure you have the proper coverage?

[Go to Close.]

Send Literature

I'd be happy to send you literature. But because our program is custom designed to meet the specific needs of our clients, and because this can result in more value for the money you spend, I'd like to ask you a few questions so I can send you the material that applies to your specific situation.

[Go to Probing Questions, and try to involve the prospect by uncovering specific needs.]

Mr./Mrs. ________, it seems that, based on what you told me, there are very definite areas where we could help you. Why don't I have *[agent name]* stop by tomorrow? He can drop off the information to you and answer any additional questions you may have.

I'm Satisfied

I can appreciate that. In fact, some of our best clients said the very same thing before we showed them how to get better coverage at a competitive price. Most of our clients in your industry have saved an average of ________percent on the cost of their *[type of]* insurance. What I'd like to do is set up a time for our analyst to come down and evaluate your present program.

[Go to Close.]

First Alternate

I can appreciate that. What is it about your present [agent, program, company] you like?

[Paraphrase answer; then add the following.]

Those are all excellent reasons. But as you know, insurance premiums fluctuate greatly from year to year, and coverages are sometimes so complicated it's difficult to know if you're getting all that you're paying for. Our agency would like to give you a free review of your current program. Wouldn't it be worth the short time it would take to make sure your program is accomplishing its objectives?

Second Alternate

I'm glad to hear that you are satisfied with your current [agent, program, company], Mr./Mrs. ________. In fact, after our specialist has shown you some of our alternatives, you may still feel that your [agent, program, company] is best. But as a [businessman/woman], you are interested in being more cost-effective. If spending a few minutes of your time could possibly save you money or help you keep your costs down, wouldn't you consider that time well spent?

[Go to Close.]

Not Ready to Make a Change

That's fine, Mr./Ms. ________. Why don't I get back to you when your policy comes up for renewal? Could you tell me when that is? Great.

[If the renewal date is not too far away, you might add the following.]

Because your policy comes up for renewal on ________, it might be a good idea to see our specialist now, just to give you an idea of some of the options you will have available for getting maximum coverage at a competitive price.

How Did You Get My Name?

I'm glad you asked me that. We go through a selective process of gathering names from special lists, including recommendations and referrals. We then match the list against a profile of those companies that would benefit most from our program. Because your company was one that qualified, I'd like to have our ________ expert come down and give you a free review of your insurance program to show you how we can benefit you.

[Go to Close.]

Expiration Date Option

Because your company was one that qualified, I'd like to ask a few questions to see if we can give you a better program than you currently have. When does your business insurance come up for renewal?

Who Is ________ Agency?

I'm really glad you asked that question. That gives me the opportunity to tell you that our agency has been providing insurance services to the local business community for ________ years, and we write insurance in excess of $_____.

I'd like to have Mr./Mrs. ________ come down and introduce himself/herself to show you in black and white what we're providing for other members of the community.

[Mention names of clients if applicable.]

I Have Enough Insurance

I can understand that the last thing you think you need *now* is more insurance, and, honestly, you may be right. When we do an evaluation of clients' needs, we very often discover that they don't need all the coverage they have. Sometimes we find out they're paying twice for the same coverage under separate policies, or we see instances where a lower deductible is actually causing them to pay more than they need to. These are the kinds of things that our professional analyst can tell you, Mr./Ms. ________. What I would like to do is to have our analyst review your situation and make sure you have only what you need. When would it be convenient for him to stop by?

[Go to Close. If closing for expiration date, add the following.]

What I would like to do is have our analyst review your program when it comes up for renewal. If you can tell me when that is, I'll get back to you at the appropriate time.

You're the Sixth Person Who's Called

I can certainly understand how you must feel. I'll bet each person that called you claimed that he had a superior program at a competitive price. Frankly, Mr./Ms. ________, they are not lying to you. Many insurance programs today have excellent features; and, depending on what you need, one company's policy may serve you slightly better than the next.

However, we have a recently developed program specifically tailored to *[the industry]*. Because it can result in a broader range of coverage without the usual added costs of special endorsements and riders, we'd like to set up an appointment for our specialist to discuss your specific industry needs.

[Go to Close.]

Not Interested

I understand that you're not interested right now, Mr./Ms. ________. In fact, after we come down and explain what we have to offer, you may still not be interested. But I do know as a [businessman/woman] that you're interested in saving money [controlling costs]. If there is the slightest chance of actually doing that, wouldn't it be worth the short time it would take seeing our specialist? After all, at the very least, you will have a free second opinion regarding your current program.

[Go to Close.]

Alternate

I can understand that you're not interested. I really wouldn't expect you to be interested at this point. But as a [businessman/woman], you're interested in getting the most for the money you spend, and that's why I'd like the opportunity to give you a free comparison when your policy comes up for renewal. If your present coverage is adequate, you will at least have the satisfaction of knowing you have the best program.

[Go to close. Note: If you can't get an appointment, try for one or more of the following: expiration date, quote information, time to call back.]

Too Busy

Yes, I can certainly appreciate that you are pressed for time. What would be a convenient time for me to give you a free review of your insurance program so that we can make sure you are getting the proper coverage at the right price? When would it be convenient for our specialist to sit down with you?

[Go to Close.]

First Alternate

I can understand that you are busy, Mr./Ms. ________. But if our specialist were to spend a short time showing you how to get coverages not normally available for your industry at competitive prices, wouldn't it be time well spent?

[Go to close.]

Second Alternate

I can certainly appreciate the fact that you are busy, Mr./Ms. ________, but we have managed to provide *[name of referral]* a remarkable amount of coverage at a competitive price. What would be a convenient time, when you are not this busy, for our specialist to come down to talk to you?

[Go to Close.]

[Expiration date and survey instructions: If the call is just to gather information, as in the case of an expiration date or survey to quote, nail down a specific time to call back.]

Worksheet
Building an Objection Response File

Use the four rules to develop responses to the following typical objections. Fill in some objections related to your own product or service, and develop responses to them.

Objection: Your price is too high.

Response:____

____

____

____

Objection: I don't need it.

Response:____

____

____

____

Objection: Send literature.

Response:______________________________________

____

____

____

OVERCOMING THE "REAL" OBJECTION

Vague forms of resistance are common. Statements such as "Well, we don't usually like to order over the phone" or "Well, I don't know . . ." are typical. When you encounter this kind of resistance, you will need to probe and get the prospect to expand a bit. Once you hear what the real objection is, paraphrase it—make sure you've gotten it clear. Then, and only then, can you respond to it.

The following is a typical "vague objection" and a possible way to handle it by paraphrasing:

OBJECTION: I'll think about it.

RESPONSE: Are you saying there's someone else you need to consult with before you decide on this?

REAL OBJECTION: No, I just feel like I need more information.

RESPONSE: I'd be happy to supply the information you need. We can set up a demonstration for Monday or Wednesday next week. How does that sound?

Figure 12-2 illustrates this process of getting to the real objections and overcoming them.

SUMMARY

This chapter presented the idea of viewing objections as opportunities to sell and close. There are four rules for developing responses to objections.

Figure 12-2. Overcoming objections.

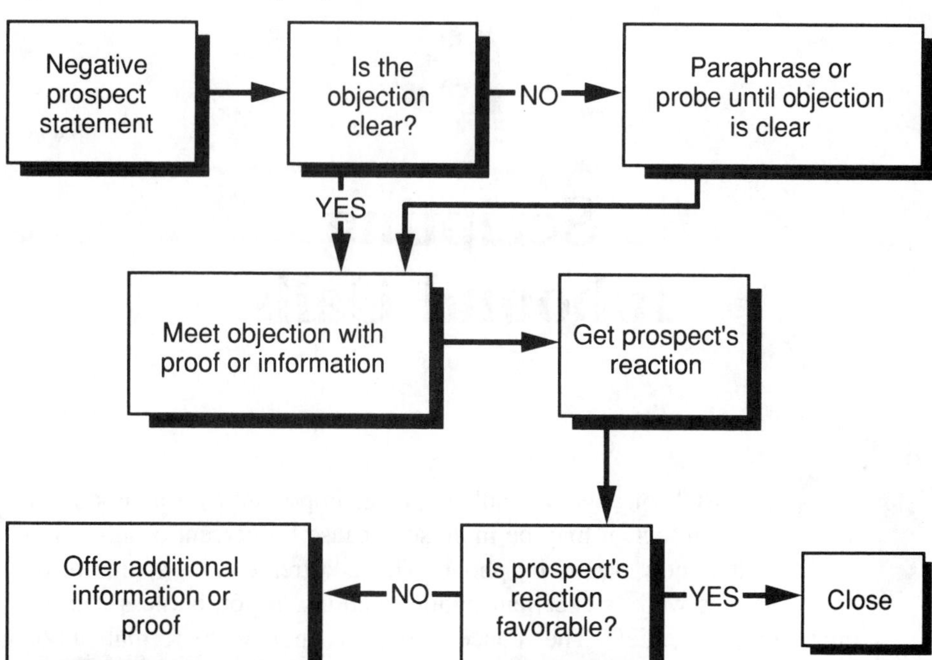

Make sure that the answers to every objection your staff may encounter follow these rules:

1. Express understanding.
2. Agree or appreciate the prospect's viewpoint—*never* argue.
3. Cite proof or offer other alternatives.
4. Get agreement and close.

This chapter also discussed some additional techniques for overcoming objections and presented a sample objection response guide covering the most common ones. Every telemarketing program should have an objection response guide similar to the sample, tailored to the objections specifically connected to the product or service. The worksheet in this chapter should help you develop your own.

CHAPTER

13

Scripting Inbound Calls

CONTROL on inbound calls is just as important as it is on outbound calls. In fact, it may be more so because 80 percent of all customer contact now occurs by phone. This is a tremendous source of business as well as excellent public relations, *if* you harness it to maximize that potential. The concern here is not with formal inbound telemarketing programs alone, but with every phone call that comes into your organization. Apply the principles behind this book's approach to formal inbound programs across the board. Every employee who takes business calls should know them and use them on every call. In this way, you will get the most out of every phone you own.

HANDLING QUESTIONS ON INBOUND CALLS

Many types of formal inbound telemarketing programs involve answering questions and providing information to support a sale. In fact, you often won't know in advance the precise reason for the inbound call. Inbound calls can go anywhere, which is why dialogue guides for inbound programs are particularly important. To get the telemarketer back in control, the dialogue guide must provide a way to get quickly to the ''real question,'' of which there can be more than one. The process for getting back to it is similar to that for handling objections on outbound calls:

1. Welcome the inquiry by saying, ''How may I help you?'' This immediately puts you in control and enables the customer to focus on the problem.
2. Listen carefully to the customer.

3. Probe for more information. Is this a customer or a prospect for up-sell or cross-sell? What needs can you identify?
4. Answer the real question.
5. Close.

The following inbound dialogue guide was developed for the inbound telemarketing department of a banking organization. It illustrates this five-step process. Look for the following elements as you read through the sample:

- Both the introduction and the transition to probing questions work together to pin down the reason for the call—early in the call.
- The guide is structured to cover every stage of the call, from introduction to close—similar to an outbound script—so that the telemarketer can get control.
- The guide anticipates a full range of specific questions and provides full information to respond to them—similar to an objection response guide.

Note also the optional up-sell/cross-sell material. This is one way to maximize the potential of every inbound call; but unless you script it and reward your employees for using it to get additional sales, you won't realize this potential.

SAMPLE INBOUND DIALOGUE GUIDE

INTRODUCTION

[Prospect calls with a question: "I saw your ad and would like some information on rates, interest, maturities, custom CD, etc."]

Good [morning/afternoon]. ____ Bank & Trust. ______ speaking. How may I help you?

TRANSITION TO PROBING QUESTIONS

[If prospect is just confirming information he/she saw about advertised CD, go to Description.]

I'll be happy to provide you with that information, but first may I have your full name . . . and your address . . . daytime phone number . . . and your home phone number?

[If it concerns a custom CD or NOW account, go to appropriate pages.]

By the way, how did you hear about us? Do you remember when you saw our ad?

DESCRIPTION (SPECIAL ADVERTISED CD)

Our advertised CD is ____ percent, and that is based on a term of ________. How much were you planning to invest? Great. The yield on this amount with your interest compounded monthly will be ____.

TRIAL CLOSE

How does this sound to you? Does the term fit your needs?

CLOSE

[If the prospect is stopping by the bank, *set up a date and convenient time for him or her.]*

In order to take advantage of this special rate, you can send in the coupon attached to our ad [or complete the application attached to our brochure] or stop by the bank and visit one of our personal bankers. Which would you prefer to do?

[If the prospect is mailing *in coupon confirming the investment, add:]*

As soon as we receive your check, we will send you a certificate confirming your purchase and a welcome kit containing information and important documentation you need.

REASSURANCE/CROSS-SELL/UP-SELL

[If prospect sounds interested, try to sell other products, such as the NOW account.]

Is there anything else I can help you with right now?
[*Optional*]
Because you are planning to invest in a CD, there are some additional benefits you get by linking your CD with a NOW checking account. For example, the interest on your CD can be deposited monthly directly into

the NOW account and accessed by simply writing a check or by using your bankcard. Would you like some information about these services?

Tell Me About Your Custom CD

Mr./Ms. ________, there are important differences between most fixed-term CDs (the most common type) and a custom CD from _____ Bank.

The first important difference is that a custom CD gives *you* the flexibility to decide when the CD matures. This can be any time you like from seven days up to ten years.

[*Optional*]

Would having that ability to pick the exact maturity date be important to you?

[Use the example if you feel the prospect does not understand the concept.]

Example

Let's say you need your funds on July 18 for a purchase you were planning to make—a deposit on a new car, a down payment on a new house. You can design your certificate to mature on July 17.

If your purchase is delayed for some reason, you can simply put your money back into a CD and set a new maturity date. In other words, Mr./Ms. ________, you will receive interest up until the time you actually need your funds.

The second major difference is that the interest rates you lock in will always be competitive because we set them by comparing the maturity date of the CD you request to the interest rate on government treasury securities of a comparable period.

We then give you a minimum of one-half to three-quarters of a percent above the government treasury securities rate. What that means to you, Mr./Ms. ________, is that you do not have to lose valuable interest while searching to find a high CD rate because ours will be consistently high. For example, today's rate on a ________ month CD would be ________ percent.

Does that sound like something that would be of interest to you? Great.

[Go to Close or offer to send some information.]

Additional Features and Benefits

1. You can borrow against the CD at market rates of interest if you need access to your money before the maturity date. The benefit of this is that you wouldn't be subject to early withdrawal penalties.
2. Small investors get the same high rate whether you invest $1,000 or $100,000.

FREQUENTLY ASKED QUESTIONS ABOUT CDs

- How is interest calculated? Interest is compounded monthly to the date of maturity. For example, $10,000 invested in a one-year CD with an interest rate of 8 percent would yield $____ at maturity. This would give you an effective annual yield of____ percent.
- *Who are you insured by?* Our bank is a member of FDIC, and your account or combination of accounts is insured up to $100,000.
- *Can I withdraw my interest monthly?* Yes. That is one of the advantages of linking our CD to our high-interest NOW checking account. Your interest will be deposited monthly directly into that account, and you can access it simply by writing a check or by using your bankcard at 2,600 cash machines nationwide.
- *When is interest paid?* You can pick one of two options. Your interest will be paid upon maturity of your CD or can be paid monthly by depositing it to a NOW checking account.
- *Is there a penalty for early withdrawal?* Yes, there is. However, the bank can make arrangements for you to borrow against your CD at current market interest rates, so that you can avoid early withdrawal penalties.

[Quote penalties only if asked.]

7–30 days = all interest earned
31–365 days = one month's interest
over 365 days = three month's interest

Tell Me About Your NOW Account

As with our custom CDs and other ________ Bank deposit services, our goal is to give you consistently higher interest than you would receive from other banks. Our NOW checking account is advantageous because it features an interest rate that is as high as a money market rate and in addition gives you the flexibility of unlimited access to your funds in terms of check-writing privileges.

Further, Mr./Ms. ________, by linking your CD to a NOW account, you have the flexibility of having the interest on your CD deposited each month directly into your account and accessing the funds by simply writing a check or through any of 2,600 cash machines nationwide.

Additional Features and Facts About NOW Accounts

1. No minimum balance is required.
2. You can write a check for any dollar amount.
3. Interest is compounded monthly.
4. The monthly consolidated statement includes CD information and all other accounts.
5. Funds are accessible at 2,600 conveniently located cash machines.
6. Overdraft protection is available.

[Go to Close.]

OTHER BANK SERVICES

________ Bank and Trust offers a full line of deposit and loan services:

- Home mortgages
- Installment loans
- Home equity loans
- CDs
- Personal savings
- NOW checking
- Direct deposit
- Automated teller machines
- Corporate accounts
- VISA and Master Charge accounts

DEFUSING HOSTILE SITUATIONS OR CUSTOMER COMPLAINTS

One of the most common inbound phone situations is the irate customer calling to complain about your product, service, or organization. Handled inexpertly, complaint calls will cost you untold dollars in lost sales, customers, and profits. Handled professionally, complaint calls can be a positive contribution to your organization. They're an opportunity to reconvert a customer and build your reputation as a responsive organization. If you track and analyze complaints, you'll be able to pinpoint weak areas in your organization and take action to strengthen them.

Essentially, the best way to handle an irate caller is similar to the approach used on any inbound call. The key to success here is first to recognize that you must defuse the anger and hostility. That is your primary objective. Until you have done so effectively, no real communication is possible.

The best way to defuse a hostile situation is to *agree with the caller's right to be angry*. Note that this is not the same as agreeing that the caller's complaint is well grounded or agreeing that your organization or product is at fault. The following example shows the distinction between the two:

CALLER: I am totally fed up to here with your company! I have written and called five times over the past ten days, and still can't get this to work properly! I am going to call your president and demand a refund!

COMPANY REPRESENTATIVE: I can understand how frustrated you must feel. If that happened to me, I'd be angry, too. I'd like to work with you to get it taken care of as quickly as possible. Can I get your name?

What the company representative has done is let the caller ventilate the hostility by agreeing he would feel the same way. Now it may be possible to communicate and get the information necessary to solve the problem. This part of the process is similar to identifying the "real question" when handling an objection. It requires probing for facts and details concerning the transaction, account, or problem so you can formulate your response. At this stage, because having to repeat the nature of the problem will often cause hostility to flare up again, it's important to keep the lines of communication open—be prepared to defuse hostile comments and feelings more than once.

After getting the facts, the next step is to communicate your response to the complaint or problem. This might include agreeing to research the problem further and call back with instructions, to exchange merchandise, or to return for a credit or refund. Whatever the commitment or agreement reached, follow-up is key. If you agree to call back with an explanation or information by a given date and time, do so. If you are providing a credit on an account or a refund, take whatever steps are necessary, right then and there.

Failure to follow through on complaint calls will not only waste the time spent on the call, it will probably cost you a customer, most of whom will then tell four or five other people about the experience. For this reason alone, it is wise to script your procedures for handling complaint calls and ensure that every employee who answers your phones knows how to use them. When you develop your script for hostile situations, keep these eight points in mind:

1. Use specific words instead of general words.
2. Deal with facts, as opposed to inferences, judgments, or generalizations.
3. Accentuate the positive, and eliminate the negative.
4. Look at the situation from the other person's point of view, because people's varying backgrounds make communication difficult.
5. Avoid "win-lose" situations.
6. Offer ideas that will help the customer solve a payment problem.
7. Listen.
8. Use feedback.

SUMMARY

Every inbound call is a source of potential business and solid public relations. Scripts for inbound calls give employees control so they can solve problems effectively and take advantage of the fact that 80 percent of customer contact is now by phone. Inbound scripts should do the following:

1. Welcome the inquiry and show that you're listening.
2. Probe for more information—is this a customer, a prospect for upsell, cross-sell? What needs can you identify?
3. Answer the real question.
4. Close.

PART

IV

Making the Best Use of Human Resources

CHAPTER

14

Designing Your Telemarketing Center

TELEMARKETING is intensive, demanding work. The physical environment you create for it will affect the success of your program in important ways. A well-designed space not only enables the work to flow more smoothly, it also has a strong, positive influence on your telemarketing staff's morale and motivation.

OPEN SPACE VS. PARTITIONED SPACE

More than once this book has emphasized how the unique characteristics of the phone affect your decisions in every area of developing and implementing a telemarketing strategy. The design of your telemarketing center is no exception to this rule. Telemarketing is filled with psychological pressure. Your staff may be making forty, fifty, even seventy-five calls a day, depending on the nature of your program. They may experience complete or partial rejection in 90 percent of those calls. So the telemarketer is handling a high level of stress.

In addition, a high volume of calls means that noise levels can become a source of distraction and further stress. As few as two or three telemarketers working close together may produce a noise level that is uncomfortable and demoralizing. Your choice is apparently between

- An open workroom, which relieves some of the pressure by allowing telemarketers to see and overhear one another
- Partitioned space, which reduces noise levels and aids concentration

In fact, by using proper spacing and modern materials, you can build the advantages of both into a ''hybrid model'' that I strongly recommend.

The case for the open work area is that people are social animals—they thrive on interaction. When interaction is enhanced by the work space, team spirit develops and seems to be almost self-sustaining. In an open environment, when one person makes a big sale, everyone knows about it right away. Also, the more experienced telemarketers can affect the technique and style of less-experienced staff—they're easy to overhear and imitate. Supervisors can monitor individual telemarketers more effectively in an open space. In addition, the open space tends to dissipate tension, which shows in voice quality and reduces performance. Ironically, the level of concentration may be greater in the open room than in the partitioned space because tension itself is a distraction.

So there are some strong arguments for the open plan telemarketing center. The main objection is noise. You can deal with this problem fairly effectively by using sound absorbent materials on ceilings, walls, and floors and proper spacing (usually about thirty square feet per person). However, this may not be appropriate in some situations, where, for example, the workstation includes a PC or computer terminal.

Partitioned spaces arranged in rows radiating from a central supervisory position can support the sort of privacy that is important in some types of telemarketing. Partitions should be no higher than forty-eight inches in order to retain the feeling of openness. Partitioned spaces also let you segregate smokers and nonsmokers more effectively than open plans do—an important issue nowadays. You may handle it by having a designated smoking area separate from the work area, or you may even be required to have a completely "smoke-free" environment.

Figures 14-1 through 14-4 show some common space plans. Use them as a starting point for your thinking on physical design. As you plan the physical environment, look for design features that support the following key factors:

- Keep noise levels at an acceptable minimum
- Maintain sightlines of supervisors
- Allow adequate privacy

LIGHTING

Lighting is a potent tool for creating and maintaining a positive attitude within your telemarketing center. Look for space and designs that maximize exposure to natural light. A view of a far-off horizon or even a small patch of nature can be very helpful in diffusing pent-up psychic energy and pressure. Even carefully selected potted or hanging plants can help in this regard.

If possible, make certain that the artificial light you do use is the soft,

Figure 14-1.

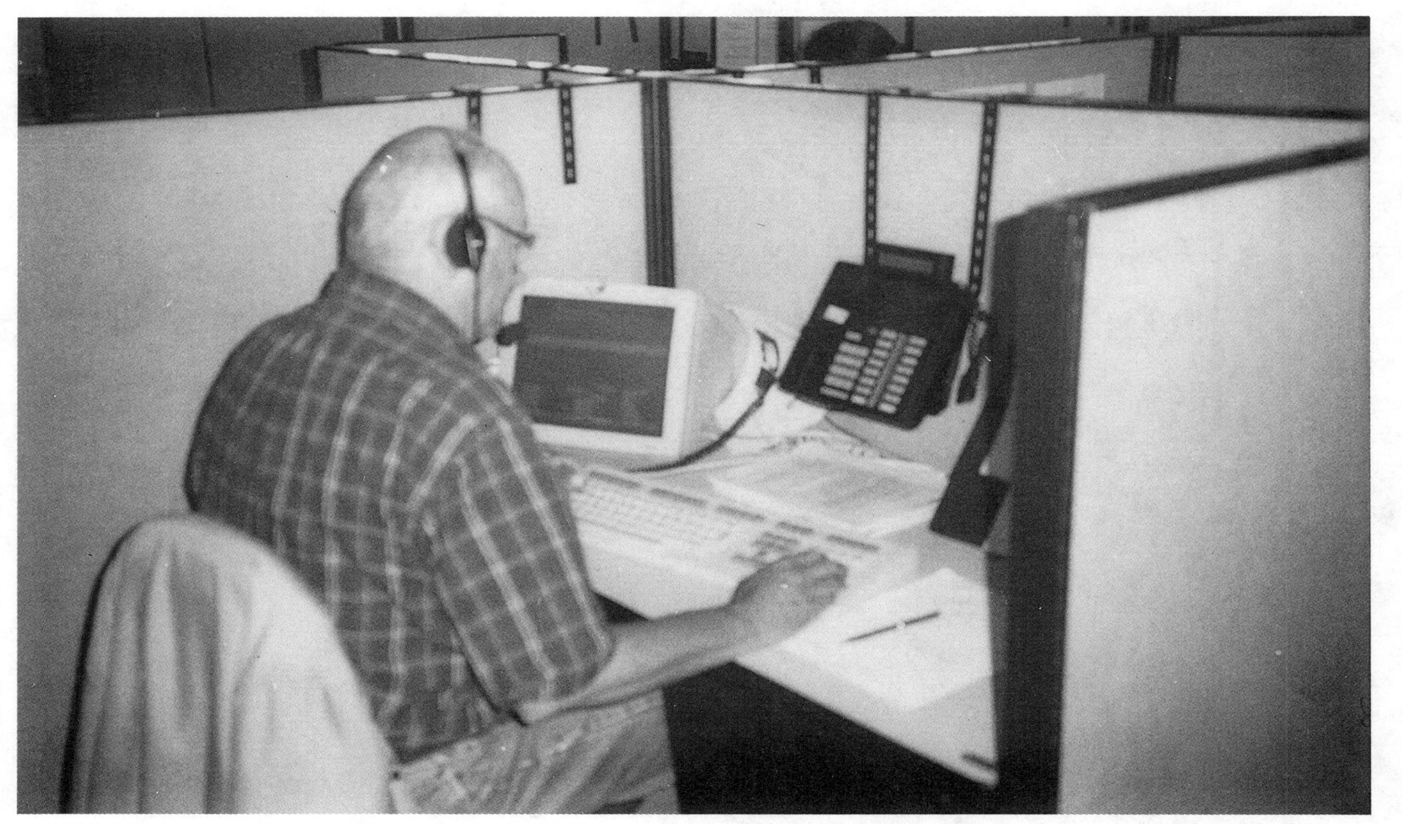

Source: Corporate Express Call Center Services.

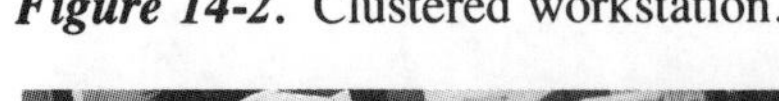

Figure 14-2. Clustered workstation.

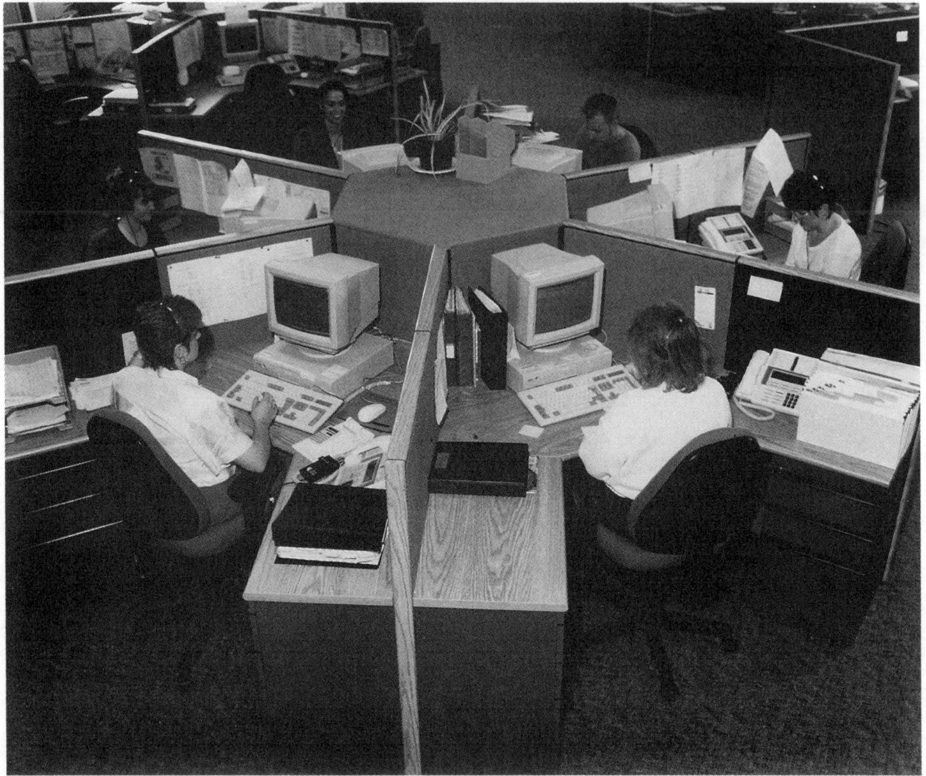

Source: The CenterCore Group, Inc.

nonglaring type. Individual lamps at each workstation are expensive, but they'll pay for themselves over and over in improved performance. Avoid overbright, overhead fluorescent lighting if you can. Studies have shown that it adds to stress, tension, and fatigue. Instead, try to combine a low level of overhead fluorescent light, natural light, and individual work space lamps.

JOB AIDS

The job aids listed below should be considered essential items.

- A comfortable desk, large enough to handle all equipment and written materials, such as script, product literature, objection response guides, and precall planners
- A desk organizer and file drawer to store written records and materials

(Text continues on page 156.)

Figure 14-3. Partitioned environment.

Source: Interior Concepts.

Figure 14-4. Telemarketing department.

Source: The Hon Company.

Figure 14-5. Headset.

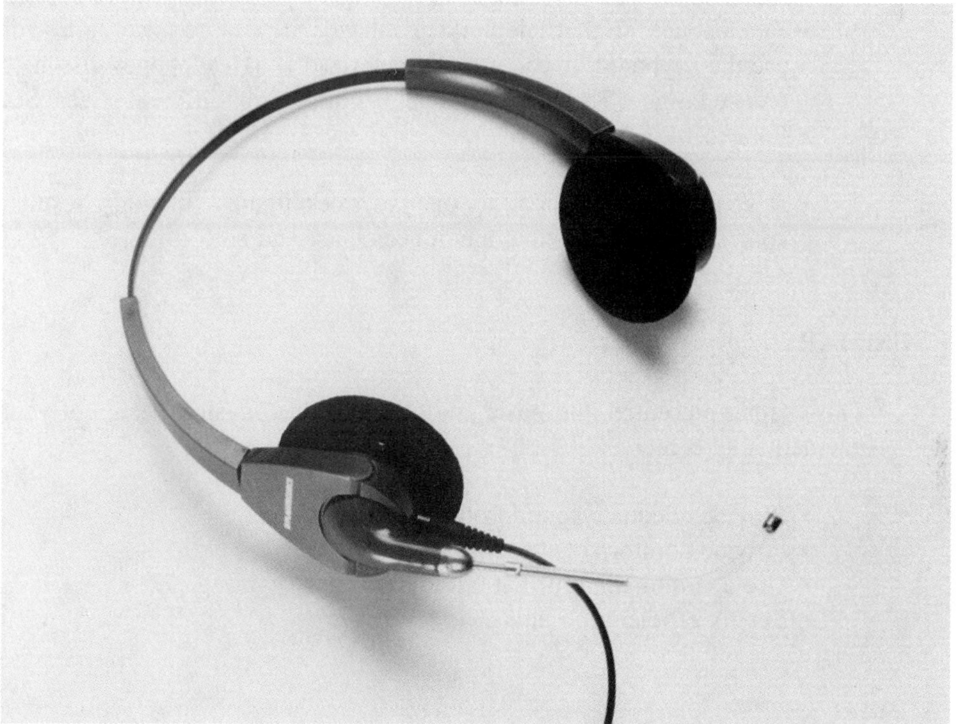

Source: Plantronics.

Figure 14-6. TriStar w/Earbuds.

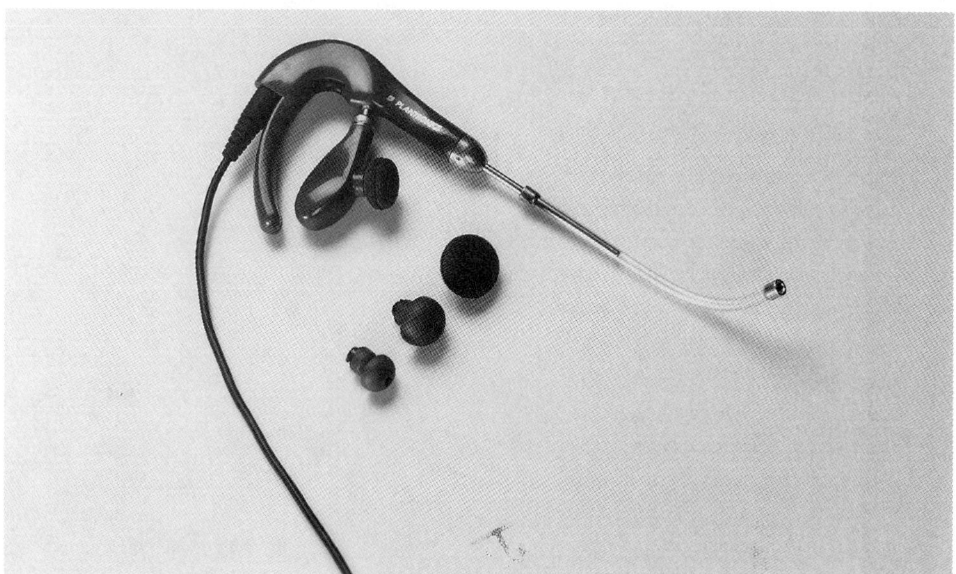

Source: Plantronics.

- An ergonomically designed chair (In view of the long periods TMRs spend seated, an investment in high-quality chairs is a wise one.)
- Headphones, so that telemarketers' hands are free to make notes (or use the keyboard, if you are computerized.) (Headphones also help reduce fatigue. They are available in a number of different styles. See Figures 14-5 and 14-6.)
- A desktop calendar
- A central posting area, to display sales figures, monthly results, contest winners, product announcements, and so forth

SUMMARY

This chapter presented four basic guidelines for the physical design of your telemarketing center:

- Provide adequate soundproofing.
- Provide comfortable spacing.
- Use a combination of natural and artificial lighting.
- Supply efficient job aids.

CHAPTER

15

Hiring Telemarketing Personnel

THE "standard" personnel screening techniques are about as useful as flipping a coin in terms of deciding who will be successful on the phone. Typically, these techniques say to look at education, job history, experience in the field, appearance, and enthusiasm during the personnel interview. Hiring telemarketing personnel demands a different approach.

DETERMINING YOUR HIRING NEEDS

You can't hire effectively until you know the skill level your strategy requires. Three factors determine your hiring needs.

1. The objective of your strategy, particularly whether it involves high-ticket/low-volume commitments or the reverse
2, The targeted audience of your strategy, especially if a particular need is known or if needs must be established on the phone
3. The relationship between your organization and your target audience

To determine your hiring needs, identify where each factor fits into your strategy, and assign it a rough "weight.

The higher on the scale of difficulty your objective is, the more your needs are weighted toward highly skilled sales professionals. If your strategy is to sell a high-ticket/low-volume product, where the prospect's needs must be clarified on the phone, you will definitely need experienced professionals, probably from the industry. If the first two factors are made

Figure 15-1. Determining your hiring needs.

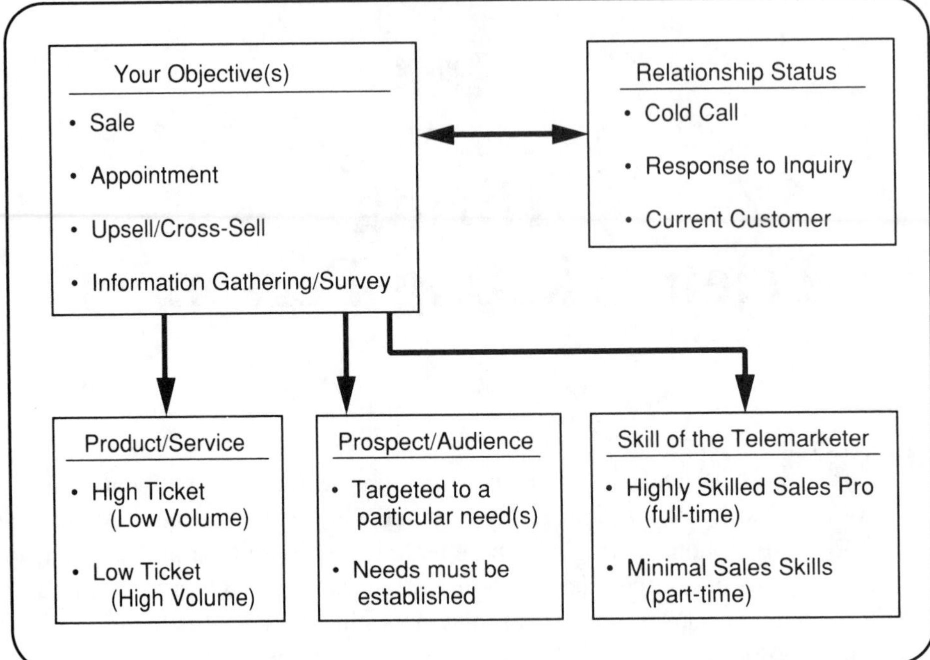

even more difficult by a weak relationship, you need to look for full-time, seasoned professionals.

At the low end of the spectrum, you may need only part-timers with minimal telemarketing skills and industry knowledge. For example, if your strategy is simply to cross-sell existing customers whose need for the product is well known, you need a much lower skill level than in the first example.

Clearly, many strategies will fall into the middle of the skill/experience range. By using these factors, you can identify your real needs before starting the hiring process and save yourself a lot of time and frustration. Figure 15-1 summarizes the relation between the three factors and the skill level required.

NARROWING THE FIELD

Once you've determined your needs in this general way, you take a second cut. No matter what general skill level you need, certain specific qualities are essential. Chief among these is voice quality. Look for people who have no strong regional accent, which might interfere with communication in different parts of the country. In addition, the ideal candidate's voice quality will convey sincere interest, not phony enthusiasm. Finally, the voice should reflect the candidate's flexibility—the ability to build rapport with people of various backgrounds—because that is what telemarketing demands. If you can identify people who combine these factors in their voices, you're well on your way to building a strong staff.

Generally, good telemarketers are good whether they are male or female. If they have the voice quality and most or all of the qualities to be discussed, gender should not be a factor in your hiring decisions. Some studies do show that people tend to buy from people who sound close to the prospect's age––within about five years. This seems to be related to the comfort level prospects feel toward the TMR, so candidates who can project the impression they are similar in age to their prospects tend to do better. This does not mean, though, that only mature TMRs will do well when calling older prospects because actual chronological age may have little or nothing to do with the age TMRs project in their voice.

After voice quality, several other factors play a role in a TMR's success on the phone. Depending on the difficulty of your program's objective, you may assign more or less weight to the following factors:

1. *Ability to handle rejection.* This quality is important in most telemarketing programs because your staff will nearly always be hearing ten "no"s for every "yes," and often even more. To avoid burnout and the resultant staff turnover, select people who can handle rejection and bounce back easily.

2. *Integrity.* Your telemarketing staff will be representing your company in the marketplace. The last thing you want in this powerful position is someone who communicates information incorrectly or in some other way damages your organization's reputation. Of course, judging another person's integrity is often a tough call—at a minimum, though, check prior references, and look for evidence that the candidate is worthy of the trust you place in him or her.

3. *Ability to handle constructive criticism.* Role playing and on-the-job coaching are the two main techniques for developing and improving telemarketing skills. This is an ongoing process, and both techniques involve careful review of performance and critical feedback. Candidates should be able to demonstrate that they can take this type of direction and criticism—basically, this means they have the willingness to confront bad habits they may have that destroy rapport and make the necessary changes.

4. *Ability to adjust quickly.* Telemarketing programs nearly always change over time. New products or services may be introduced; new scripts must be learned; new lists targeting prospects in a different part of the country may be used. Hence, candidates should be able to adapt quickly to changes in their working environment.

5. *Ability to deal with the pressure of rapid pacing.* Generally, tele-

marketing staff are required to meet certain call per hour and contact per hour standards. How TMRs handle this pressure determines whether they have the staying power to succeed. This is one quality where prior telemarketing experience is a useful indicator.

6. *Ability to get along with difficult people.* Telemarketing is a people job, often involving an interruption of a prospect's routine. Candidates should be able to project patience, empathy, and understanding of the prospects' needs when ''difficult'' situations arise—because they certainly will.

7. *Persistence.* Sales won't always be made on the first call, and maybe not on the second or even the third. But the best telemarketers have the persistence to keep calling back and to keep answering objections until the sale is made.

The closer you can get to these ''ideal'' qualities in hiring decisions, the more successful your telemarketing program will be. The best sources of candidates for TMR positions, depending on the nature of the program, may be the following:

1. *Actors.* Traditionally, actors are an excellent source of telemarketing candidates because they have trained voices, are familiar with role play, and are experienced in giving the same performance repeatedly. If you can offer a flexible working schedule, actors are one of the best sources for locating TMR staff.

2. *Graduate students.* Grad students are often a good source, especially for business-to-business telemarketing where some type of subject area expertise may be useful. For example, computer science grad students may be skilled at selling software and business students at selling office products. Generally, grad students are comfortable with the language such scripts use and are confident enough to build trust and rapport with prospects quickly. Their longevity on the job is usually limited by the length of their degree program, which may be two or three years. Night students can be scheduled for daytime shifts to make calls during business hours, and day students can be scheduled for days they do not have classes. Telemarketing programs may also successfully function as preliminary employment programs for graduate students who are subsequently recruited as permanent employees.

3. *Retirees.* Retired businessmen and women often have a wealth of experience and skill that can be used effectively in a telemarketing position. They can be particularly good candidates for part-time positions.

4. *Persons reentering the work force.* Employees who have left the workplace temporarily—to rear children, for example, or because of illness—may be unable to return to their former jobs but often have excellent business skills that can be applied in a telemarketing environment.

5. *Physically disabled persons.* The physically disabled may be perfectly suited for telemarketing work. Often, they are highly motivated and have the persistence to overcome obstacles that make for success as a telemarketer.

6. *Entry-level sales personnel.* Some companies use the telemarketing program as an entry-level job for candidates who will ultimately be promoted to other areas of operation. In this way, the telemarketing program becomes part of an overall staff development plan, enabling the company to promote from within.

STAFFING GUIDELINE FORMULA

As a general rule-of-thumb, use the following guidelines when determining the number of telemarketing personnel to hire.

For Business-to-Business Telemarketing

- A telemarketing rep can reach four-to-six prospects per hour.
- A telemarketing shift averages five hours.

For Consumer Telemarketing

- A telemarketing rep can reach ten to fifteen prospects per hour.
- A telemarketing shift averages four hours.

These averages must also take into account the amount of other work the reps are responsible for and whether they are full-time or part-time.

WHERE TO ADVERTISE

Where do you look for these ideal candidates, and how do you get them to break down your door for an interview? The answer is, you don't. You don't want to *see* candidates; you want to *hear* them. You next step is to advertise and "look for" candidates *over the phone*. Personal interviews come later. Here's some sample advertising copy, which you can adapt for your own needs:

Telemarketing/Inside Sales

Ground floor opportunity to join our newly formed Telemarketing Department. ABC Co., a leader in providing services to the industry, is looking for a few intelligent self-starters with excellent speaking voices and the ability to talk to our customers and prospects on a professional level. Prior industry experience not required. Prior telemarketing experience essential. Excellent salary, bonus, and benefits. Call Joe Smith, 9 A.M.–1 P.M., at 667-7777.

University theater departments and theatrical trade papers are the best places to advertise for actors. For graduate students, post notices at the student activities office and the campus job placement office, and advertise in the campus newspaper. Retirees can be reached through local newspapers as well as retiree organizations and clubs. Finally, telemarketing recruiting and employment agencies now exist in many areas. These may be particularly useful for specialized kinds of telemarketing staff.

PRESCREENING CALLS

When the calls start coming in, you'll need to be prepared to make the most of them. Depending on your area, you may get a surprisingly heavy response. Do some up-front screening before going through the telephone interview. Make up an ad response/prescreen form before you start taking calls. You can use the sample in Figure 15-2 or adapt it to fit your needs. The idea of using this form is to make sure you record essential data at the time of the call, when your memory is freshest. This is your source for calling back candidates you want to interview personally with the twenty-seven–point hiring profile. Tell applicants what types of calls they would be making, the hours, and the pay. Make sure they are still interested in the job. Some applicants will disqualify themselves at this point. For those who do not, set up telephone interviews.

Figure 15-2. Ad response/prescreen form.

Name/Address/Phone	*Diction/Artic. (+/0/–)*	*TM Exper. (Yes/No)*	*Best Time to Call*

USING THE TWENTY-SEVEN–POINT HIRING PROFILE

Figure 15-3 shows the Phone For Success(TM) twenty-seven-point hiring profile, used to select thousands of successful telemarketers for many industries. You can use it with confidence that the ratings you derive are a sound basis for making your hiring decisions.

Ten of the twenty-seven points are connected with voice quality—diction, articulation, volume, rate, and tone. This is absolutely key. The other major categories are rapport and prior telemarketing experience or prior industry experience.

1. *Voice quality.*
   a. *Pronunciation and choice of words:* As you question the candidate, listen closely. Ask yourself, "Do I have any difficulty understanding this person? Some? None at all? Does the candidate slur words, use slang, or have an accent that would give our customers difficulty? Does the candidate project professionalism in his or her choice of words?" Give a score of 0, 1, 2, or 3, with 0 the low score and 3 for truly outstanding clarity, expression, and choice of words.
   b. *Volume:* Give a score of 0 if you have to strain to hear the candidate or if he or she is too loud for your comfort. Give a score of 1 point if the tone is moderate—neither too soft nor too loud.
   c. *Rate of speech:* If you find the candidate talks either a great deal more slowly than you do or noticeably faster, give a score of 0 here. If you have no problem with the rate of speech, give a score of 1 point.
   d. *Tone:* This is a critical category. You can award up to 5 points to the candidate who projects enthusiasm, professionalism, and confidence. If you hear timidity, nervousness, or lack of interest, lower the score accordingly.

2. *Rapport.* The second major area the profile helps you rate is rapport. You can award up to 10 points in this area. This is a major predictor of success on the phone. Listening for rapport is more than listening for voice quality alone, though the two are usually present together.

Ask yourself, "Is this person actively trying to build my confidence and trust? If I were a prospect, would I find this person believable? Does he or she ask relevant questions about the job? The organization? Am I hearing someone sell me on his or her strong points?"

3. *Prior telemarketing experience.* The scale asks you to consider a candidate's prior telemarketing experience. Generally, assign them 1 point for up to six months experience, 2 points for twelve months, and 5 points for more than a year of experience. Ask the candidate his or her prior

Figure 15-3. Twenty-seven-point telemarketing hiring profile.

Name ______________________ Telephone ______________

Street Address ______________________________________

City-State-Zip ______________________________________

1. Voice Quality (10 points total)

A. Pronunciation and choice words (0-3 points)
Diction, articulation, ease of expression ________

B. Volume (0-1 point)
Too Soft? Too loud? Appropriate level? ________

C. Rate of Speech (0-1 point)
Too Fast? Too slow? Normal? ________

D. Tone (0-5 points)
Timid? Confident? Enthusiastic? ________

2. Rapport (10 points total)

A. Was this person interesting to talk to? (0-3 points)
Did you want to know about him/her?
Was he/she engaging? Likable? ________

B. What kinds of questions did he/she ask? (0-3 points)
Intelligent? Probing? ________

C. How would you feel buying from this person? (0-4 points)
Caring? Trustworthy? Inspires confidence? ________

3. Prior Telemarketing or Industry Experience (0-7 points total)

A. Up to 6 months Telemarketing (1 point)
B. 6-12 months Telemarketing (2 points)
C. Over 1 year Telemarketing (5 points)

Choose One (0 if none) ________

Describe past experience ______________________________

D. Prior industry experience (2 points) (0 if none) ________

Describe past experience ______________________________

References ______________________________________

____

____

Interview Date: ______________ **Time:** ________ **Total Score:** ________

PHONE FOR SUCCESS™
181 Hudson Street • New York, NY 10013 • 212-431-6700

experience because the type of telephone work may or may not be close to what you need. Adjust the score accordingly.

4. *Prior industry experience.* Lastly, add up to 2 extra points if the candidate offers some experience with your industry or a related one.

TIPS FOR TELEPHONE INTERVIEWING

It's useful to have a list of questions ready. This will help you keep the conversation on track and ensure that you get the information you need. The following questions will "open up" candidates and get them talking:

What was it about the ad that attracted your attention?

What do you like about selling?

What do you dislike?

What do you think are your strong points in terms of telephone communication?

What are your weak points?

How do you handle rejection?

Tell me about your past telemarketing experience.

If I called up your boss today, what would he say about you?

How much money do you expect to earn this year? In five years?

You may not use all these questions, or you may have some that relate more to your organization or your particular type of telemarketing program. The main point is to be prepared so the conversation generates the information you need.

Note on Taping

It's a good idea to get permission to tape sixty seconds of the interview so that afterwards you can replay it to help you reevaluate the candidate. You may find that you have many qualified candidates who score high on the twenty-seven–point profile. Listening to a candidate's taped conversation may help you in your final decision.

After You Hang Up

After completing the telephone interview, find out the best time to call the candidate back and record it. Conclude the call by letting the candidate know that you will be in touch. After you hang up, tally the scores in each category. As a rule of thumb, 17 is a good candidate, and 20 is outstanding. You may want to invite those who fall in the middle range (15–16) to your office to read a script for you before making a final determination. Anyone who scores below 15 is not worth seeing personally.

THE PERSONAL INTERVIEW

Personal interviews should largely be used simply to confirm the impression you received on the phone. They are also a good opportunity to explain the pay, incentives, and benefits your program offers, as well as the performance standards (see Chapter 17).

If you have an applicant with a questionable rating, you may want to have him or her go through a script with you, using a phone extension. This is fairly high pressure and will reveal whether the voice quality and persistence telemarketing requires are really there.

SUMMARY

Hiring good telemarketers is a process that involves the following steps:

- Determine your hiring needs.
- Narrow the field.
- Advertise.
- Prescreen on the phone.
- Evaluate applicants using the twenty-seven-point hiring profile.
- Confirm your decisions in person.

CHAPTER

16

Training Telemarketing Personnel

REMEMBER, to get the most out of your investment in telemarketing, you need to shape every component of your strategy with the unique characteristics of the phone in mind. Training your telemarketers is no different. Whether you are implementing an outbound or an inbound telemarketing program, you need to use your awareness of the phone as you design your telemarketing training.

And there is no reason why you can't design and implement your own training; this chapter will help you do so. No one knows your needs and your strategy better than you do. The guidelines in this chapter will walk you through this process. If you don't want to take the time to develop your own training, this chapter provides a useful basis for evaluating "off-the-shelf" training and for customizing a training package for your own specific needs.

I have developed the training principles and practices presented in this chapter over fifteen years in telemarketing. It is the essence of the Phone for Success(TM) training program. Phone For Success has effectively trained thousands of participants to handle the demands of telemarketing professionally because it is based on what we know about the phone as a communication medium—its unique characteristics and demands. Consequently, it addresses key training issues:

- *Fear of phoning.* How can your telemarketers overcome the psychological barriers to interrupting and summoning a prospect to the phone? How can they do it day after day?
- *Telephone time management.* How can telemarketers set individual goals that mesh with your overall goals, in a team selling approach?
- *Product knowledge.* How can telemarketers quickly develop a

knowledge base they can use on the phone, particularly to communicate a sophisticated product or service?

- *Getting field sales reps to love the phone.* Many sales executives want field sales personnel to make their own appointments, even when they have separate telemarketing support. Yet most outside salespeople fear the phone and lack the discipline and organizational skills to use it well.

Training in these areas—along with essential listening skills and sales techniques—give telemarketers and outside salespeople an ''edge'' on the phone. They are more confident, more organized, and more in control; and it shows in their performance numbers.

ADVANCE PLANNING

Before starting training, develop a training plan that specifies your goals and the equipment you'll need. Your training goals follow from your strategy. First, summarize the strategy itself, for example, ''Our strategy is to make 500 calls per week to decision makers in the banking industry and to set appointments with them for field sales personnel to demonstrate our software products.''

Training goals are *behaviors that support your strategy.* For this reason, it's best to state your training goals in terms of what participants will be able *to do* after training. For example, at the end of training, you will be able to do the following:

- Get through to decision makers 90 percent of the time
- Use listening techniques to ''see with your ears''
- Get your prospect's attention within twenty seconds
- Handle objections successfully
- Ask relevant questions that establish rapport
- Listen for the prospect's needs, and relate only benefits that match them
- Close effectively using three basic techniques
- Make an appointment with one out of every five prospects
- Manage your limited sales time efficiently

EQUIPMENT

The following is a list of basic equipment. You may want to add or delete materials to fit your needs.

- A tape player and blank tapes—for warm-up, listening, and voice quality exercises
- A speakerphone setup in the training room—so the group as a whole can benefit from each participant's practice exercises
- "Mock problem" outlines—to use for warm-up exercises
- Role play outlines—both related and unrelated to your product
- Role play scenarios—based on specific objections or specific types of personalities your telemarketers will encounter on the phone
- Role play evaluation forms—to record comments on practice exercises
- Scripts, objection response guides, and separate product knowledge materials (if necessary)
- Tapes of an outstanding presentation and a poor presentation—for critique sessions
- Tapes of outstanding voices—from old radio programs, for example

I discuss how to use the equipment and materials in each stage of the training sequence later in the chapter.

DEVELOPING THE TRAINING SEQUENCE

An interactive approach that emphasizes role play to develop confidence as well as competence is a good training technique. It allows moving quickly from role play to actual calls, and the more time spent on actual calls, the more effective the training. The training sequence discussed is suggested as a starting point. You may want to alter it to meet your specific needs. If your concern is getting field salespeople to use the phone effectively, see "Getting Field Salespeople to Love the Phone" later in this chapter.

Introduction

Trainees are usually nervous about the training and about the job. Your goal during a brief introduction is to start channelling that energy into the training process. It's a good idea to begin with a short company orientation and then follow with the strategy summary (the short description of what the telemarketing program is to accomplish).

Then fill in details about how the program fits in with your organization's broader marketing plan for your product or service and the key role that each telemarketer will play. Conclude your introduction with a short review of the product or service itself, including specific features and benefits.

A good transition to the training itself is to present the three key aspects of the telephone as a communication medium (see Chapter 1):

1. It summons a participant.
2. It is audio only.
3. It is interactive.

Warm-up Exercises

Some warm-up exercises that help release some of the nervous energy and focus trainees on the process of communication are a good way to start the training. One called ''the interview'' pairs off participants and allows two minutes for one in each pair to interview the other as though he or she were a reporter for the local paper gathering information for a short news report. After the ''reporters'' give their reports, each pair switches roles.

Another warm-up exercise is the ''mock problem.'' A mock problem is an artificially created situation, usually between two people, each of whom has a conflict or problem to resolve. Because neither person is aware of the other's role, conflict will also emerge as each person tries to accomplish his or her assigned goal.

The purpose of both warm-up exercises is to demonstrate the dynamics of communication and how easily ideas are miscommunicated. The need to listen fully and consciously—rather than simply to think about what *you* want to say next—is the point this type of exercise demonstrates. Here's an example of a mock problem:

> *Instructions:* Have trainees form pairs for this exercise. Assign each individual one of the characters. Tell them, ''Your goal in playing your character will be to resolve your character's conflict to the best of your ability.'' Then instruct each individual separately from his or her partner as follows:
>
> *Trainee 1 (employee):* You don't think your boss is paying you enough money. You have been thinking about asking him for a raise for two weeks, and you've decided to confront him today.
>
> *Trainee 2 (boss):* As you were checking your records, you discovered serious discrepancies in the figures. You think your employee might be stealing money from you. You don't want to accuse him, but you want to talk to him about what's going on.

In this situation, one person will usually assert himself or herself more aggressively and get control. The point of the exercise is that the one who gets control is the one who gets his or her message across. Control is what telemarketing is all about. How to get it on the phone is a major focus of the training.

Script Writing

Before beginning role play exercises, I often take trainees through the process of developing a script for the product themselves. More than anything else, this process will acquaint them with every aspect of the product and stage of the call. If you have the time to take trainees through this process, do so. (See Chapter 10 for the steps required for script development.)

Role Play Exercises

Once you've broken the ice with the warm-ups and familiarization with the script, it's important to move quickly into role play exercises—first using some role plays unrelated to your product, then using your own scripts. The role plays are critical because they focus on the actual communication task trainees will be performing, such as probing and paraphrasing. Paraphrasing is one of the most difficult skills to teach, so spend as much time as possible covering this critical area.

Two role plays you can use or adapt for your training to get trainees practicing phone skills without the pressure of having to work with a particular script follow.

Role Play 1

Service: Photo checks, premium item free with $500 balance

Instructions to Trainee: You represent the Bank of Transylvania. You are going to call a list of current checking account customers. The purpose of your call is to get your current customers to keep a minimum balance of $500 in their checking accounts. You are going to offer them checks with their own photograph on them as an incentive. The customer must come to the bank to take the photograph and deposit the money.

A $25 charge will be deducted from the account if the balance is not maintained. Your objective is to have the customer make an appointment to see a bank officer for the purpose of depositing a minimum of $500 into the checking account.

Features	*Benefits*
1. Checks provide identification	1. Instant credibility
2. Color photograph on the check	2. Prevents stolen checks
3. Checkbook comes in a variety of colors	3. Peace of mind
	4. Convenience for check cashing

Role Play 2

PRODUCT: Pocket electronic dictionary

Setup: The pocket electronic dictionary has been on the market for six months. In that time, the Japanese have begun marketing the product. Why should I buy your electronic dictionary?

Instructions to Trainee: You represent Bright Ideas Unlimited, a mail order electronics firm. You are working from a list that has been mailed a brochure about your product line. Your prospects may or may not have in fact seen the catalog. The brochure may have reached the circular file long before reaching your prospect. Under the most ideal circumstances, he or she may have glanced over it briefly.

The brochure was accompanied by a letter from the president of Wizard Electronics, which featured a few special new items. One of them was the pocket electronic dictionary. However, no price reduction was offered.

Your objective is to sell the dictionary to the executive for personal use, as a valuable tool for his or her secretary, or as a gift item for a client or friend.

The price was $200. However, if purchased within the next thirty days, there is a 15 percent discount, bringing the price down to $170.

Price: $200

Discount: two or more, additional 10 percent off, good for thirty days

Features	*Benefits*
LED display	Easy readability
20,000 entries	You won't need another dictionary
Small size	Can be taken with you
Guides to spelling	Improves your writing
Pronunciation guide	Saves time
Synonyms, antonyms	Your own personal teacher
Easy instructions	

To develop your own role play outline, you need to focus on accurately reproducing the realities your telemarketers will encounter on the phone. One of the best ways to begin writing a role play is to tape some of your test calls. These tapes will give you a good representation of many situations telemarketers will have to handle. They should tell you how to structure your role plays to cover all aspects of a moderately difficult call.

To prepare to run a role play exercise, you need to develop two sets of instructions. The instructions for trainees who will play the role of prospects should include specific product knowledge questions you've encountered during the test calls. The instructions for trainees playing the telemarketer role should include explicit requirements to paraphrase product knowledge questions and to ask the probing questions as indicated in your script. (Leave objections and handling objections to a later stage of the training.)

When trainees begin to role play using your actual script, they will need to have a reservoir of product knowledge to draw on. (In fact, it is often helpful to have trainees develop their own scripts for this purpose.) Product knowledge fact sheets are good supplements to the question/answer format of the objection response guide. You will need to judge whether your product or service is more sophisticated and requires a more elaborate product knowledge manual. If it does, make a formal presentation with a question and answer period part of the training at this point.

You will also need to evaluate each trainee's performance in the role play exercises so you can focus the remainder of the training on specific needs. This is the function of the critique sheet in Figure 16-1.

Figure 16-1. Critique sheet for role plays.

1. Introduced self and company properly		(Y)	(N)
2. Gave good reason for calling		(Y)	(N)
3. Initial statement	strong	adequate	weak
4. Asked for prospect's time if appropriate		(Y)	(N)
5. Smooth transition to probing		(Y)	(N)
6. Used probing questions	strong	adequate	weak
7. Uncovered relevant information and significant needs	strong	adequate	weak
8. Paraphrased effectively	strong	adequate	weak
9. Handled objections	strong	adequate	weak
10. Presented benefits enthusiastically	strong	adequate	weak
11. Closed	strong	adequate	weak

12. Comments:

____

____

____

____

Role Play Critique

Once the training group has gone through the initial role play exercise, go through the critique sheet with each one. The purpose of the critique is not to focus on negatives; telemarketing training needs to concentrate on *positive feedback.*

The critique sheet will show areas that trainees need to focus on; handle this by working with the group to come up with alternatives (e.g., "What else could you have done at that point in the call?"). It's important to avoid getting hung up on negatives without offering or discovering a positive way to handle some part of the call. At this point, it's often useful to play a tape of an actual call by your best telemarketer.

Handling Objections and Fear of Phoning

At this stage of the training, participants should be fairly comfortable with role playing phone techniques, so they can begin role playing with actual scripts, which emphasize typical objections they are likely to encounter. This is also often when you'll begin to confront the very common reaction of "fear of phoning."

If trainees have already experienced or heard everything that prospects can throw at them, they'll be able to respond without fear on the phone. To accomplish this effectively, do intensive role plays, incorporating every objection and question discovered during the test phase (see Chapter 18). This approach gets trainees comfortable with using the objection response guide and the actual script they'll use on the phone.

Objections aren't the only part of telemarketing that causes fear of phoning. The final role plays you use should concentrate on recognizing the personality types telemarketers will encounter on the phone. The training needs to provide the same type and range of experiences that actual phoning involves. Handling it in training really helps trainees overcome fear of phoning on the job.

Overcoming fear of phoning may start in training, but TMRs also need ongoing support to keep it from becoming a problem. And it does become a problem, even among experienced telemarketers. Fear of phoning is basically fear of being rejected.

So you need to monitor on-the-job performance carefully and look for signs that your telemarketers are avoiding the phone—perhaps putting off the first call of the day or making fewer calls per hour. Use weekly meetings to pinpoint the cause and identify solutions other telemarketers are using to overcome the problem.

Role plays 3, 4, and 5 were developed to help trainees practice handling different personality types on the phone. They should give you a starting point to develop your own, based on the types of personalities your own program will involve.

Role Play 3

Personality type: Cautious

Position: You own ten Gold Eagles and one Chinese Panda

Situation: Your spouse recently died and left you $150,000 to invest. So far, you have placed all these funds in a CD, which matures next month. You would like to know how much of your money should be in precious metals, stocks, bonds, etc. A friend of yours told you that precious metals are not a good risk because there is currently very little inflationary pressure in the marketplace. Besides, you don't feel confident doing this kind of business over the phone.

If asked, you might consider a gold accumulation plan.

Role Play 4

Personality type: Skeptical

Position: You have just been promoted to the position of purchasing agent for your company but you have very little experience in purchasing.

Situation: Your company needs a new photocopier. Every day you are flooded with calls from sales representatives trying to set up appointments to see you and sell all sorts of office equipment. You are skeptical to do business with a perfect stranger over the phone.

If a sales representative calls who sounds like he or she knows what he or she is talking about *and* he or she sounds sincere, you will agree to a sales presentation.

Role Play 5

Personality type: Laid back

Position: You are the accounts payable clerk for a small manufacturing company.

Situation: The president of your company does not like to pay the company bills within 30 days. His float averages 90 days. All day long, you are bombarded with phone calls from vendors demanding payment.

The president has just allocated $10,000 to pay the most "pressing" invoices. Explain to each collections department agent what your policy is. Agree to send a check only if the agent makes an excellent case for getting paid immediately.

Voice Skills

Any telemarketing training program must provide trainees the opportunity to recognize the voice quality they bring to the job and work on areas that need improvement. I usually start this stage of the training by playing tapes from classic radio programs (such as "Superman," "The Shadow," or "The Hindenburg Disaster"), because they powerfully convey a rich experience, primarily through the human voice, in a few minutes.

Professional telemarketers need to be able to project their voices in the same powerful way. To do this, they need some of the same techniques for developing their voice quality that great actors use. Most of us are simply not aware of our voice quality and of how we sound to others. For most of us, that's OK; but for telemarketers, it won't do.

Two people using the same script can get very different results because one has recognized the voice quality required and worked to build it, and the other hasn't. Four aspects of voice quality must be worked on in training:

1. Tone
2. Diction
3. Volume
4. Rate

Tone. Tone is probably the most important. It is "how you say what you say." Most of us don't speak or understand German, but no one has trouble understanding the aggression in Hitler's speeches—hearing a tape of one of his speeches is hearing an unmistakably *agressive* tone. Tone in a telemarketer's voice tells the prospect just as much. Trust, confidence, and enthusiasm are the elements that build rapport and are conveyed through tone.

Diction. Diction tells the prospect a great deal about you. In field sales, if you were making a sales visit, you would wear clothing suitable to the environment. Likewise, on the phone, your diction should not be a distraction. Work on recognizing slurred speech and eliminating slang or filler words.

Volume. Today's telephones are well amplified, so shouting isn't necessary. Likewise, too low a volume is irritating and self-defeating. Tell trainees to talk at their normal volume, as if the prospect were seated directly across the desk from them.

Rate. A good rule of thumb is to listen to the prospect and talk just slightly faster than he or she does. Most people are comfortable speaking at about 180 words per minute. Because most trainees have no idea what this rate actually sounds like, have them self-evaluate their rate—and other aspects of voice quality—by using the following voice quality evaluation.

Voice Quality Evaluation.
Instructions: The following paragraph is about 180 words long. Read it aloud and time yourself. When you are able to complete it in one minute, tape your performance. Then use the voice quality checklist to evaluate your tape. The results are often surprising.

Voice Quality Self-Test

Our company is really a people company. It's a growing organization because it's committed to meeting important business needs. We maintain high standards of performance and service in a variety of ways. One of the most important is our "Management Involvement Program." MIP seeks to recognize the contributions of every employee at every level of the company. It works through organized groups consisting of managers, supervisors, and line employees from every department in the company. These groups meet regularly to discuss their operations and to identify solutions to problems. Leadership of the groups revolves among all employees within each group. Every participant speaks as an equal. Very often, the MIP groups assign a task force to brainstorm about a specific problem. Sometimes the task forces cross departmental lines if the problem seems to involve several departments. We've found that the MIP is an effective way to remove obstacles to performance. It has improved communication between departments. And it has really built the strong sense that we're a team, working together to keep our organization ahead of the competition.

Voice Quality Checklist

Instructions: As you listen to your tape, grade each aspect of your voice. A total of 15 points is possible. If you score 10 or above, your voice quality is excellent. A score of less than 10 suggests you need to improve in some area(s).

Tone (0–6 points possible):

Friendly______	Pushy______
Sincere______	Timid______
Phony______	Confident______

Diction (0–5 points possible):
Mumbled______ Distracting______

Volume (0–2 points possible):
Too soft______ Too loud______

Rate (0–2 points possible)
Too slow______ Too fast______

After the self-test of voice quality, you may want to listen to individual tapes and reevaluate them using the checklist. Comparing the trainee's evaluation with another's evaluation is often a revealing exercise and can pinpoint specific aspects of the voice that need improvement.

Telephone Time Management

The final stage of training, prior to monitored calling to actual leads, focuses on a crucial telemarketing skill: time management. Any telemarketer who lacks the techniques of telephone time management is operating at half-speed. Emphasize establishment of a calling rhythm at the beginning of the workday and sticking with it.

Precall Planning. Start every day with a plan, including clear, personal goals. Some telemarketers set goals for their first calling hour (e.g., to set a specific number of appointments or reach a certain number of decision makers). If and when they make their goal, they reward themselves in some way. The goals and rewards must be individualized. The important thing is they are meaningful to the telemarketer.

Mental Warm-ups. Whether the goal is actually met is less important than the process of goal setting and striving. It takes organization and a positive mental attitude to do it successfully on the job. So it is important that trainees—especially field salespersons being taught telemarketing techniques—develop and practice a mental routine before they ever pick up the phone for the first call of the day. This routine before the first call is like the warm-up exercises that runners perform before an event:

- Organize your materials—callbacks, new leads, report forms, scripts, and objection response guides you know you will need.
- Clear your mind of everything—the problems you had yesterday, the party you went to last night, etc.
- Concentrate exclusively on your personal goal for the hour or the morning.
- Make the first call of the day.

Sustaining the Momentum. Once trainees understand the importance of starting off the morning with a personal goal in focus, they need to know how to keep the momentum going throughout a long and often frustrating shift or day. This is especially important for training field salespersons to use the phone to set their own appointments. Here are some tips:

- Never allow more than one minute between one call and the next.
- Never stay on hold more than thirty seconds—hang up and call back.
- Never make more than three calls to the same lead—the chances are, if you haven't gotten hold of the prospect after three tries, you're not going to.
- Never leave your phone number with a prospect's secretary—callbacks are rare. If they do call back, you are not in control.
- Terminate nonproductive calls quickly but tactfully (for example, "I know you're busy, and I don't want to hold you up. Thanks for your time.").

Monitored Calling

The final phase of the training sequence is monitored calling to actual leads. In a two-day training program, monitored calling usually begins by the morning of the second day, although this may vary somewhat—actual calling may begin sooner when retraining experienced telemarketers or later if the first day sequence has a lengthy product knowledge component. The key point is that telemarketing training should emphasize time on the phone, in actual calling situations, as much as possible.

The focus of actual calling is to work on polishing techniques learned in training. It is a good idea to tape the initial calls and play them back for critique with the telemarketer. As with the role play critiques, the critique of monitored calls should emphasize the positive. The negatives will be obvious enough to the trainee. The point of going over the tapes is *recognition* of an alternative way to handle a given situation.

The individualized coaching during the actual calling stage builds on the confidence that role playing develops. So the more time you can devote to actual calls and coaching, the more polished the posttraining performance will be. If a pattern develops in the training group (e.g., difficulty getting through to decision makers or closing), regroup and go over alternative solutions for the entire class.

If trainees are experiencing different types of problems on different stages of the calls, have them listen to recorded conversations in which the specific aspect of the call was handled well. The key is to quickly recognize problems, redirect trainees to an alternative, and get them back on the phone. Trainees may also be seated with an experienced telemarketer for a while to listen for specific alternatives to the problem they were experiencing.

Supervised Calling

Typically, the entire second day of training is spent in actual calling. Try to duplicate on-the-job conditions as much as possible (e.g., distribute actual leads, provide activity report forms, and work with trainees to form specific personal goals).

On the second day of actual calling, you will normally need to provide close supervision and coaching to "fine-tune" some points with trainees. Again, your actual training agenda may vary somewhat, depending on the prior experience of the staff you are training and particularly on the amount of time you need for product knowledge orientation.

Wrap-up and Evaluation

End with a brief summary of the key points and have trainees fill out a short training evaluation form. These evaluations are important and often provide useful feedback for subsequent training. Training should be ongoing, based on consistent monitoring and intervention for individuals who need it.

GETTING FIELD SALESPEOPLE TO LOVE THE PHONE

Most people in sales are familiar with the "80/20 rule": Salespeople spend 80 percent of their time looking for customers and 20 percent of their time actually selling. A separate telemarketing group focused on generating appointments for field sales visits can increase actual selling time dramatically and so is an efficient use of marketing resources. However, there is a significant body of argument that says, even if you have telemarketers developing leads for field sales, the outside sales rep ought to be on the phone generating appointments. (No one argues anymore that face-to-face calls should be made *without* appointments. Just knocking on random doors is an inefficient use of a trained sales rep's time.)

The bottom line is that field salespeople live or die by having enough high-quality leads. Yet most companies that put their outside salespeople on the phone experience disappointing results. Despite the incentives, the pep talks, and the analyses of how phoning for appointments can build commission income, *field salespeople resist using the phone.* The following scenario often unfolds:

1. The salespeople sit down to make calls.
2. They proceed to take care of yesterday's business, make service calls, make personal calls, read the newspaper, have a cup of coffee, go to the bathroom, and return and shuffle through a stack of lead cards, looking for someone to call. An hour elapses in this way.
3. They finally dial and make a contact.
4. They are rejected.
5. They repeat many of the time-consuming actions in step 2.

In this way, the typical face-to-face sales rep will make four or five calls a day, resulting in zero appointments. Ultimately, he or she concludes that the phone doesn't work, is a great waste of time, and the sales manager is crazy to insist on it.

There are basically four reasons for this behavior: (1) fear of rejection, (2) lack of organizational skills required for success on the phone, (3) poor understanding of the telephone as a communications medium, and (4) failure to develop and use the selling skills—*different from face-to-face selling skills*—that the telephone requires.

Fear of Rejection

In field sales, where perhaps four to six sales visits are made in a day, the absolute number of negative responses is fairly low and spread out over the course of a day. Face-to-face salespeople are usually able to handle this level of rejection. However, most are simply not accustomed to the volume of rejection that sustained telephone selling involves—in a four-hour shift, a telemarketer may experience rejection five to ten times every hour, twenty to forty times per shift. Field sales reps will do almost anything to avoid this.

Lack of Organizational Skills

Most outside salespeople are bright, quick, creative thinkers. They do not enjoy regimentation and discipline. Yet success on the phone depends heavily on planning, goal setting, and discipline—*before* a single call is made. Prospect cards must be collected and organized; clear, *hourly* goals must be set; and a strong script with primary and secondary objectives must be adhered to. This disciplined approach is radically different from that typically taken prior to a day of face-to-face sales calls. Few outside salespeople are ready for it, unless they've been trained to do it; consequently, most hate the phone.

Poor Understanding of the Telephone

Outside salespeople love visuals. They are accustomed to getting visual cues in person and are well prepared to respond to them. Even their training programs have accustomed them to repond visually, stressing the use of role play and videotape to develop their sensitivity to visual cues in selling.

In contrast, the audio-only quality of the phone frustrates and inhibits outside salespeople. They feel like they're flying blind—and most are. Most cannot "see with their ears" without proper training or use a script effectively. Most don't even know why a script is necessary to sell on the phone.

Failure to Develop Telephone Selling Skills

Training of outside salespeople should concentrate on *changing behavior* using constant positive feedback. Focus on specific ways that selling on the telephone differs from selling face to face:

- *Getting through to the decision maker*—most face-to-face selling just doesn't require this skill.
- *Introductory skills and pacing* in telemarketing—the first fifteen seconds of the call are critical to success. A telephone sales call typically lasts only a few minutes. Compared to an in-person call, this is rapid indeed, and most field salespeople are not accustomed to handling it.
- *Presenting only relevant features and benefits*—Most field salespeople say too much on the phone and still fail to get their message across. The reason is they're selling the product, not the appointment. The difference is not automatically clear to them unless they are trained to see it and practice it.
- *Voice and listening skills*—Instead of giving and getting visual cues, as in face-to-face selling, the telemarketer must listen for cues and has only his or her voice to convey the message. Again, the difference in behavior is critical and comes only with training and reinforcement.
- *Telephone time management*—Telephone time management involves not merely precall planning and knowing the script, important as they are, but *behavioral discipline:*
  - — Preparing leads, so calls can be made in quick succession
  - — Allowing no more than sixty seconds between calls
  - — Never staying on hold for more than thirty seconds
  - — Never leaving a phone number because no one calls back and because you don't control the call if they do.

— Telephoning without interruption for any reason *for two-hour periods*
— Setting daily goals instead of the monthly goals more common in face-to-face selling.

These behaviors are *habits of success* in a telemarketing environment. They do not occur "naturally" to anyone, least of all to face-to-face salespeople.

FIELD SALES TRAINING IMPLEMENTATION PLAN

Here are the steps in the Phone for Success™ basic approach to training field salespeople in using the telephone:

1. Set aside separate days or mornings—at least four hours—for appointment calls during each week, and require *all sales personnel to get on the phone.*
2. Get the sales group to agree to the day or morning selected and buy into the program.
3. If possible, select a single large room where the entire sales staff can assemble for the calling.
4. Set a goal for the day(s) and a total goal for the week—put a chart or some other visual up on the wall where everyone can see the progress made toward the daily goal.
5. Appoint a supervisor from the sales group—this should rotate weekly through the group and is important for monitoring and coaching.
6. Use the scripting materials in Chapter 11 to train the group to develop their own script—they don't like accepting someone else's verbiage.
7. Require each salesperson to stay on the phone for a minimum of two hours, without getting up for any reason.
8. Require a minimum of twenty calls and six contacts per hour, knowing that they will be rejected thirty to fifty times in that period.
9. *Positively* reinforce the value of getting rejected—every rejection means you're closer to the goal of having enough appointments for the week. Sales trainer Tom Hopkins actually puts a dollar value on rejection—i.e., if four appointments result in one sale worth a $1,000 commission, and it takes 100 rejections to get four appointments, *every rejection is worth $10!* This is looking at rejection positively, not negatively.
10. Design group—not individual—incentives for each day. Make sure

that everyone can win. These can be small amounts—the dollars are less important than getting into the spirit.

11. Forbid any other type of call or activity during appointment-setting hours—no service calls, no inbound calls, no personal calls.
12. Require casual clothing for the session—no one is going to make a sales call or visit a client.
13. Prepare and give a pep talk at the beginning and end of each two-hour calling segment.
14. Look for opportunities to provide coaching—ten-minute sessions with individuals who are struggling or having problems to get them back on track.
15. Install appropriate monitoring equipment so supervisors can listen for problems and intervene.
16. Install taping equipment so managers or supervisors can review "good" and "bad" calls and let new people hear them. The review creates discipline among the staff and can help train new personnel or those having problems.
17. Post this rule in large, clear lettering: NO CALLS, NO APPOINTMENTS.

This approach is designed to *change behavior*. It can be adapted to any organization that uses outside salespeople. It has been tremendously successful in getting field salespeople on the phone, making their own appointments, handling the rejections involved and ultimately making more sales.

SUMMARY

The training approach described in this chapter emphasizes getting trainees on the phone early in the training process, using actual scripts and actual leads. To make the transition from the training environment to the job environment, role play is used to overcome fear of phoning. This chapter also presented a number of tips on telephone time management.

The key point about training field salespeople to use the phone effectively to generate sales appointments is that it changes behavior. It focuses on training field salespeople to use the phone as an important source of income, instead of letting it be a waste of time and a source of frustration and rejection. There are four key reasons most field salespeople cannot use the phone effectively:

1. Fear of rejection
2. Lack of telephone organizational skills
3. Poor understanding of the phone as a communications medium

4. Failure to develop telephone selling skills, as distinct from face-to-face selling skills

The following training checklist for a two-day telemarketing training seminar can be adapted to most situations:

Training Checklist

- ☐ 1. Introduction/company orientation
- ☐ 2. Product knowledge introduction
- ☐ 3. Warm-up exercises
- ☐ 4. Script writing (optional)
- ☐ 5. Role plays (unrelated to your product)
- ☐ 6. Critique
- ☐ 7. Role plays (using your script)
  - a. Selling benefits
  - b. Closing
- ☐ 8. Critique
- ☐ 9. Script walk-through without objections
- ☐ 10. How to handle objections
- ☐ 11. Role play (script with objections)
- ☐ 12. Role play (personality types)
- ☐ 13. Voice skills
- ☐ 14. Tips on telephone time management
- ☐ 15. Monitored calling/coaching

CHAPTER

17

Compensation and Morale

NO factor is more closely linked to the morale of your telemarketers than compensation. Telemarketing programs that have well-thought-out, realistic compensation plans usually maintain high morale and productivity levels over time and avoid the common problems of ''burnout'' and rapid turnover.

PLANNING YOUR COMPENSATION STRUCTURE

No matter how carefully you've selected and trained your staff, boredom and ''burnout'' will eventually affect your telemarketers. This can lead to unacceptable turnover and productivity problems, so it really is critical to plan ahead. The most basic strategy is to develop and implement an equitable and financially realistic compensation schedule. The following guidelines should be helpful in this regard.

Step 1: Calculate Sales-to-Cost Ratio

Your first step is to calculate the basic amount you can afford to pay. Don't borrow figures; determine your own, based on your own costs and profit margin. Most telemarketing operations use a baseline sales:cost ratio in the range of 22 to 25 percent. This ratio includes costs associated with direct mail, plus overhead and labor, taken as a percentage of the unit price of the product or service. After deriving this basic percentage, you know what you can pay while realizing a given profit.

Step 2: Evaluate What You Need to Pay

Factors to be considered in determining what you need to pay include the following:

- The relative difficulty of your program's call objective
- The amount of training and knowledge required
- The number of daily calls needed to meet sales objectives
- The labor pool available for your specific type of telemarketing program
- The compensation being offered by companies

Be conservative at this point, until you have some historical data to work with. If you initially think that the job to be done requires compensation that would raise your sales ratio above the 22 to 25 percent range, don't immediately assume that you should jump to the upper limit—say, 30 percent—allowed by your profit margin. If you do so and then later find out that other costs are higher than expected, you will be putting your program in the hole. Start at the low end; then, if other cost projections hold up in relation to sales, raise compensation accordingly.

Step 3: Plan How to Pay

Most telemarketing programs that employ full-time staff use a base salary plus commission structure. Programs employing part-timers normally offer a base hourly wage plus a commission or bonus for each sale, order, or appointment scheduled. Assuming that you are using full-time people and that your product is fairly sophisticated, you may decide on a relatively low salary plus a commission designed to double the salary if minimum sales targets are met.

Commission percentages may be graduated after the minimum is reached so that each additional sale nets more to the telemarketer who makes the effort. Some plans have several "plateaus"—for example, if the product is priced at $375, a 10 percent commission might be paid if the minimum target of three sales per day is met. The next plateau might be 15 percent on the next five sales and then 20 percent on any sales above that. Some programs pay a 5 percent bonus to telemarketers who meet or exceed targets for two months in a row. These percentages are just samples. You will need to develop your own based on your cost factors and margin of profit.

It is essential to review your compensation schedule regularly. You may need to change your initial commission percentages, offer additional bonuses, or adjust the plateau points. As with any type of incentive program, commissions must be based on known, reachable objectives. Don't offer commissions you know you'll never pay. Until your program is well established and you can predict with certainty what your costs and sales volume will be, avoid using a draw against commission approach because it adds another pressure factor few new programs can manage well.

Step 4: Decide When to Pay

Decide how frequently you will pay, and then be sure to stick with it. If salaries are paid twice a month, commissions once a month, and bonuses quarterly, be sure your telemarketers understand this schedule at the outset. If commissions are determined on the basis of product shipped and not orders written for a given time period, say so at the time you hire. And if you use an order verification system that may result in lowered commissions, be sure to tell your telemarketers about it in advance. Be prepared to substantiate orders that are refused.

Be prepared to pay salaries, commissions, and bonuses *promptly,* when due. When all is said and done, what keeps your staff on the phone and selling, putting up with rejection and stress, is the thought of the check they will get for doing so. If you delay paying your telemarketers, you sabotage your program.

Finally, if you employ both field sales and telemarketing staff to sell the same product or service, pay the same commission per sale to both. That you pay less to telemarketers will soon ''get around'' and will substantially damage morale.

MAINTAINING MORALE

There is no way around the fact that telemarketing is stressful work. Many questions are naturally passing through the telemarketer's mind:

What kind of person will I be talking with?
Am I going to be rejected?
Can I make this sale?

Handling these mental questions every day is bound to wear down even the most enthusiastic telemarketer at some point. Just think about it for a moment. Imagine yourself in a phone booth at a busy airport. Frenetic activity bustles all around you, and the air is charged with the pressure of people ''getting somewhere.'' During the next six hours, you must make fifty or sixty calls, knowing that many will result in rejection. Yet, to meet your goal, you must project confidence and enthusiasm in every call, hour after hour, day after day.

In this environment, discouragement is going to set in at various points. When it does, you'll see your volume of calls slide, your conversion ratio fall, and profits drop. Frequently, you'll see telemarketers avoiding the first call of the day and stretching the time between calls well beyond the minute maximum.

Managers have various tools available for handling this situation *before* it becomes a productivity problem. Your compensation plan is basic to good morale. In addition, you need to review your plan regularly to make sure its incentive structure is realistic and effective. Other useful morale-building strategies include changing the pace, adding a manager, holding staff meetings, and providing executive support.

Changing the Pace Often

One of the best ways to boost morale and build an energetic selling atmosphere is to run productivity contests and games. The rewards from these morale-building programs should be available in the short term, though the contests can be continuing.

An extremely effective morale-building program for the inbound sales reservations staff of a major cruise line worked like this: The staff of fifty was split up into five teams of ten people each. Each team was represented by a different ship on a magnetic map of the world. Each team's sales moved its ship ahead on the sailing route around the world. Whenever a ship made a "port of call," the team members earned a gift that represented the port—this might be a sack of oranges for a Florida port, a bag of coffee for Rio, or a TV when the ship arrived in Japan. Figure 17-1 shows the "game board" for "Ports of Call." This simple game kept interest levels high and eliminated absenteeism. Productivity skyrocketed as teams began to "close in" on a port. Basically, this program worked because of two factors:

1. It provided frequent rewards of different, sometimes surprising, values.
2. It provided a longer term frame of reference—something that telemarketers often lose as they focus on daily and hourly goals and frustrations.

Another approach is to use surprise contests in which you award small cash bonuses on the spot to anyone who meets a certain performance level during the day. For example, you might announce that anyone who does 5 percent over his or her prior day's sales gets $25 cash. You'll have to figure out the specific percentages and cash awards that make sense for your environment, but the idea is to use surprise contests to liven the atmosphere and provide a change of pace.

Figure 17-1. Ports of Call game board.

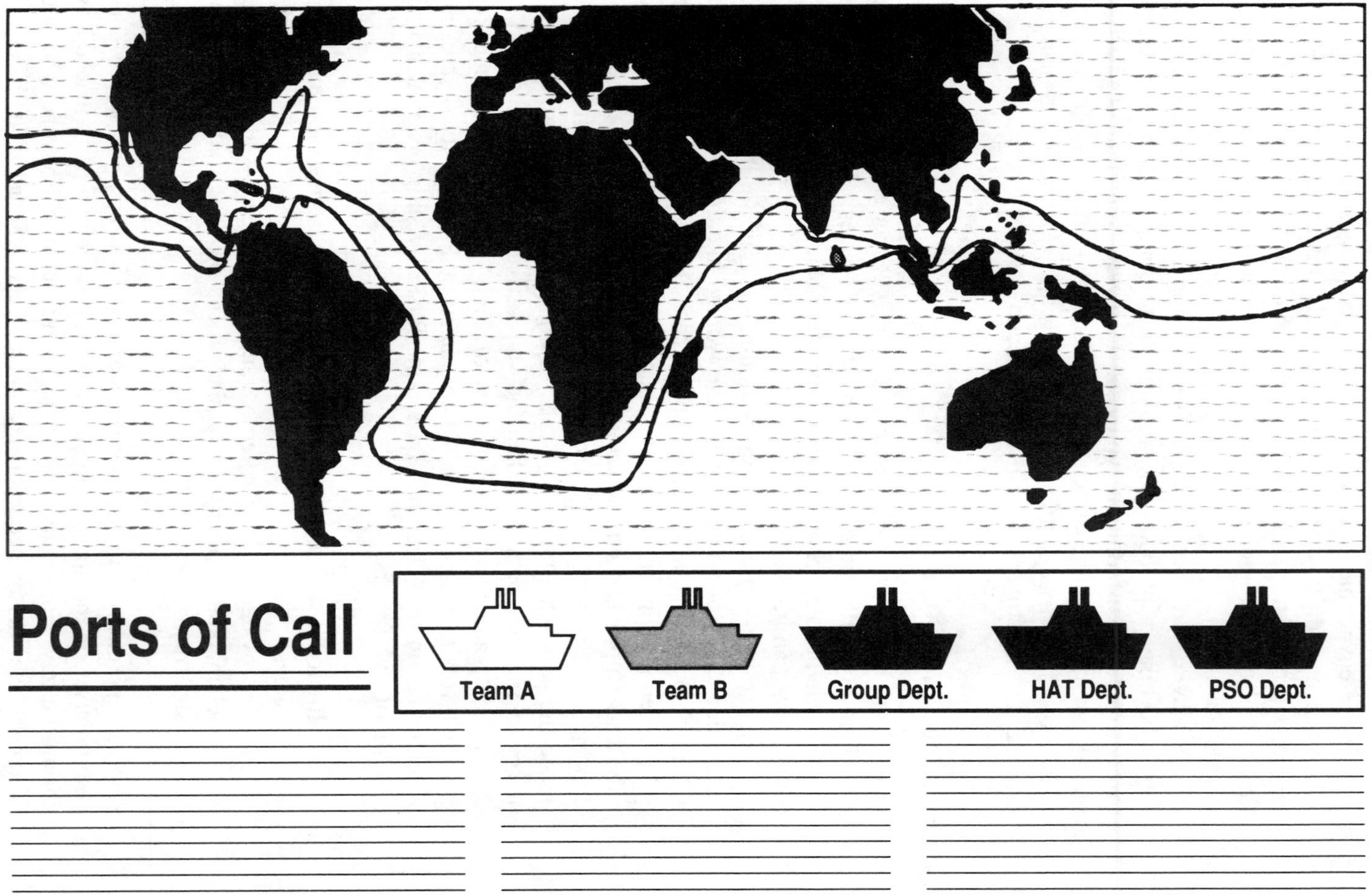

The rewards don't always have to be cash. A pair of movie tickets, free video rental certificates, tickets to sports or other events, dinner tickets, and so forth all work well. Remember to keep the goals realistic—don't offer surprise awards for achieving unproven call objectives, and time your announcements so the goals are reachable in a short period.

Surprise contests offering near-term rewards do help change the pace and relieve some of the stress in a telemarketing environment. But bear in mind that "one-winner" games will eventually lose effectiveness. Mix in a liberal number of "no-loser" games, such as "the fishbowl": Every time a telemarketer makes a sale or schedules an appointment, he or she gets to pick a slip of paper from the fishbowl. On the slips are amounts ranging for $1 to $5. Slips are picked at random, and everyone is capable of winning something. Other variations are the bingo game and the poker game. In the latter, every sale entitles the telemarketer to pick a card from the deck. The best three hands win a prize.

Don't forget the purpose of all of these short-term incentives and contests: to raise morale and inspire interest. They should not be used to encourage "dog-eat-dog" competition. This only increases pressure and leads to further demoralization. What you're looking for is creating a roomful of winners. If you design your incentives so that everyone can win, you'll win, too.

The Role of the Telemarketing Manager

At some point as you develop your program, you will need to bring in a telemarketing manager to handle day-to-day operations. This person plays a key role in maintaining morale.

Especially at the beginning of the day, but also at various points throughout the day, it's important for telemarketers to sense the manager is available, watching and listening—but not looking over the telemarketer's shoulder. "Management by walking around" is an excellent morale builder at the same time that it lets the manager pick up impressions and information.

Another helpful technique is for the manager to review daily call logs. This allows the manager to pinpoint potential problems and plan early responses. If a problem is revealed, it's important that criticisms be handled in a positive way. The most useful approach is to recognize what isn't working and direct the telemarketer to alternatives that do work. The manager also needs to keep on top of the situation and review it again in a reasonable amount of time. People will nearly always agree to work through a problem if the manager's basic stance is one of support and developing solutions.

Never bring in as manager someone who has not been a telemarketer. Unless he or she has experienced the intense pressure and frustration inherent in the job, your manager will never understand the needs of the staff. The motives that underlie their behavior as well as the methods that help them do a better job will simply be a mystery.

In addition, the manager should be sensitive to the facts of a professional telemarketing environment and to the feelings of confinement and pressure it generates. You need someone who knows the importance of balancing the stress of selling with short breaks, unregimented lunch hours, and other methods of relieving pressure. He or she should be comfortable using morale-building methods to support the telemarketing staff and creative enough to develop new variations that fit specific situations.

The manager must also be flexible. Telemarketers do need organizational limits (e.g., set working hours), but within those limits, the manager needs to be able to promote a climate of freedom in which individual work styles are allowed. A highly regimented management style is generally not successful for telemarketing managers.

Holding Regular Staff Meetings

One of the most useful morale builders is a short, five- or ten-minute meeting each morning. The morning meeting is an opportunity to reiterate goals, brush up on fundamentals, reemphasize important product benefits compared to the competition, let off steam, and ventilate frustrations. These are ''warm-up'' meetings to get the staff primed for the job that day. Beyond that, you can use them to get at the sources of frustrations or specific performance problems. Sometimes it may be an objection that is hard to answer. At other times, it may be the strength of the competition. Often other staff members will contribute solutions they've used in the same situation—an excellent way to build teamwork while solving practical problems.

Regular meetings can also provide valuable feedback about the market's response to your product or service. They can be mini-training sessions to introduce new products, services, scripts, and so forth. And this brings up an important point. Over time, you will most likely phase in new products and services. Make an effort to introduce them and train the telemarketers about them in a formal way. Suddenly switching staff to a new product—before they've had time to assimilate the details and learn scripts—is extremely demoralizing. Sometimes it is useful to select some of your top performers to learn a new script first, before introducing it to the entire sales force.

Providing Strategic Executive Support

As an executive, you can support morale. For example, your telemarketing department should be fully integrated into your enterprise, both physically and organizationally. The telemarketing center should not be physically isolated from the heart of your company. The implication of physical isolation is that the leadership level of your organization wants to be disassociated from it. In large organizations, it's particularly important to send a positive message to the telemarketing staff by locating the telemarketing center in a prominent place.

Organizational integration of telemarketing is another way to support morale from a "big picture" standpoint. Involve telemarketers in the organization. Plan for the staff to participate in new product seminars. Invite their feedback in regular sessions. Provide methods for them to develop within the telemarketing group—as team leaders, product specialists, supervisors, and managers—as well as outside of telemarketing. Develop career paths from telemarketing to other functions within the organization so telemarketing people know they are on an equal footing with others regarding opportunities.

These steps at the strategic level will strongly counteract the tacit understanding—formerly quite common—that telemarketing is a kind of "fly-by-night," short-term operation. It will also dispel the expectation that telemarketers are simply low-level employees, likely to leave the job in a few months anyway. People tend to strive toward the expectations set for them. To build and maintain morale in your telemarketing program, set your expectations high.

SUMMARY

This chapter addressed two important human resource issues in telemarketing: compensation and morale. These issues are especially important in telemarketing due to the extraordinary rejection and burnout that telemarketing reps experience every day.

The most important aspect of compensation is planning its structure. The steps involved are:

1. Calculate your sales to cost ratio
2. Evaluate what you need to pay
3. Plan how to pay
4. Decide when to pay

The section on maintaining morale provided specific examples that you can implement immediately. Among the general guidelines offered are changing the pace, holding surprise contests, adding a telemarketing manager, holding regular staff meetings, and providing strategic executive support.

PART

V

Managing Your Telemarketing Program

CHAPTER

18

Testing Every Step of Your Program

CHAPTER 12 showed that testing your script is a critical task in implementing your strategy. It allows you to develop a file of objections and polish your responses to them. But the script isn't the only aspect of your strategy you need to test, and objections aren't the only information you can collect by testing. Properly planned and executed, test calls will generate an abundance of useful data—about your market, your customers and prospects, and your product or service.

TEST VARIABLES

In addition to testing a new script to help develop your objection response guide, there are several other variables it's important to test:

- Your list
- Your offer
- Your calling hours

The more variables you test, the more certain you can be of your program's financial feasibility. Testing for the variables listed allows you to project your program's overall ROI with reasonable confidence and shows you which elements of your strategy need adjustment or "fine-tuning" so you will meet your revenue goals.

You don't necessarily have to test your program yourself. There are any number of contract telemarketing services in most major cities that will make test calls for you for an hourly fee. As with any other business decision, you will need to investigate this thoroughly. Make sure you understand clearly what you will get for each hour of calling time. If your offer is sophisticated or complex, try to meet the telemarketing staff yourself. This way you can make a judgment as to their competence to project your offer over the phone.

However, if your offer is relatively simple, designing and conducting test calls yourself is a fairly straightforward process consisting of four steps.

Step 1: Developing Test Data Sheet

In telemarketing testing, as in any other type, you test for one variable at a time—holding all the others constant. Your first step is to decide which variable you will test first—the list, the offer, or calling time, for example—and to create a *test data sheet*.

You will use the test data sheet to record the information collected from your test calls. Figure 18-1 shows a sample test data sheet. You can use this basic design or adapt it to meet your own needs and situation. It

Figure 18-1. Sample test data sheet.

PROJECT NAME: ____________________

	Scrn Out	*Wrong # No Ans.*	*Not Avail*	*Not Int*	*Send Lit*	*CB*	*Yes*
Time Called: __________							
Name __________							
Title __________							
Company __________							
Street __________							
CSZ __________							
Phone: ( ) __________							
Time Called: __________							
Name __________							
Title __________							
Company __________							
Street __________							

	Scrn Out	*Wrong # No Ans.*	*Not Avail*	*Not Int*	*Send Lit*	*CB*	*Yes*

CSZ__________________

Phone: (   )____________

Time Called:____________

Name__________________

Title__________________

Company_______________

Street__________________

CSZ__________________

Phone: (   )____________

Time Called:____________

Name__________________

Title__________________

Company_______________

Street__________________

CSZ__________________

Phone: (   )____________

Notes ____

TOTALS: ____

provides space to record the prospect's name, phone number, and address for each test call. You may want to add space to record the decision maker's title or department if identifying those details is important for your strategy. Or you may wish to record your test calls by the hour to measure productivity for different calling times (morning, afternoon, or evening), as shown in Figure 18-2.

Across the center of the form is a series of column headers designating different call outcomes. Again, you may want to change some of these to more accurately reflect your call objective. At the end of each call, simply check off the appropriate column. At the completion of test calling, you can easily count and total the checkmarks for each category.

It is always good practice to include a "notes" area so you can record comments, questions, and information that don't fit into one of the categories. This kind of information is extremely useful for developing your objection response guide, revising your script, and evaluating your offer.

Testing does represent a cash outlay, so you will want to set some limits. A basic guideline is to make enough calls to produce at least 50 positive responses on a medium- to high-ticket item. For a low-ticket item, make enough calls to get 125 positive responses. Another guideline is to limit the test calls for each variable to 200. A third guideline is to set 500 as the limit to test the overall feasibility of a given strategy.

Obviously, how many test calls to make is something of a "gray area." It is at least partly a function of the financial resources available and partly of how much certainty you need before you proceed with full-scale implementation. The previous guidelines should be considered minimums. You will need to use your own judgment and knowledge about your situation to decide when to stop test calls and evaluate results.

Step 2: Analyzing Test Data

Analysis of your test data should follow three basic steps:

1. Cumulate the totals for each column of your test data sheet, and enter them along the bottom.
   - Number of contacts with decision makers (completed calls)
   - Number of call attempts (dials)
   - Number of sales/appointments
   - Number with no interest in offer
   - Number that wants literature sent
   - Number of wrong numbers or no answers
   - Number not available (in meetings, out)
   - Number of times screened out by reception staff
   - Number to call back for a decision

Figure 18-2. Sample test data sheet for recording calls by hour.

PROJECT NAME: ______________________

LIST: ______________________________

	Scrn Out	*Wrong # No Ans.*	*Not Avail*	*Not Int*	*Send Lit*	*CB*	*Yes*
8 A.M.–9 A.M.							
9 A.M.–10 A.M.							
10 A.M.–11 A.M.							
11 A.M.–12 P.M.							
12 P.M.–1 P.M.							
1 P.M.–2 P.M.							
2 P.M.–3 P.M.							
3 P.M.–4 P.M.							
4 P.M.–5 P.M.							
5 P.M.–6 P.M.							
6 P.M.–7 P.M.							
7 P.M.–8 P.M.							
8 P.M.–9 P.M.							

Notes ______________________________________

____

____

____

TOTALS: ______________________________________

You may also want to cumulate other totals, such as the number of times certain kinds of objections occurred. However, the main thing is to be able to calculate your sales per calling hour and your contacts with qualified decision makers per hour. Other areas, such as testing the offer, the list, and calling time, are important because these factors affect the sales and contact rate per hour.

Before comparing your test results with the following guidelines, note that it is impossible to say in hard numbers what sales results to expect or find acceptable. Several variables prevent this (e.g., business-to-business sales vary a great deal from business to consumer sales). Even within the area of business-to-business sales, the nature of the product itself and the call objective can produce fairly wide variations in results. For example, appointments generated per hour can vary greatly between selling office products and a complex software product.

2. Calculate the following percentages:

Test Percentage	*Standard Percentage*
Completed calls/total calls, or presentations per hour:	Four–six/hour

The standard of four to six presentations per hour seems to hold up across most business-to-business telemarketing programs, provided there are no extreme call objectives (e.g., selling a $100,000 computer system).

Calls screened out/total calls:	No more than 20 percent

This is a function of your TMRs' ability to penetrate screens.

Wrong numbers and no answers/total calls:	No more than 10 percent

This is a function of your list quality.

Send literature/completed calls:	20 percent

Unless your call objective is to mail a catalog or brochure and then follow up with a second phone call, be careful of any percentage much higher than 20 percent. You don't want a telemarketing program that consists of mailing literature.

Not available/total calls:	30 percent

This "standard" will depend on the universe of prospects you are calling. Some groups, like purchasing agents, are nearly always available. Others, like sales executives, are often tied up in meetings.

3. Compare the percentages you calculate from your test data to the "standard percentages."

Step 3: Evaluating Test Results

For the first ratio (completed calls/total calls), the standard guideline is 40 percent. If your calculated percentage is noticeably lower than this, you need to isolate the reason. Run a second series of test calls using a sample from the same list but focused on a single time of day. Record the resulting percentage of calls completed. Then test another list sample using the same calling hours as on your original test. In this way, you should be able to decide whether your list or your calling time is the factor to change.

The ratio of requests for literature to completed calls should be about 20 percent. If your percentage is much higher, you need to improve your script and retest it. This might also be a function of your training. Requests for literature should be handled as objections to be overcome. (See Chapter 12.)

In business-to-business telemarketing, wrong numbers and no answers usually mean out of business. If your percentage exceeds the standard, you may need a new list. You might also seek a refund on your rental payment for your first list.

Both the "decision maker not available" and the "decision maker requests callback" categories should total about 30 percent of your completed calls. If your percentage is much higher, you need to find out why. Retest your calling time.

Clearly, the closer your test results are to the standard guideline percentages, the more likely your program is to succeed as is. Most telemarketing programs do require some modification, however; so don't be surprised if your test results send you "back to the drawing board." Revising your script, changing your calling hours, or obtaining a higher quality list are small investments compared to the lost revenues if your telemarketing strategy fails to meet its objectives.

What you're really comparing in a test is not your results against some arbitrary standard, but your results against your own experience. You may need to run "split" tests to determine where and when your specific program will generate the best response for your investment. Hence, in a way, every program establishes its own guidelines and standards.

When establishing your initial guidelines, check with your outside sales force if you have one. Usually, they've been in contact with your prospect audience and can help establish what you can expect.

Always have at least two TMRs making calls to the same list to make sure it isn't the TMR who is affecting results. As you get more TMRs, you'll be able to establish incentive guidelines.

Step 4: Calculating ROI

Your testing program will give you important productivity information for fine-tuning your script, list, offer, calling hours, and so forth. More important is the fact that you can use test data to project your cost of sales, sales per hour, and return on investment. The following example assumes you have made 500 test calls at the rate of 15 call attempts per hour

Call attempts	500
Out, not available, screened out	300
Prospects reached	200
Requested literature	40
Asked to be called back	40
Not interested	90
Yes response	30
Order cancellations	3
Net orders	27

Assuming that these calls sold a $400 product, the 500 calls have yielded $10,800 in gross revenue (27 orders × $400). This yields the following statistics:

Total sales per call	$ 21.60
Total sales per completed presentation	54.00
Total sales per calling hour (33 calling hours)	$327.00

Hourly operating costs will vary, depending on the type of program. For example, telemarketing personnel selling a complex product on the phone will be compensated more than those who are setting appointments. Phone usage costs will vary with the places called, among other factors. But using the *average* cost of $40 per calling hour, the thirty-three-hour test would have cost roughly $1,320 for phone, labor, and overhead. This represents an ROI of over $8:1.

Certainly, under a slightly different scenario, the ROI could improve. For example, if the forty prospects who requested literature were called back, such callbacks might have increased the sales per hour. Or such callbacks might have resulted in higher returns. Also, many different results are possible, depending on the list used, how well targeted it is, how well targeted the decision makers are in terms of their buying authority, and so forth. Another variable that will certainly make a difference is packaging the offer differently to produce a higher average order size. To understand how some of these variables can affect test results, let's vary the assumption and look at a second testing scenario.

Assume again that the calls are designed to sell a $400 item, but are made using a different list, with the following results:

Call attempts	500
Out, not available	150
Prospects reached	250
Requested literature	60
Requested callback	40
Not interested	135
Yes responses	15

Under this scenario, more prospects were reached (250 versus 200 in the first test), but the rejection rate was higher (135 not interested versus 90 in the first test). Because more prospects were reached, you would expect a higher number of "not interested" responses, but not necessarily a higher *rate* of rejection.

One explanation might be that the second list was less well targeted in terms of need for the product than the first list. For example, the first list might have targeted purchasing agents for whom a decision to order $400 worth of industrial chemicals is a daily occurrence, and price is the key factor in the decision. The second list may have targeted engineers, who actually use the product and so have a definite need for it, but who are harder to reach and less accustomed to buying by phone. Before making a judgment about the worth of the second list, consider the following:

- What could have happened is that though orders were fewer, they had a higher average dollar value.
- You still don't know whether the "requested literature" category would have raised total sales.
- You don't know whether the return ratio would be higher or lower than the first test—possibly the purchasing agents have not yet had feedback from users of the chemical on the shop floor that would affect this key number.
- Finally, although the first list may give a higher ROI, the second list still may be useful as a secondary focus of a telemarketing program.

TESTING OTHER ASPECTS OF YOUR PROGRAM

Beyond considerations related to the list, it's important to test aspects of your offer because different buying inducements, such as discount pricing for purchase of related products or flexible payment terms, can substantially affect sales ratio and ROI. You may find that some offers are simply not worth telemarketing.

For example, Macmillan Publishing tested a telemarketing program to sell a reference work to school libraries. Initial average sales were $85 per hour; costs ran $40 per hour. This produced an ROI of about two to one. Possibly this would have been a profitable offer for a direct mail campaign, but the numbers did not support a telemarketing program for this offer in this form. But when the offer was reformatted and the book was packaged with five similar reference works, the package, sold at a discount over prices for the individual titles, raised the average order to $500. Though this sale required two hours of calling time on the average, the resulting ROI of $6 to $1 was profitable for Macmillan. Repackaging the offer and rethinking pricing turned a disaster into an effective telemarketing campaign.

In product sales, it is essential to establish a returns policy. However, your policy on returns can have important impact on sales per hour because it can function as a buying inducement for purchasers by phone. This is another aspect of your offer you should test.

One of the keys to telemarketing success is scripting. Hence, script testing should be part of your test calls, focusing on determining the most effective introductions, probing questions, and closes for various audiences. For example, you may feel that the best way to capture attention when selling copiers to office managers is to emphasize a common problem—like paper jamming—in your introduction. But this might not work at all effectively with a purchasing agent or an executive whose main concern is price. Similarly, asking a general probing question such as "What are the three key features you'd have to have in your ideal copier?" might open up an office manager quite effectively, but strike an executive decision maker as a waste of valuable time. Probing strategy must vary with the audience and can be determined and perfected only through testing. The same is true of the close. Will you seek a commitment on the first call or close on the second, follow-up contact? Do you need risk-relieving terms, or can you close for a firm order with minimum risk relief? These questions can be answered only by running well-designed tests and carefully analyzing the results.

Clearly, this type of statistical analysis allows you to set reasonable sales goals and monitor your progress accurately. Just as clearly, you will need to have a system in place to manage your statistical data base as it develops.

SUMMARY

This chapter presented the key variables you need to test before you implement your telephone program on a large scale. It provided a sample *test data sheet* and standard guidelines to use in evaluating your test results and showed how to calculate relevant sales and cost statistics based on your test calls.

The following are the *most important data* your test calls should generate:

- Number of call attempts (per calling hour)
- Number out, not available, screened out
- Number of prospects reached
- Number that requested literature
- Number that asked to be called back
- Number not interested
- Number of yes responses
- Number of order cancellations
- Number of net orders
- Total sales dollars per call
- Total sales dollars per completed presentation
- Total sales dollars per calling hour
- ROI

CHAPTER

19

Collecting and Managing Telemarketing Information

TIMELY information is the key to controlling your telemarketing program. A system that gives you up-to-date information—on productivity, sales, costs, etc.—allows you to make the changes your telemarketing program will require over time, *before* they cut into your profits. Among other things, it will tell you where to focus your program and who your top producers are.

Telemarketing—even in the test phase—produces a great deal of data, which you must then "massage" to tell you what you need to know. To control your program effectively, you need an information system that performs these critical functions:

1. Captures the data in timely fashion
2. Manipulates the data to produce relevant productivity statistics and other output, such as follow-up letters
3. Interfaces with other systems, such as order entry, invoicing, and inventory

This chapter shows you the basic units of a telemarketing information system. The model forms and procedures presented were developed for a number of different clients, and you can adapt them for your own requirements.

Although most programs these days are automated, managers who have been through the conversion process, advise getting every phase of the manual information and control system working perfectly *before* automating. A vice-president, who manages telemarketing for a well-known financial services company that started with six people on the phone and went through an eighteen-month automation process based on growth projections of forty to fifty TMRs, says:

> If you can't get it right manually, don't even try to automate. What you really want to do is simulate manually what you want automation to accomplish for you. And if you can't do [that] manually, it gets very complicated when you try to automate. Most (automated) systems have more bells and whistles than you could ever use in a lifetime. You get very carried away with it. So I would really recommend to anyone developing a telemarketing program, do it in stages, and get your processes working well manually, *then* start deciding what you need to automate. Otherwise, automation is a never-ending, and very expensive process, which can consume your bottom line.

Initially, a manual system is usually adequate for most start-up telemarketing operations, though PC-based telemarketing software is available for a few hundred dollars. The key is to keep in mind where you want and expect to be six months out, twelve months out, twenty-four months out from your start-up date. As your program develops, you will at some point need to automate—not only to manage the volume of data, but also to keep your cost of handling the data reasonable. Telemarketers who are filling out forms and reports are losing valuable production time.

SOME BASIC TOOLS

Telemarketing information systems basically require the following kinds of records: (1) prospect information, (2) call activity, and (3) work flow management. Your program may require additional files, but these three are pretty basic.

Prospect Information Records

Prospect information records store the history of all telephone contacts with a prospect. These records can vary in format, depending on the call objective, but basically they should include the following data:

- Telemarketer's name (TMR)
- Contact name and title
- Company name
- Company address
- Company telephone number and extension
- Initial contact date
- Follow-up contact dates
- Order history
- Notes or remarks

You can use the notes/remarks section to note problems or personal comments on the prospect. On subsequent calls, these notes are very useful in building the relationship with the prospect.

In developing prospect information files for clients, I often color code the prospect card to separate major, intermediate, and minor accounts. You can also use a numeric or alphabetic sequence to rank them. This makes it easy to distribute the prospect cards equitably and helps telemarketers manage their time better. In addition, if you use a two-part carbon form for your prospect card, you can file the carbon in a chronological "tickler" file for a callback. Another approach is to flag the card with its callback date and file it alphabetically.

Figure 19-1. Prospect information card.

TMR ____________

COLOR CODE

Company Quick Printing ①2 3 Date 11/30 1 2 3 Date ___
A Ⓑ C A B C

Contact Bruce Gogel Title V.P. Phone (210) 123-4567

Address 290 Stoney Clove Lane

City/State/Zip Citichester, N.Y.

Parent Super Fast Affiliate ABC Paper

Other Contacts Dara Lasky

# of States/Active 3 Loss Ratio 0 Best Rating 1

Date	ACTION/REMARKS
2/15	On Vacation call back 1/10 to set appointment
1/10	Set appointment for next week 1/16. He just got appointed to senior V.P.

Figure 19-1 shows a fairly typical prospect information card, using a simple basic design. In Figures 19-2 and 19-3, the sample is much more elaborate, providing an area for survey and competitive data as well as evaluative data. The figures are filled in with the type of information telemarketers might typically collect.

Figure 19-4, the Dun's sales tracker, is provided courtesy of Dun's Marketing Services. The "tracker" format is extremely useful in telemarketing because it allows you to mail at your own pace and follow up with local telemarketing to obtain survey data. When you buy a list in this format, Dun's will print basic Dun and Bradstreet information on the left-hand portion of the form. The telemarketer can fill in customer survey data in the center. The survey questions can be changed to fit the product or service. On the bottom of the form are labels for follow-up letters or mailings. Figure 19-5 shows the rear of the tracker form, which provides space

Figure 19-2. Prospect information card (front).

PROSPECT INFORMATION CARD

INITIAL CONTACT DATE: 3/15/ TMR LL | PROJECT: Film Cds | AIRPORT: JFK | CODES (circle): (A) B C

NAME: Marc De Hove TITLE: TRAFFIC MGR

COMPANY: Apex Film Co. TELEPHONE: (213) 114-1878

ADDRESS/CITY/STATE/ZIP: 1401 Riverside Drive, San Francisco Ca. 95014

FREQUENCY: (Daily) Weekly Monthly Less OUTB. INB.

WEIGHTS: (1-50 lbs.) 51-200 over 200

COMPETITION: EM (FE) AB Airline Other

ORIGINS: JFK, LAX, CHI DESTINATION: London, UK

REMARKS: Is going to give us his next shipment to try us out

commitment overnight fulfillment No E.P.S. Yes

rates $10 under 1 pound WWD No other

Figure 19-3. Prospect information card (rear).

FOLLOW UP CALL #	DATE	USED (1)	USED UNSAT. SERVICE (2)	USED UNSAT. RATES (3)	ROUTING NOT HONORED (4)	THIRD PARTY ACCOUNT (5)	NO CONTACT	CALL BACK DATE	REMARKS
1	3/21		✓						didn't pick up fast enough
									but said he would try again
2	4/1	✓							very happy this time
									is going to give us
									more shipments

DATE	# SHIPMENTS/WT.	DATE	# SHIPMENTS/WT.	DATE	# SHIPMENTS/WT.
3/22	1/10 pounds				
3/28	1/7 pounds				

to record follow-up and sales activity. This is an excellent format for supporting field sales with telemarketing and direct mail.

Call Activity Records

Each telemarketer on your staff should log daily activity records. At a minimum, your daily activity log should provide the following production totals for a given time period:

- Number of hours worked
- Number of dials
- Number of complete calls
- Number of no answers, wrong numbers
- Number of sales or other commitments

This log is your primary tool for keeping your finger on the productivity of your telemarketing program. Design it carefully to ensure that you

(Text continues on page 215.)

Figure 19-4. Dun's Sales Tracker (front).

DUN'S SALES TRACKER™

PRODUCED EXCLUSIVELY FOR USE BY: FACSIMILE DEALERS

D-U-N-S NO.	DATE	JOB NO.	SEQUENCE NO.	SALESPERSON
01-050-0108	04/24/	J9DX	436	

COMPANY NAME	STATUS	INITIAL CONTACT DATE
CASTLE CORP	HO	

ADDRESS	COUNTY	USER/INFLUENCER NAME/TITLE
549 OLDHAM ST	ERIE	

CITY, STATE, ZIP
OUTWAY NY 10498

DECISION MAKER/TITLE

CONTACT/TITLE

C.E.O. R T DREWERY PR
MICHAEL WEINSTEIN VP FINANCE

OVERALL EVALUATION

☐ HIGH POTENTIAL ☐ MEDIUM POTENTIAL
☐ LOW POTENTIAL

EMPL. HERE	TOTAL EMPLS.	SALES VOLUME
61	140	$7,730,000

PRIMARY SIC	SECONDARY SICS	
3552	3566	3562

LINE OF BUSINESS	TELEPHONE NO.
MFG IND MACHY	(317) 435-0041

PRODUCTS:

QUOTE:

COMMENTS

PARENT: THE OUTWAY CO
ULTIMATE: B & J MACHINERY CORP.

SURVEY DATA

1 ARE YOU PRESENTLY SENDING DOCUMENTS OVERNIGHT?

2 CARRIER PRESENTLY USING/# OF DOCUMENTS PER NIGHT?

3 DO YOU PRESENTLY HAVE FACSIMILE EQUIPMENT?

4 PRESENT FACSIMILE BRAND, MODEL, QUANTITY?

5 WHO MAKES FINAL OK ON OVERNIGHT MAIL/OFFICE EQUIP?

COMPETITIVE INFORMATION

↓ FOLD HERE AND PEEL BACK

R T DREWERY PR CASTLE CORP PO BOX 3537 OUTWAY NY 10497	MICHAEL WEINSTEIN VP FINANCE CASTLE CORP PO BOX 3537 OUTWAY NY 10497
DIRECTOR OF PURCHASING CASTLE CORP PO BOX 3537 OUTWAY NY 10497	OFFICE SERVICES MANAGER CASTLE CORP PO BOX 3537 OUTWAY NY 10497

DUN'S MARKETING SERVICES

Source: Dun's Marketing Services, a company of The Dun & Bradstreet Corporation.

Figure 19-5. Dun's Sales Tracker (rear).

DATE	CONTACT	STATUS
10/19	R.T. Drewery	FOLLOW UP ☑ 30 DAYS ☐ 60 DAYS ☐ 6 MONTHS ☐ ______ ACTIVITY ☐ PRESENTATION ☑ DEMO ☐ PROPOSAL ☐ NO INTEREST EST. TIME OF PCHSE. ☐ 30 DAYS ☐ 60 DAYS ☑ 6 MONTHS ☐ 1 YEAR
		FOLLOW UP ☐ 30 DAYS ☐ 60 DAYS ☐ 6 MONTHS ☐ ______ ACTIVITY ☐ PRESENTATION ☐ DEMO ☐ PROPOSAL ☐ NO INTEREST EST. TIME OF PCHSE. ☐ 30 DAYS ☐ 60 DAYS ☐ 6 MONTHS ☐ 1 YEAR
		FOLLOW UP ☐ 30 DAYS ☐ 60 DAYS ☐ 6 MONTHS ☐ ______ ACTIVITY ☐ PRESENTATION ☐ DEMO ☐ PROPOSAL ☐ NO INTEREST EST. TIME OF PCHSE. ☐ 30 DAYS ☐ 60 DAYS ☐ 6 MONTHS ☐ 1 YEAR

COMMENTS

10/19 R.T. not ready to purchase. Wants to discuss with controller.

PURCHASE ______________________

DATE ____________

COMMENTS ______________________

Source: Dun's Marketing Services, a company of The Dun & Bradstreet Corporation.

get the level of detail you need—hourly results, for example, may be as important to you as daily totals.

The daily call activity log should enable you to spot trends in individual performance so you can intervene early. You can also design it to help you see geographic trends or variances in productivity by time of day. Figures 19-6 through 19-10 show sample outbound and inbound daily activity logs. Use these as models in designing your own. For most telemarketing programs, it is useful also to cumulate the daily totals into weekly and monthly "roll-up" reports. In this way you can build a valuable historic file.

Figure 19-6 shows a typical daily activity log covering an eight-hour calling shift. Figure 19-7 provides a format for recording outbound call activity, separating new calls from follow-ups. The figure shows the simple "hash marks" a TMR makes to fill it out, with the lower area used to enter calculated totals. Figure 19-8 provides another variation for recording daily calls, outcomes, and calculated totals.

Figure 19-9 provides a sample daily report to record inbound call activity, and figure 19-10 is a form designed to convey a monthly cumulation of all activity, by telemarketer. It is useful for determining and comparing production rates and sales generated by each individual.

Work Flow Management Records

Earlier in this chapter, I present the idea of using prospect information cards to build a tickler file of chronological callbacks. This is a typical telemarketing "work flow management" tool and a relatively simple solution to keep track of leads. Because telemarketing is used for so many purposes, though, we need to look at a few additional parts of the workflow process.

If you are planning an outbound strategy involving invoice or approval sales, using a *confirmation letter* can help you manage the work flow as well as build the relationship with the customer. A confirmation letter should go out the day the customer makes the commitment on the phone.

Basically, a confirmation letter summarizes the conversation—the item purchased, the terms, shipping date, address, etc.—and reminds the customer when to expect another call. Most of the body of the letter can be stored in a word-processing system; the telemarketer need only submit the particulars for a specific customer. These specifics are then plugged into the body of the letter by your word processor.

One copy of the letter can go to the telemarketer as a record of the sale. Another copy can go to your order fulfillment group or department. The original should be signed personally by the telemarketer. Figure 19-11

(Text continues on page 219.)

Figure 19-6. Daily activity log.

DATE 1/27/ TELEPHONE REP. D. Lasky PROJECT Direct Mail Followup HOURS WORKED 6

TIME	# CALLS	# CONV.	COMMITMENT TO PROGRAM			FOLLOW UP CALLS	CALL BACKS	SEND CATALOG	SEND OTHER LIT.	REF. TO DSM	MISC.	REMARKS
			strong	med.	weak							
9-10	HHT IIII	III	I		II		I		III	I		
10-11	HHT HHT IIII	I			I							Everyone seems to be in a meeting
11-12	HHT HHT	HHT	III		II			IIII	I	II		
12-1			LUNCH									
1-2	HHT HHT HHT	I		I					I			Most prospects seem to be at lunch
2-3	HHT HHT II	IIII		III	I	I		II	I			
3-4	HHT HHT	HHT I	III		III							
4-5			LEFT FOR DENTIST APPOINTMENT									
TOTALS												

Figure 19-7. Daily call tally report-outbound.

Rep. J. L. Day Mon Date 2/26/

	New Calls						Follow-up Calls					
Time	Call Attempts	Call Me Back	Closed/ Supplies	Send Literature	Made Appointment	No Interest	Call Attempts	Call Me Back	Closed/ Supplies	Send Literature	Made Appointment	No Interest
9-10 am	HHT HHT HHT ||	||	||	||||	|	HHT						
10-11 am							HHT HHT ||	|	|||	|	|||	|
11-12 pm												
12-1 pm												
1-2 pm												
2-3 pm												
3-4 pm												
4-5 pm												
5-6 pm												

Total Hours Worked 1

Total Presentations 10

Presentations/Hour 10

Total Hours Worked 1

Total Presentations 8

Presentations/Hour 8

Figure 19-8. Daily call activity report—outbound.

TMR: ______

DATE: ______

PROJECT CODE: ______ PROJECT CODE: ______

	NEW CALLS								FOLLOW-UP CALLS							
RESULT	CALL ATT.	INCORR-ECT INFO.	CALL ME BACK	CLOSED CONTR.	SEND QUOTE	SEND LIT.	MADE APPT.	NO INT.	CALL ATT.	INCORR-ECT INFO.	CALL ME BACK	CLOSED CONTR.	SEND QUOTE	SEND LIT.	MADE APPT.	NO INT.
9-10																
10-11																
11-12																
12-1																
1-2																
2-3																
3-4																
4-5																
5-6																
TOTAL:	*	*	*	*	*	*	*	*	*	*	*	*	*	*	*	*

HOURS WORKED: ______ HOURS WORKED: ______

OF PRESENTATIONS: ______ # OF PRESENTATIONS: ______

PRESENTATIONS/HR: ______ PRESENTATIONS/HR: ______

Figure 19-9. Daily call activity report—inbound.

DATE: 11/30/ REP.: Lucy L.

RESULTS

	CALL ME BACK	CLOSED CONTR.	SEND QUOTE	SEND LIT.	MADE APPT.	NO INTEREST
9-10	ll	l	ll	ll	l	ll
10-11	l	ll	llll	lll		l
11-12	lll	l	ll	l	l	lll
12-1	ll	ll	llll	l		
1-2						
2-3						
3-4						
4-5						
5-6						
TOTAL:	* 8	* 6	* 12	* 7	* 2	* 6

shows a sample confirmation letter from an appointment-setting program developed for an insurance company.

You may not always be confirming an appointment or a sale in your follow-up. For example, you may simply send a short note or postcard to every prospect you contact or to everyone who requests a brochure. This follow-up should review the key benefits discussed on the phone and alert the prospect to your next call. You can retain a copy for your tickler file so that you make the scheduled second call on time.

My company developed an outbound appointment-setting program for a large data-processing services firm that employs 600 field sales representatives nationwide. Using a "team sales approach," we assigned telemarketers to support two or three sales representatives. One problem was how

Figure 19-10. Monthly telemarketing statistical report.

For Month of: SEPTEMBER TMR: AMANDA BECK Project: BOOK CLUB Total Hours Worked: ______

Date	# Hours Worked	# Calls	# Conversations	# Sales	# Follow-up Calls	# Call Backs	# Send Lit.	Comments
1	6	24	6	1	3	4	5	

Figure 19-11. Confirmation letter.

[Your Company Name]

[Date]

Mr. Martin Stone
787 Baxter Boulevard
Harvey, IL 90017

Dear Mr. Stone:

I enjoyed discussing your Business Insurance needs on the phone with you the other day. As you requested, I've enclosed brochures on the Small Business Owners Policy. I'm sure you will find that the SBO Series is a truly comprehensive package of coverages, and offers extras that valued customers like you won't find elsewhere.

I know you are involved in some important business decisions right now, so I certainly appreciate the time you are taking to see me at 8:00 p.m. on Thursday.

Good luck with your new business venture. I'll look forward to meeting you on the 24th.

Sincerely,

Susan B. Sales
Commercial Lines Manager

to ensure that the appointments produced by telemarketing were given to the assigned sales representative in timely fashion. Part of the solution was to develop an appointment calendar form, reproduced in Figure 19-12.

Another solution to managing work flow is to use multipart forms that combine the lead management function with the work flow function. Figure 19-13 shows this as a four-part form. The original remains in the alphabetic lead file. When an order is placed or literature requested, the second copy goes to the fulfillment department. When a sales appointment

(Text continues on page 224.)

Figure 19-12. Field sales representative's appointment calendar.

FS Rep. J. Smith

Week of 1/3/

Time	Monday	Tuesday	Wednesday	Thursday	Friday
9-9:15 am					
Co. Name Address Area	XYZ Co. 292 Park St. Ramsey		Acme Trucking 450 Bellview Nanuet		
11-11:15 am					
Co. Name Address Area	AL Assoc. 340 Main Woodmere				
1-1:15 pm					
Co. Name Address Area					
3-3:15 pm					
Co. Name Address Area					

Week of 1/9/99

Time	Monday	Tuesday	Wednesday	Thursday	Friday
9-9:15 am					
Co. Name Address Area				Harry's Supp. Broadway + 7th Fort Lee	
11-11:15 am					
Co. Name Address Area				Print Shop Ink 2 Irvine St. Fort Lee	
1-1:15 pm					
Co. Name Address Area				Getty Pub Rel. 106 Arthur Fort Lee	
3-3:15 pm					
Co. Name Address Area					

Figure 19-13. Four-part combination lead management/work flow form.

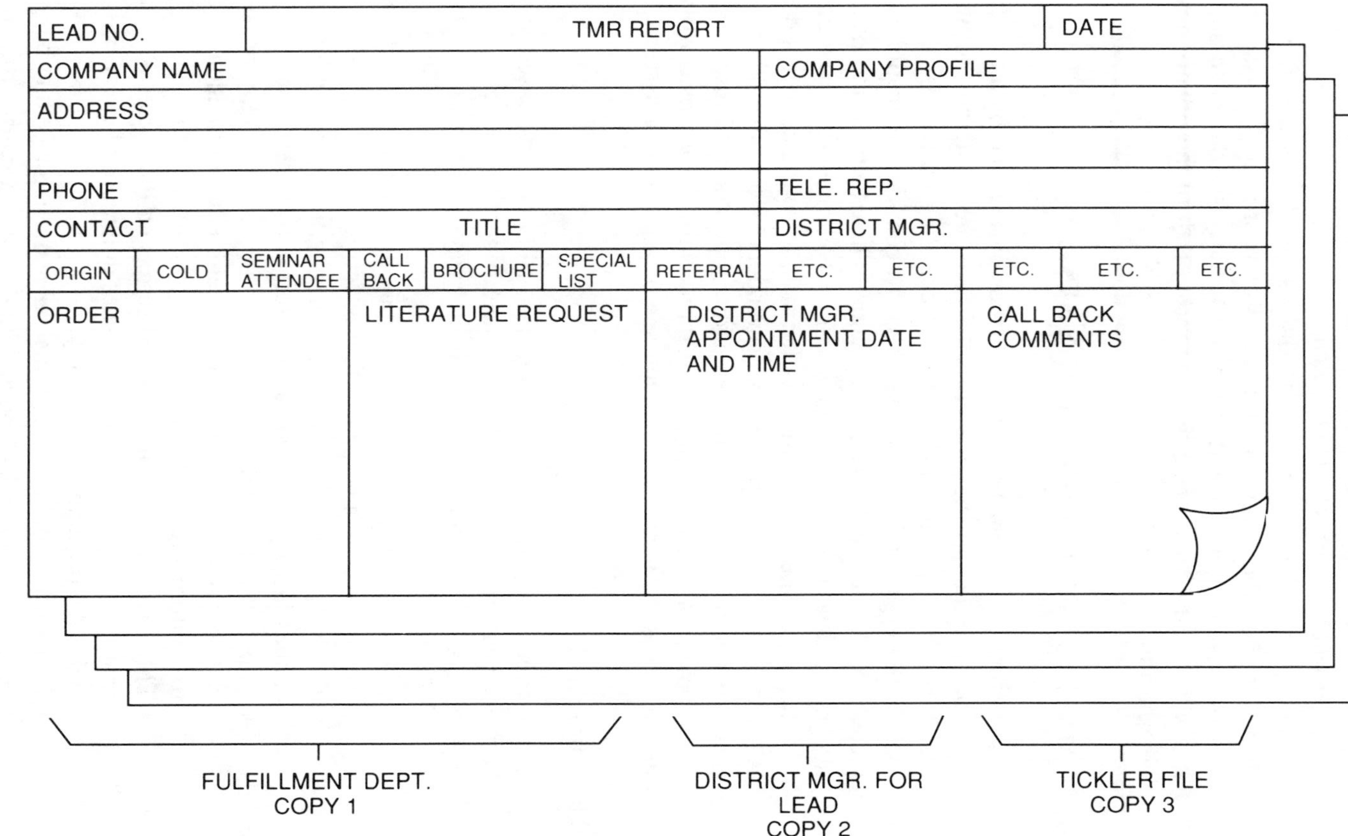
COMBINATION PROSPECT/WORKFLOW DOCUMENT/ORDER FORM
AND TICKLER FILE SAMPLE-(TYPE OF BUSINESS GOES HERE)

LEAD NO.	TMR REPORT	DATE

COMPANY NAME	COMPANY PROFILE
ADDRESS	
PHONE	TELE. REP.
CONTACT TITLE	DISTRICT MGR.

ORIGIN	COLD	SEMINAR ATTENDEE	CALL BACK	BROCHURE	SPECIAL LIST	REFERRAL	ETC.	ETC.	ETC.	ETC.	ETC.

ORDER	LITERATURE REQUEST	DISTRICT MGR. APPOINTMENT DATE AND TIME	CALL BACK COMMENTS
FULFILLMENT DEPT. COPY 1		DISTRICT MGR. FOR LEAD COPY 2	TICKLER FILE COPY 3

is scheduled, the third copy is sent to the manager of the field sales territory. The fourth copy is used by the telemarketing department as a tickler file copy when a callback is scheduled.

You can use or adapt any of the sample letters and forms in this chapter to meet the specific requirements of your strategy. After you have developed your program and the manual systems required to support it, you will want to consider automating most or all of these work flow management functions.

AUTOMATING YOUR INFORMATION SYSTEM

Automating your telemarketing information system can be a complex process, but it need not be mysterious. There are numerous software and hardware vendors in the marketplace. Depending on the size of your operation and organization, you may need to consider compatibility of any system you select with existing systems. Then there is the question of integrating data-processing systems and telecommunications systems.

I can give you basic guidelines for making your automation decisions. What questions should you be asking vendors? How have other organizations handled automating their telemarketing programs? I also discuss new developments in telemarketing automation, particularly those involving the integration of the telecommunication and data-processing systems.

Why Automate?

The ultimate benefit of automation is, of course, increased sales. But how does automation deliver that ultimate benefit? Automated telemarketing enhances TMR productivity in several ways:

- TMRs can automatically access your customer or prospect data base, so their time is not spent filling in forms.
- TMRs can display customer purchasing history and prior telephone contact history, so each call is direct and to the point.
- TMRs can take orders over the phone more quickly because they can get pricing information, customer credit information, and inventory information—at a keystroke.
- TMRs can access multibranched scripts on their screens, so they are prompted to get every possible sales dollar out of every call, as well as handle objections effectively.
- TMRs need not waste time dialing numbers or getting busy signals because programmed "power dialers" can do this for them.

Beyond supporting increased sales, there are other common benefits of automating:

- *Improved customer satisfaction.* TMRs who quickly and efficiently get the right information during the call will improve customer satisfaction with your organization.
- *Enhanced fulfillment.* By automatically generating postcall confirmation letters, order-processing documentation, and delivery labels and by scheduling follow-up contacts, an automated system improves fulfillment time and quality.
- *Better management of your telemarketing personnel.* Automated telemarketing systems generate reports that allow you to analyze your staff's performance, calculate commissions, improve staff scheduling, and pinpoint training problems.
- *Better business planning.* Telemarketers using an on-line system can modify the data base during the call. Subsequently, managers can use periodic and ad hoc reports generated by the system to more accurately analyze the impact of advertising and promotion campaigns, to forecast sales, and to get a better handle on complaints. The same data bases can be used to develop lists for follow-up mail or phone campaigns focused on up-selling or cross-selling.
- *Cost containment.* Generally, automation should enable you to do more with fewer TMRs and clerical staff. Controlling people costs is a major benefit of the automation decision.
- *Information sharing.* Other departments (accounting, inventory, order processing, and marketing) can use the information generated by an automated telemarketing system.

An industrial products firm that carries over 2,000 safety equipment products in its line uses its automated telemarketing system to supply TMRs pricing of any 1 of those 2,000 products, calculate price breaks for volume orders, check inventory, recommends substitutes when inventory of a particular item is out, access credit information through the accounting system, and perform billing, order processing, and fulfillment. Every data base and function needed to sell products and generate revenue can be integrated within the telemarketing system.

Ultimately, automation of telemarketing can and should give you complete control of the sales and marketing process. It should increase the productivity of any user, from TMR to company president.

System Options

Amazingly, these productivity benefits can be obtained from simple, off-the-shelf systems costing only a few hundred dollars. The same benefits are also delivered by systems costing many thousands of dollars. To help you figure out which of these extremes—or which choice in between—is best for you now and which will serve your needs down the road, I talked with several experienced telemarketers who had been through the system selection process. The following is a distillation of their main points:

1. *Start by carefully analyzing your business.* How do your telemarketers interact with your market? How do you want them to be able to interact? Are they just generating leads? Are they sending them on to field sales reps in remote locations? Will they do order processing? Do they need to interact with other computer systems in your organization? What sort of existing system support and maintenance expertise do you have? Will there be a "learning curve" as the data-processing staff learns to support and maintain the telemarketing system? What about growth? How many people are you going to have on the phone?
2. *Investigate vendors who already have clients in your industry.* You want to work with vendors who understand your business and can talk your language. Get the names of client references and check them carefully, including, if possible, on-site visits. You'll get a lot of good ideas and will be able to question and evaluate vendors more effectively.
3. *Don't try to automate overnight.* If you do, your system may be up and running quickly, but down the road, you may find that adding users is expensive, system maintenance is eating up your resources, or interface with existing systems requires extensive custom programming—again an added expense. It may be better, in fact, to automate only certain telemarketing functions initially, and gradually add on other functions as the need arises and the cost can be justified.

Any system you select may be a compromise in terms of its ability to serve current telemarketing needs, grow with future needs, and interface with existing systems and in its maintenance and support requirements.

For this reason, you need to be aware of what your current environment is in terms of all these factors before you talk with vendors. As important, you need to *project what your environment will be* by the time you install whatever automated system you select. One approach to determining this is to assemble a *task force* of individuals familiar with your organization's data-processing and telecommunications systems and requirements, along with marketing, accounting, and other functional areas affected by the decision. Gathering their input and developing comprehensive automation goals based on it will take time, but this is probably the best investment you can make. Finally, remember to get your telemarketing system defined and running well manually before you invest in automation.

Once you begin the research process, you'll find an amazing number and variety of software and hardware available to you. The following sections outline the major systems options you may consider.

Off-the-Shelf Software: PC - Based. "Off-the-shelf software" means software that will support some but not all telemarketing functions without any need to modify the programming. It is generally the lowest in initial cost, easy to learn and use, and hence capable of quick start-up, especially if it runs on hardware you already own.

For a *single-user* environment, a PC-based off-the-shelf program may be all you ever need—and if a one-person operation is all you anticipate your telemarketing program will involve, perhaps a PC-based off-the-shelf program is the right choice. But be careful—you may find it a waste of money if, after running the system a few months, you find you need capabilities it just cannot deliver. Also, security of your data—including customer files, prospect files, and purchasing history—is generally at a high risk in a PC-based system because files are easily copied onto diskette. Data security is usually tighter on minicomputer and mainframe programs, where levels of data access can be controlled electronically.

If you plan to have two or more people on the phone, you will want to investigate LAN-based telemarketing software. LAN means "Local Area Network," and it refers to microcomputers configured together so that they can share data bases. This tends to give managers better access to data and hence better control. For example, both single-user and multiuser systems may produce sales forecasts based on TMR data input. The difference between them is that the single-user software will generate a forecast based on the data stored in a single microcomputer; if you've got more than one user, you will have to manually compile the forecasts produced. A multiuser system will generate such a consolidated report automatically, based on inputs by all users.

Though more expensive up front than a single-user system, a LAN-based system sometimes actually costs less per user as users are added. Here are some other advantages of LAN-based telemarketing systems:

- They can accommodate single users as well as growth of six or more users, depending on the system selected.
- Unlike single-user systems, they will automatically compile data collected by all users and produce reports and statistics useful for analyzing performance and productivity and for forward planning.
- They have data base management and on-screen scripting capabilities similar to those available on minicomputer and mainframe systems.

Once you need more than five or six users, it becomes quite expensive to add users to a LAN-based system, and a minicomputer-based system may be justified. Also, one of the major disadvantages of LAN-based telemarketing systems is that they are not as good as more expensive options in terms of communicating with other data bases and computer systems within your organization. If you foresee needing this capability of integrating telemarketing systems with others, you may not get your money's worth out of a LAN-based system. To accomplish this type of integration, your system must be designed with "open architecture." "Openness" means how easily two (or more) different computer systems can share information and instructions. Some, though not all, *minibased* telemarketing systems offer open architecture.

Minicomputer-based Software. Minibased systems are more expensive than single-user or LAN-based systems in terms of both software and hardware. But again, "expensive" is a relative term. How many users will you have, needing what types of capabilities? A key advantage of such minibased systems is that there currently exist some excellent, well-thought-out software packages, and the vendors can *customize* the basic package to meet individual needs. For example, most provide an array of standard reports and statistical analyses, but your particular organization or type of telemarketing may require a special report. Vendors of minibased telemarketing will—for a fee—customize their software to produce such reports (see Figures 19-14 through 19-17).

In addition, minibased systems can do most of the tasks you will want to do when your telemarketing program grows beyond five or six people. They can handle more information, and handle it more efficiently, than single-user or LAN-based systems. Minisystems can be made to communicate with your other data bases and existing computer systems. Some of these support features, like "predictive dialing," are capable of interfacing effectively with your telecommunications system. If you anticipate needing this type of capability, your investigation should probably focus on a minibased system.

Mainframe Solutions. You can run telemarketing software—off-the-shelf or customized—on your mainframe computer. However, you will probably want to carefully investigate your mainframe's processing capacity because telemarketers need rapid response time since they are on the phone with customers and prospects and require nearly instant access to data. For this reason, if you take this route, you may want to investigate your firm's network capacity and the potential use of a server dedicated to a telemarketing application.

Integrated Systems. You really can't develop and run a cost-effective telemarketing program without educating yourself about the technologies available to support and streamline your program. Thus,

Figure 19-14. Sample 1: automated telemarketing report.

REP-1 **PROGRESSIVE SOLUTIONS, INC.**
5.0 **FOLLOW-UP SCHEDULE BY TSR**

REPORT DATE: 7/15/ **TIME:** 17:35:23

COMPANY NAME ADDRESS CONTACT, TITLE	F/U DATE F/U TIME	PROSPECT ID SEARCH NAME SALES REP	MAIL CODE INDUSTRY PHONE NO.
Coast Realty Management Co. 45 Santa Monica Blvd. Los Angeles, CA 90220 Allen Karp, President	7/17/88 16:00	213-875-7555 karp molloy	VIP's Banking 213-875-7555
Patrick & Sons 700 Lakeshore Drive Chicago, IL 30012 Ed Patrick, Partner	7/29/88 11:00	312-822-8100 patrick molloy	VIP's Software 312-822-5575
Belsher Manufacturing 850 Bayou Street New Orleans, LA 30021 Debra Summit, Vice President Marketing	7/30/88 09:00	504-321-8877 summit molloy	AAPA Marketing 504-321-8877
Unique Marketing Concepts 1500 Wabash Street Chicago, IL 10025 Irving Kindelberger, President	7/31/88 09:00	312-988-5233 kindelberger molloy	AAPA Advertising 800-448-3233

REPORT CRITERIA: Molloy's follow-ups

Source: Brock Control Systems, Inc.

I'll briefly outline some of the important automation options available. Essentially, they concern coordinating all components of your telemarketing system–processors and data bases–with those of your telecommunications system–Private Branch Exchanges (PBXs), Automatic Call Distributors (ACDs), and the telephone network. (See also Chapter 20.)

Figure 19-15. Sample 2: automated telemarketing report.

CAM-6 **PROGRESSIVE SOLUTIONS, INC.**
5.0 **CAMPAIGN PERFORMANCE REPORT BY TSR**

Report Date: 7/15/ **Time:** 19:10:37

TSR			
gibson	# SALES	$ VALUE	% SALES
	7	8,973	% 1
	# QUOTES	$ VALUE	% QUOTES
	24	28,781	% 3
	# INTERESTED	% INTERESTED	
	439	56	
	# NOT INTERESTED	% NOT INTERESTED	
	93	12	
	# SENT LITERATURE	% SENT LITERATURE	
	220	28	

Report Criteria: Customer Upgrade Campaign—June Results

Source: Brock Control Systems, Inc.

Some of the more advanced telemarketing centers have integrated systems capable of gathering information about the caller *from the telephone network.* This technology, called *Automatic Number Identification* (ANI), enables TMRs to know the identity of an inbound caller before answering the call. Through ANI, the caller's record is retrieved from the data base and sent automatically to the TMR's screen along with the call. The TMR can review the data before or during the call, and hence can respond to the customer's needs more promptly and efficiently. In addition, TMR time is not used to enter data (already existing in the data base), but in communicating with customers.

ANI also enables TMRs to call back customers who hang up because it can capture the phone number from which the call originated. Another application of ANI is as a dealer locator. For example, a prospect who wants information on a specific product calls an 800 number. While the call is being routed, the prospect's phone number is compared with a data base holding all the company's dealer locations. By the time the TMR answers the phone, a list of dealer locations near the prospect has already

Figure 19-16. Sample screens showing performance monitoring and prospect notes.

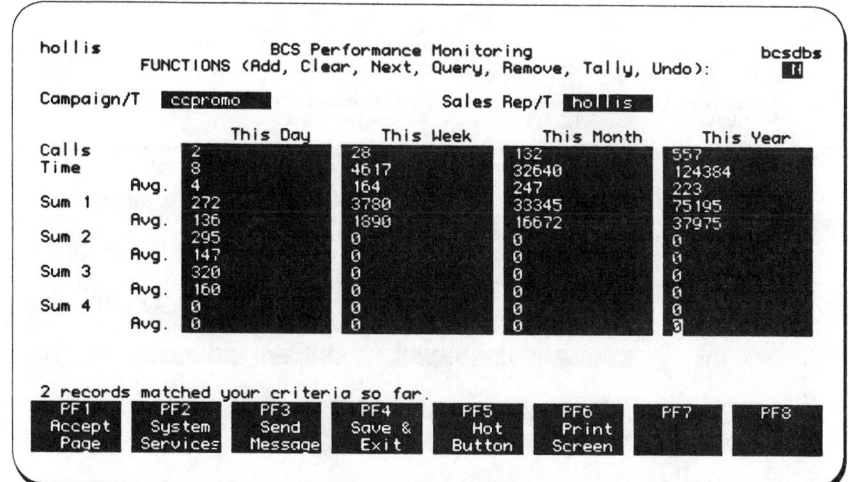

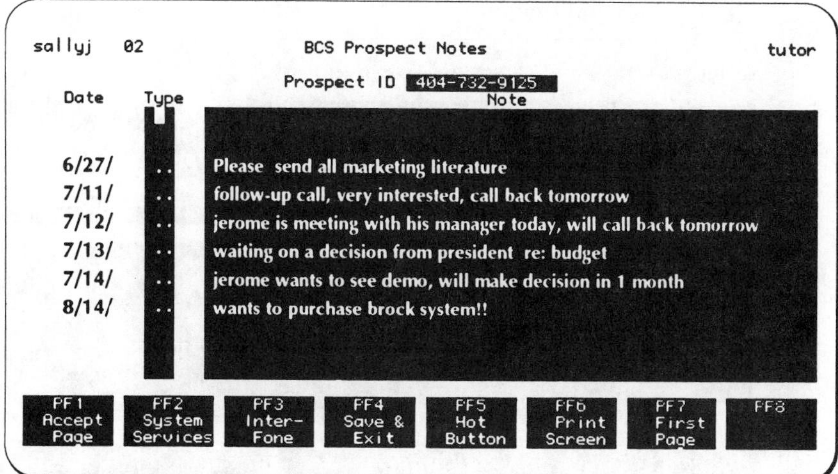

Source: Brock Control Systems, Inc.

been sent to his or her screen. The TMR can then immediately tell the prospect where to see a demonstration or make the purchase.

Another example of how integrated systems enhance the productivity of telemarketing programs is *Outbound Call Management Dialers (OCM)*. There are two types of OCM technologies on stream now: predictive and preview.

Predictive OCM basically automatically dials outbound calls from a stored list. The technology predicts when a TMR will be free to handle a call, based on parameters set by the telemarketing manager—how much talk time a TMR uses, how much time a TMR requires between calls, and

Figure 19-17. Sample screen showing sales information and prospect tracking.

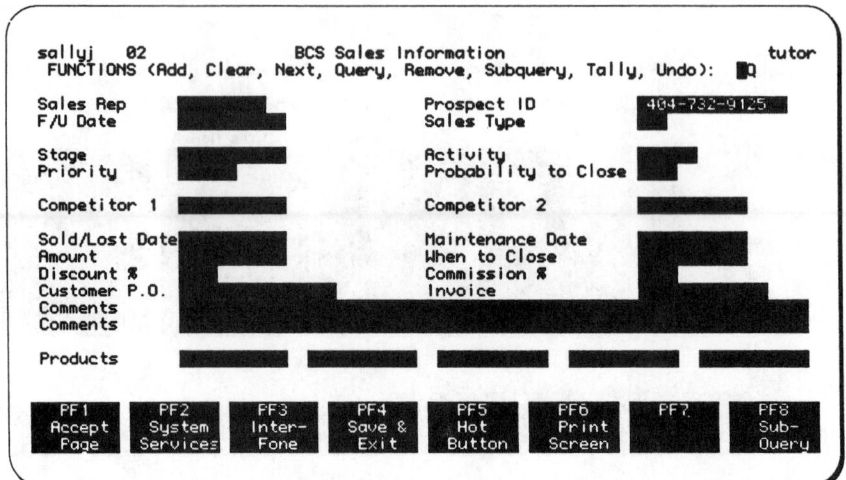

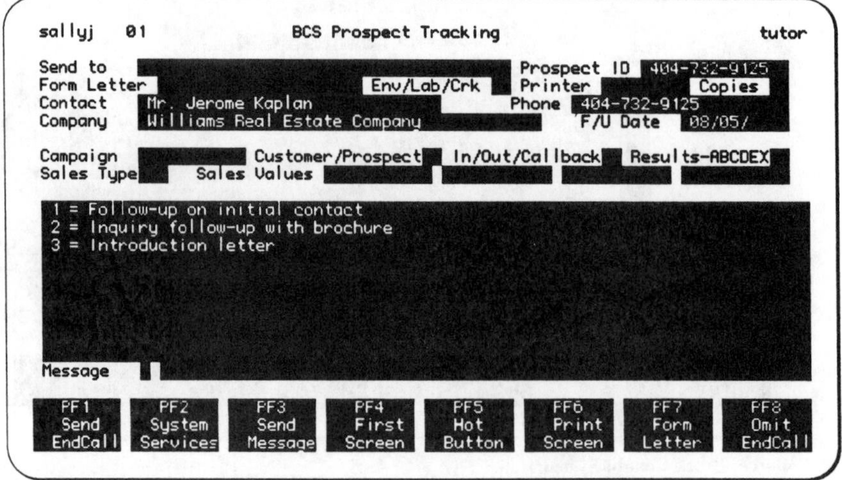

Source: Brock Control Systems, Inc.

so forth. OCM can tell whether a dialed number is busy or is not answered and hence passes on only "live" calls to the first free TMR. You can imagine the savings in TMR dialing time and the productivity gains that predictive OCM allows. It is especially efficient in telemarketing programs that require large-scale calling where basically the same thing is said on every call—surveys, fund raising, subscription sales, and the like.

Preview OCM is an application suited to low-volume telemarketing programs, especially where the TMR must see customer information before talking with the customer, as in account management. Pressing a function key on the computer keyboard makes the system automatically dial the customer's number after the TMR has had an opportunity to review the customer's data on the screen. Figure 19-18 is a sample report generated by OCM software.

Automating the Key Information Tasks

The following are the critical functions that any automated system ought to handle.

Managing Prospect Profile Data. The heart of any telemarketing operation is its prospect file. An automated system should capture the same information as a prospect profile card and store it in a central electronic data base. The telemarketer can then display the data on a workstation screen quickly and easily—often with just a keystroke.

Managing Call History Data. The automated system should allow telemarketers to record notes on conversations with each prospect and store them in the data base. When recalling the prospect for a follow-up, the system should retrieve the prospect record and display the most recent comments first.

This is an important function to look for in considering any telemarketing software. Notes of past conversations should be on the screen when the telemarketer makes the call. This way no time is wasted trying to recreate past conversations. The telemarketer is immediately oriented to where the prospect is in the sales cycle by the time the prospect is on the line.

Managing Multiple Contacts. Often telemarketers will have many contacts within a prospect organization. For this reason, an automated system should be able to keep separate records and notes on each. In addition, you should look for a method of following up each contact within the organization at different times in the sales cycle. In other words, you want the capacity to tie additional contact records to a main organization record and also to prioritize the secondary records.

Managing Daily Call Activity Data. One of the most time-consuming telemarketing tasks can be recording daily call activity. Yet this information is vital for measuring the productivity of your telemarketing program, as well as for forecasting future sales. Any automated telemarketing system you consider should be capable of the following call activity functions:

1. *Dial automatically.* When the telemarketer pulls the prospect record, the software should dial the number and record the time spent on the conversation.

Figure 19-18. OCM report.

Report Generated
Sat, Sep 17,   at 01:08

National Office Products, Inc.
Weekly Campaign Performance
For the Week Ending Sep 16,
Time Interval: 0:00–23:59
Selection: Campaign(s) 01

Campaign Name: Renewals

Sales Rep Name	*Duration Active (hh:mm)*	*Numbers Dialed*	*Names Contacted*	*Contacts Per Hour*	*Success Contacts Per Hour*	*Total Units*	*Units Per Hour*	*Total Sales*	*Sales Per Hour*	*Allocation of Time (Percentage)* Avail	Talk	Wrap
Hanson, H.	17:18	560	447	26	14	362	21	$3,620	$209	12	76	12
Hobbes, T.	17:06	554	445	26	13	332	19	$3,320	$194	13	70	17
Holcomb, J.	16:57	531	418	25	13	332	20	$3,320	$196	10	80	10
Lawrence, H. L.	17:19	611	480	28	13	332	19	$3,320	$192	14	75	11
Moore, M.	17:15	536	438	25	14	368	21	$3,680	$213	11	79	10
Robertson, R.	17:15	552	457	26	13	338	20	$3,380	$196	12	71	17
Rodriguez, R.	17:15	566	445	26	13	350	20	$3,500	$203	11	79	10
Samuels, S.	17:01	520	429	25	13	349	21	$3,490	$205	11	71	18

Totals:	*Duration Active (hh:mm)*	*Numbers Dialed*	*Names Contacted*	*Success Contacts*	*Total Units*	*Total Sales*
	137:26	4430	3559	207	2763	$27,630

Sales Rep Average	*Duration Active (hh:mm)*	*Numbers Dialed*	*Names Contacted*	*Contacts Per Hour*	*Success Contacts Per Hour*	*Total Units*	*Units Per Hour*	*Total Sales*	*Sales Per Hour*	*Allocation of the (Percentage)* Avail	Talk	Wrap
	17:11	554	445	26	13	345	20	$3,454	$201	12	75	13

2. *Record call results.* At the end of the conversation, the software should prompt for standard result codes, such as "send literature," "call back," and so forth. With a keystroke, the telemarketer should be able to select and record the result code for each call. This is a good deal less time-consuming than writing the information down.

3. *Use a tickler system.* The software should automatically display each telemarketer's callback commitments at the beginning of each shift or log-on. Typically, you will need a one-line listing by account of currently scheduled callbacks, previously missed follow-ups, then newly assigned calls. You will also want a means of prioritizing calls to balance the load over the course of the shift.

Further, when each call is dialed, busy signals and "no answers" should be recorded and a follow-up code assigned for another day. After successful calls, the system should prompt for a follow-up call date so the call can be automatically scheduled.

4. *Handle literature requests.* The capability of branching quickly from the prospect profile screen to a literature request menu is important for many telemarketing programs.

At the literature menu, the telemarketer should be able to select from a menu of literature or follow-up letters. The prospect's name and address are then automatically merged to the selected letter, which is printed and sent to literature fulfillment

5. *Handle objections.* Any telemarketing software should enable you to automate your objection response guide. The telemarketer should be able to display instantly the answers to typical objections, as well as questions on the product, the competition, and so forth.

6. *Generate management reports.* Any software you consider should generate management reports as a by-product of the telemarketers' daily input to the system. Telemarketers should not have to spend time requesting reports—they should be on the phone making calls. You and your managers should be able to access the following types of reports:

- Individual performance for various time periods
- Individual account activity
- Statistical summaries on group performance, leads, campaigns, and results
- Ad hoc reports of your own design

Script Development. Finally, your automated system should give you the ability to put your script on the screen as well. In this way, you can use the software to train new telemarketers and get them productive sooner.

You have much to choose from in deciding on the automated telemarketing system that meets your specific needs at the specific time you decide to make the move. Keep in mind that you don't necessarily have to automate every aspect of your program at the same time. You may need the flexibility of building your automated support gradually. Many systems now on the market enable you to take this phased approach.

Figure 19-19 shows some intermediate steps you may take as you move in phases from a small-scale manual operation to a completely automated account management system. As it also indicates, management control in telemarketing is a function of information availability. As you enlarge your program and the volume of your data increases, automated support of your information needs lets you capture a larger and larger portion of your potential revenues.

SUMMARY

This chapter has focused on how you control your telemarketing program. It looked first at manual information systems and provided examples of effective forms, particularly for start-up programs.

Figure 19-19. Management control—a function of information availability.

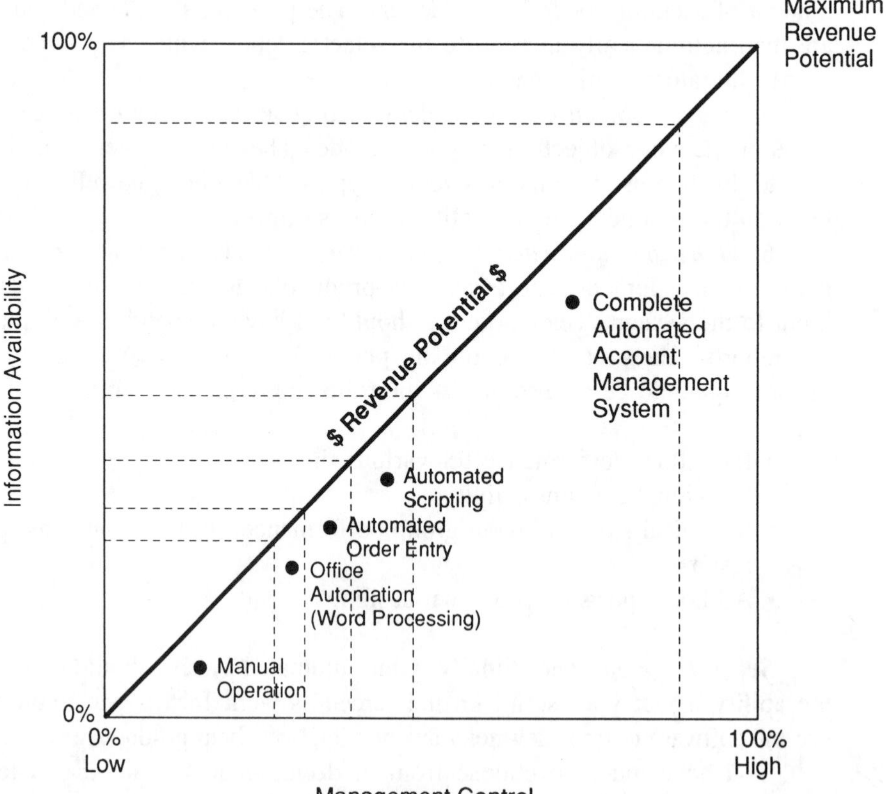

Source: Richard T. Brock and Sam L. Gallucci, Brock Control Systems, © 1988. Used with permission.

At some point, your program and its growing information management requirements will force you to consider automating your system. This chapter looked at how to approach this task, described current system options, and discussed some future applications available through integration of computer and telecommunication systems.

There are five key capabilities you need to consider as you look at the telemarketing software now available.

1. Managing prospect profile data
2. Managing call history data
3. Managing multiple contacts
4. Managing daily call activity data
   — Dial automatically
   — Record call results
   — Tickler system
   — Handle literature requests
   — Handle objections
   — Generate management reports, standard and free form
5. Develop scripts

CHAPTER

20

Telecommunications Equipment and Services

FOR most start-up outbound telemarketing efforts, a telephone and someone to make your calls will be all you need. This basic system will allow you to see where your real needs lie before diving into a myriad of options that could prove more confusing than helpful.

The real trick is to begin with the minimum and then to define your sales goals and expansion strategy. The key to your equipment and service needs is not in technology, but in your analysis and understanding of your own operation. Where is it now? Where it will be next year? You need to be asking questions like the following, and then analyzing your answers, *before* talking with vendors:

- Approximately how many calls will you make each day?
- Where will you be calling (time zones)?
- What time will you be calling (day, evening, weekends)?
- How many telemarketers do you plan to hire?
- What type of call will they make (average call length)?
- How large is your prospect/customer base?
- How many prospects/customers do you plan to sell to?
- What kind of reporting will you need?
- In what ways will your telemarketing department interface with the rest of the company?
- Is your operation going to be inbound, outbound, or both?
- Are you planning to be open twenty-four hours a day?
- What features are you going to need (conferencing, monitoring capabilities, predictive dialing, call waiting, call forwarding, etc.)?
- What types of long-distance services will you need (800, 900, WATS, etc.)?

As you expand, you will begin to consider how advanced technology can make an impact on your operation, allowing it to run more smoothly and more efficiently. As you look over the vast number of exciting options available, keep in mind these critical requirements that your telecommunications investment should meet:

- Cost containment
- Increased productivity
- Stronger management and supervision
- Improved marketing strategies

For most small- and even medium-sized telemarketing programs, your own analysis plus information gathered from various telecommunications vendors, equipment suppliers, and industry trade journals should be adequate for deciding among alternatives. As your operation grows and you anticipate substantial capital and operating outlays, you may decide to bring in an expert in telecommunications.

As with computing technology, the telecommunications field is evolving so rapidly that a complete survey is not possible. But this chapter acquaints you with the basic terminology relating to current equipment and services options and urges you to develop expertise within your organization to deal with these issues. You will have to make choices at some point; they should be informed ones that contribute to your bottom line.

The discussion that follows deals primarily with outbound telemarketing. But more and more operations are incorporating both inbound and outbound functions, so it includes some equipment and services that reflect this trend.

TELEPHONE SYSTEMS

When you move beyond the "plain old telephone," you will be offered an exciting array of telephone equipment, systems, and features.

PBX (Private Branch Exchange)

Originally, PBX referred to any switching system on a telephone customer's premises that required an operator to interconnect calls among extensions and between the building or organization and the outside world. The term "PBX" (or PABX, Private Automated Branch Exchange) is now used to describe all private switching systems.

Every PBX has four parts: (1) a switching mechanism enabling connections to be made among inside users and between them and the outside network; (2) a set of signals for ringing, dial tone, busy, and intercom connections; (3) the trunk circuits that connect the PBX to the central lines of the local telephone company; and (4) the attendant console and telephone "station" sets. An operator uses the console to complete transfer calls, page users, "bridge" internal conference calls, etc. "Station" sets are phones connected to the PBX through which users make and receive calls.

A PBX enables you to minimize the number of lines needed to handle your call volume while maximizing the use of telephones and personnel. This can be important in terms of controlling both telephone and labor costs.

Key Systems

A key telephone system differs from a PBX in several ways. Usually, it is smaller, and, each telephone is equipped with buttons (keys) so users can select lines to make an outside call. In a key system, the caller selects the line; in a PBX, the switch does this, eliminating the need to dial 9 to get an outside line. Another difference is that in a key system, all incoming lines are generally common to all sets. Finally, because more than one line terminates in each set in a key system, a TMR can answer more than one call at a time by depressing the "hold button." Hybrids combine some characteristics of key and PBX systems. Some key systems look very much like PBXs but do not offer the same array of features.

Both the PBX and many key systems offer the following features. You will not necessarily need all these, but it is important to know what is available.

- Conference calling
- Call transfer
- Speed dialing
- Speakerphone
- Call waiting
- Intercom
- Music on hold
- Automatic redial
- Toll restrictions
- Call detail recording
- Least cost routing
- Battery backup
- Call forwarding
- Automated attendant
- Voice mail
- Automatic Call Distributor (ACD)

Centrex

Centrex is a business telephone service available through your local telephone company. It offers many of the same features as a PBX, except that the master switching device is located at the telephone company's central office, eliminating the need for a switch on your premises.

Because the telephone company houses the equipment, Centrex is generally extremely reliable and has the added advantage of allowing your company to grow quickly without having to reinvest in new systems. Although it can also be an economical choice (for operations that have to hook up several stand-alone systems among multiple locations in the same city), Centrex may also be more expensive depending on your specific needs.

Automatic Call Distributors (ACDs)

ACDs have created a revolution in the way inbound calls are handled and managed. An ACD does two things very well: (1) It allows you to control how calls are received, delayed and distributed to your staff. (2) It provides the information tools—called reports—to help balance the level of service against the demand. ACDs offer three major benefits to telemarketers:

1. Increased sales and enhanced goodwill—because your TMRs are more accessible to your customers and prospects
2. Improved productivity—because calls are allocated efficiently, so fewer TMRs can handle the volume, and fewer lines are needed
3. Better decision making—because ACDs generate reports that tell you the where, when, why, and how your business is coming in, so you can spot opportunities, plan campaigns, and allocate your resources better

Figures 20-1 and 20-2 show a sample of the sophisticated reports an ACD system can generate.*

Uniform Call Distributors (UCDs)

A UCD offers many of the same functions as an ACD, but generally at a lower price. Like the ACD, it can handle a high volume of incoming calls quickly and efficiently while keeping callers informed of the status of their calls. Originally only available on large PBX systems, these features are now available either as a stand-alone item or incorporated into an electronic key system.

A UCD system works as follows: when a caller reaches the designated group, the UCD delivers the call in a predetermined, specific order and rings that station.

UCDs generally do not have advanced reporting capabilities that ACDs

*The material about ACDs has been adapted from "Using Your Chance to Sell and Service," *Inbound/Outbound Magazine,* May 1989, pp. 26–27.

Figure 20-1. Sample ACD report—Teknekron Infoswitch.

Report Generated
Fri, Sept. 16,

National Office Products, Inc.
Daily Agent Activity
For the Day of Sept. 16,
Start Time 08:00 End Time 10:15
Selection: Agent(s) = (01)

Agent Name: Kali Generic

Type of Event	*Completion Status*	*Event Time*	*Duratn Talk (sec)*	*(Seconds) Wrap Hold*	*Call Origin*	*Call Dest*	*Number Dialed*	*Wrap-Up Data*	*Did Nbr*	*Rte Nbr*
Incoming	Completed	07:19	19		L-1172	P-1191			3000	10
Incoming	Wrap-up	07:23	197	19	L-1172	P-1191		2110	3000	10
Intraflow	Completed	07:25	148		L-1197	P-1191			3310	31
Incoming	Completed	07:36	400		L-1146	P-1191			3000	10
Incoming	Completed	07:44	183		L-1149	P-1191			3000	10
Incoming	Completed	07:49	427		L-1149	P-1191			3001	10
Incoming	Wrap-Up	07:56	427	68	L-1149	P-1191		2110	3001	10
Incoming	Completed	08:00	114		L-1136	P-1191			3008	14
Incoming	Completed	08:05	81		L-1104	P-1191			3001	10
Incoming	Wrap-up	08:06	81	5	L-1104	P-1191			3001	10
Intraflow	Completed	08:12	193		L-1152	P-1191				04
Intraflow	Wrap-up	08:15	193	36	L-1152	P-1191				04
Consultation	Completed	08:16	8		P-1143	P-1191	2191			
Consultation	Wrap-up	08:16	8		P-1143	P-1191	2191			
Internal	Completed	08:18	9		P-1143	P-1191	2191			
Internal	Wrap-up	08:18	9		P-1143	P-1191	2191			
.	.	.	.	.	.	.	.		.	.
.	.	.	.	.	.	.	.		.	.
.	.	.	.	.	.	.	.		.	.
Outgoing	Wrap-up	10:59	63	1	POS 91	LINE 68	912195551234			
Mis-dialed		10:59			POS 91		2136			
Intraflow	Completed	10:59	30		LINE 59	POS 91				05
Incoming	Completed	10:59	227		LINE 47	POS 91			3001	10
Incoming	Wrap-up	11:03	227	18	LINE 47	POS 91		2117	3001	10
Agent sign-off		11:04			POS 91					

Figure 20-2. Graphic for ACD report—Teknekron Infoswitch.

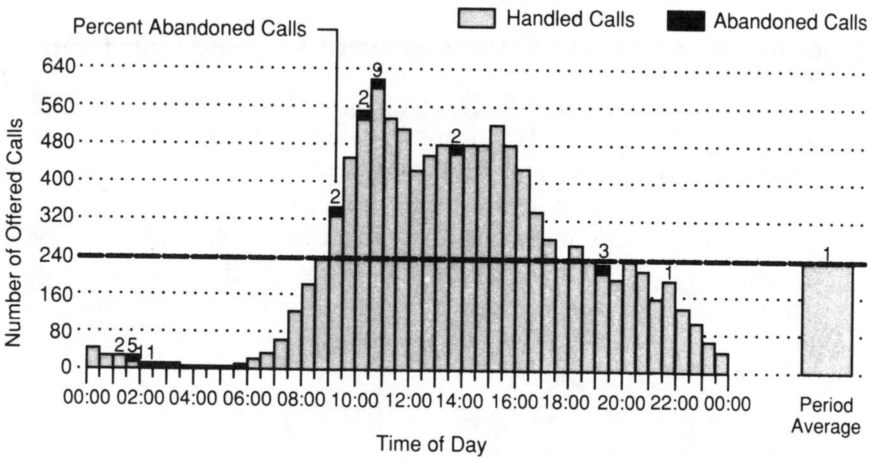

provide. UCDs, if they provide reporting features at all, usually produce less detailed summaries.

Monitoring Equipment

Although many states have laws limiting monitoring, many feel that such supervisory attention is essential for ensuring quality communication and identifying training needs. Usually, the monitoring function is an integral feature of an ACD system. Most ACDs come with a management station that allows the supervisor to key into an extension undetected and without affecting the quality or volume of the line. Some have a display that indicates the agent's name, the line status (whether or not the agent is talking), and the time elapsed. From this indicator, the manager can decide which conversation he or she wishes to monitor. Another available ACD feature alerts the monitor to the "wrap-up" or final stages of a call, thus allowing spot checking of the "sale."

For telemarketing operations without monitoring capabilities, special equipment utilizable on 90 percent of all existing phone systems may be purchased. From a designated phone, a security number that allows access to various preprogrammed extensions is dialed. By hitting the pound key (#) and an extension number, the supervisor can monitor calls simply by moving from one extension to the next. Although this equipment cannot provide the display information noted above, it does have remote capabilities from any touch-tone telephone either inside or outside the company.

The "silent monitoring" devices mentioned here have generated a great deal of controversy. Chapter 21 discusses this topic in more detail. Check with legal counsel or the attorney general's office in your state before embarking on a monitoring program.

Voice Response Units (VRUs) or Automated Response Units (ARUs)

Automated voice response systems transform any touch-tone telephone into a computer terminal. When a caller dials into the system, he or she is prompted by a prerecorded digitized voice that gives a menu of choices. By pressing different numbers on the touch-tone pad, the caller is able to input and retrieve information from the host data base. The system responds with a recorded phrase corresponding to the caller's specific needs. In this way, data entry, transaction processing, and information retrieval are conducted via the telephone instead of by individual computer terminals.

The benefits of an automated voice response system are as follows:

- The system responds twenty-four hours a day, seven days a week at no additional cost.
- Because processing time is reduced, so are telecommunication costs.
- By decreasing the need for human operators, VRUs and ARUs reduce overhead costs

Typical applications for the system include the following:

- Account status information
- Sales/order entry
- Banking information
- Airline reservations
- Telephone directory assistance
- Mortgage information
- Loan information
- Crew scheduling
- Package tracing
- Dealer locations

Automatic Dial Recorded Message Players (ADRMPs)

ADRMPs are computers that store the telephone numbers of lists of prospects and/or customers, automatically dial them in a random or preprogrammed mode, and deliver a prerecorded message. ADRMPs can reach a large number of people in a short time at a dramatically low price. Because many of the systems allow interactive conversations, they can also be utilized in such areas as surveying, market research, and opinion polls.

ADRMPs have worked successfully in the following situations:

- Announcements of new products, businesses, or services
- Advising customers of pick-up or delivery information

- Alerting customers to the recall of a product (Car companies and drug firms have used ADRMPs to notify of potential danger.)

ADRMPs have gotten a lot of negative publicity because consumers have complained of being bombarded by repeated automated offers for products they don't want and because they cannot terminate the call. Manufacturers have responded by modifying equipment so that it disconnects. However, because more and more legal questions are surfacing regarding use of ADRMPs, you should seek legal counsel if you are considering them.

LEASING VS. PURCHASING A TELECOMMUNICATIONS SYSTEM

Most equipment suppliers offer both lease and purchase options. The question becomes what is best for your situation. As usual, the answer is "it all depends." One consideration is the rate at which you anticipate your program will grow. How large and sophisticated a system will you need five or ten years down the line? If you purchase a system too early, you run a definite risk of buying too small, too large, or too outdated a system. Thus, if you are starting a program from scratch, you should probably lease equipment until you have developed some baseline data on growth. If you lease a system, avoid a long lease and try to get an escape clause in the contract.

If your program has been in existence for some time, and you plan an expansion, this might be the time to consider purchasing. However, you will want to consider how long it will take you to amortize such an investment as well as the effect of any existing tax regulations. If, after weighing these considerations, you believe you should purchase, then a careful review of available options and costs is in order.

First, talk with representatives of various vendors. Their presentations and written materials will help refine your thinking. Ask questions, and makes notes as you would in comparing bids on any other type of capital investment. Obtain customer references, and take the trouble to follow them up. The process may be time-consuming, but it is time well spent.

If you decide to purchase, here are some tips to keep in mind before selecting a vendor:

- Make sure you are comparing "apples with apples" when weighing features.
- Price is not necessarily the main consideration. It's more important to feel confident the vendor will be responsive and reliable and can

keep the system functioning on a day-to-day basis with minimal downtime.

- Be sure to look closely at service warranties and training programs.
- Make on-site visits to users, and talk with someone who works with the system daily. When you speak to references, ask them why they chose the vendor and whether they would do so again.

CHOOSING A LONG-DISTANCE SERVICE

If your business is selling over the phone, *consistent quality* of transmission and *reliability* should be your priorities. With many long-distance carriers in the marketplace, service can vary considerably. Major differences in quality may be due to how the network is managed, switching and call-handling equipment, type of network (fiber optic, microwave, satellite, etc.), or whether the facilities are analog or digital. Again, talk to users and try the network. You may also want to sign up with two carriers to compare their services.

There are basically two types of long-distance services: switched and dedicated. A switched service allows you to simply dial anywhere in the world. All you need is the telephone line provided by your local telephone company. Switched long-distance services are divided into two general areas: Direct Distance Dialing (DDD) and Wide Area Telecommunications Service (WATS). What distinguishes them is how they are billed.

DDD is the most expensive type of long-distance service because it is billed using only two criteria: time of day and distance. Because there are no setup or monthly charges, DDD may be the best way to test or start your telemarketing program. Using information from the detailed billing statements, you can easily weigh the merits of more cost-effective options for the future.

WATS-Type Services

WATS (Wide Area Telecommunication Services) was originally offered only by AT&T as a dedicated service to large long-distance users. Today, the term WATS is often used by AT&T and by many long-distance companies to describe most volume discounted services (both switched and dedicated).

WATS discounts are based on time of day, day of week, duration of call, and total number of hours billed. Switched WATS services also bill for a one-time order charge (or setup fee), monthly service, installation, a per line charge, and/or a minimum usage charge.

Dedicated WATS Services

Dedicated WATS, offered by AT&T and other major carriers, is a higher volume, higher discount service. It is usually one way (outbound or inbound 800), interstate (outside your home state), or intrastate (within your home state) and dedicated to long-distance usage only. Dedicated WATS lines are separate from your regular office telephone lines and should be purchased according to your telemarketing needs.

Discounts for dedicated WATS are based on the total number of hours of usage, time of day, distance (sometimes in mileage bands), day of the week, type of WATS (intrastate or interstate), and duration of call. Because they are dedicated lines, carriers charge for installation, in addition to a per line, monthly service, and minimum usage guarantee fee.

Other Dedicated Services

Depending upon your calling patterns, your telemarketing group might be able to take advantage of other specialized dedicated services, such as FX (Foreign Exchange), TIE lines, and T-1. All these services are offered by AT&T and many other long-distance carriers.

FX Service. If you have a high volume of calls going to or from a particular city, you might consider FX services. An FX line is a dedicated line that either (1) enables you to be in New York, for instance, and make local calls in, say, Cleveland or (2) allows your customers to call you in New York from Cleveland and pay only for a local call. In other words, you can have a local number in a distant city without having an office there. You are generally billed a fixed monthly fee plus a local charge for each call.

TIE Lines. A TIE line connects one office (PBX) to another in a distant city. If you make many calls between branch offices, a TIE line may be cost-effective because you pay only a fixed monthly fee.

T-1. A T-1 is a dedicated circuit made up of twenty-four separate channels (lines). Companies that have a very high volume of telecommunications traffic are the primary users of this service.

Inbound WATS

First introduced by AT&T in 1967, 800 ("toll-free") services have increased dramatically in the last ten years. Popular for customer services, banking by phone, providing information, ordering by mail, ordering from catalogs, and especially responses to commercial television advertising, 800 services are now available through most long-distance companies. Recently, they have become so inexpensive that some families have installed 800 numbers in their homes so their kids can call home from college!

Inbound 800, like outbound WATS, is a volume discount service that is sensitive to time of day, distance, and volume. Dedicated 800 is available within your state (intrastate), within a few state area, nationwide (interstate), international, or any combination of these. AT&T's new Advanced 800 Service offers the following options:

- Single 800—gives you one 800 number regardless of the call's point of origin (within or outside your state)
- Customized call routing—allows you to route your 800 calls by area code (East Coast calls can be routed to your East Coast location; West Coast calls can be routed to your office on that coast. This can cut costs and speed up handling.)
- Call prompting—combines an automated attendant feature (enabling callers to route their calls to a particular extension or department by pressing the touch-tone key pad) with 800 service

AT&T 800 Readyline

AT&T's 800 Readyline is a toll-free inbound service that allows you to handle 800 calls on your company's regular, non-800, telephone lines. Smaller businesses thus have the option of using their existing lines more flexibly and efficiently without the cost of a dedicated service. Sprint, MCI, ALLNET, and other companies are now offering similar services.

900 Service

900 services have created new entrepreneurial opportunities for marketing companies and information providers. Essentially, they allow you to advertise a 900 number, attach a host of creative messages to that number, and have the phone company act as your collection agent.

Originally a long-distance extension of local 976, 970, and 540 services, 900 numbers are now used in such diverse areas as opinion polling, response to special TV promotions, weather offerings, restaurant information, and sweepstakes. Savvy marketers have put DJs, record artists, and actors on prerecorded tapes to promote everything from records to movies to television programs. Cereal companies have even used 900 services to get kids to call in and play interactive games to promote their cereals. Some companies are thinking of switching from an 800 to a 900 number, thus converting their free informational service into a new revenue stream.

There is even a 900 service that, for $10, will teach you how to make money from 900 services!

AT&T and the major carriers, like MCI and Sprint, offer 900 services. You are charged a fixed rate for the first minute and a lesser rate for each additional minute, and callers are billed on their regular telephone statement. In addition, there could be a surcharge on any revenue collected on your behalf, though limits are set. Be sure to check maximum rates with your carrier.

USEFUL QUESTIONS

Regardless of your telemarketing objectives, work with the two lists of questions that follow. The first is designed to help you better understand your business needs now and in the future; the second is to help you interview a long-distance carrier.

Needs Analysis Questions

1. How many hours of long-distance calling (outbound/inbound) will I actually be using?

Inbound Hours	*Outbound Hours*
0–50	0–50
50–100	50–100
100–200	100–200

2. How many hours of long-distance calling do I anticipate utilizing in six months, one year, etc.?

Inbound Hours	*Outbound Hours*
6 months	6 months
1 year	1 year
2 years	2 years

3. How many calls per hour do my telemarketers actually make?

Number of telemarketers:	____
Actual number of calling hours:	____
Calls per hour:	____

4. What is the average duration of each call?

(Note: Most companies bill in six-second increments but have a thirty-second call minimum billing.)

5. What time of day are my calls made?

Hours	*Number of Calls*
Daytime (8 A.M. to 5 P.M.):	____
Evening (5 P.M. to 11 P.M.):	____
Night (11 P.M. to 8 A.M.):	____
Weekends and holidays:	____

(Note: Because long-distance carriers differ about which hours of the day are discounted, check carefully with each to determine the most appropriate.)

6. Where do my telemarketers call? What cities do they call most frequently?
7. What area codes are called most frequently?

Questions to Ask Long-Distance Carriers

1. *Which of the services below do you offer and what are your rates?*

   OUTBOUND
   - ☐ DDD (switched services)
   - ☐ WATS
     - Switched
     - Dedicated
     - International calling
   - ☐ FX services
     - What cities?
   - ☐ TIE lines
     - What cities?

   INBOUND (900)
   - ☐ Switched
   - ☐ Dedicated

   INBOUND (900)

2. *What kind of discounts do you offer?*
   - ☐ Time of day
   - ☐ Volume discounts
   - ☐ Distance sensitive
   - ☐ Special city rate
   - ☐ Multiple locations

3. *What are the billing increments?* (Ask this question for each service in which you are interested.)

- ☐ Six-second billing
- ☐ Thirty-second billing

4. *What is your minimum billing per call?*
5. *What kind of call supervision do you have? Do you bill for completed calls, or do you bill on a timed basis?*
6. *Do you have any redundancy capabilities built into your network?* (For example, alternate routes to the same city).
7. *What is your network comprised of?*

Percentage of Network	
Fiber optics	____ %
Microwave (analog)	____ %
Microwave (digital)	____ %
Satellite	____ %

8. *Describe your rate structure.*
   - ☐ Volume discounts
   - ☐ City-to-city discounts
   - ☐ Time of day discounts
   - ☐ Discounts for multiple locations
   - ☐ WATS (switched access)
   - ☐ Dedicated WATS
   - ☐ FX
   - ☐ Tie Lines
   - ☐ T-1

9. *What are your setup charges?*
10. *Are there any monthly charges for higher volume services (especially dedicated services?)*
11. *How do you handle credit for calls, misdials, wrong numbers, and busy signals?*
12. *What are your rates for directory assistance?*
13. *Do you have any calling cards?*
14. *What kind of management reports are available?*
    - ☐ By time of day
    - ☐ By date
    - ☐ By project billing or account codes
    - ☐ By individual user
    - ☐ By call duration
    - ☐ For each mileage band
    - ☐ For international calls
    - ☐ For frequently called numbers
    - ☐ For long-duration calls

Figure 20-3. Sample management report—Allnet.

ESP can be shipped to any person at any location you request - not just to your billing address and payables department.

Your report description and the month it covers are listed on each page.

The exact date and time your report is run is listed on each page.

This sample report is summarized by store location. You choose both the format and the information options you need, creating your own customized ESP.

ESP

Allnet

ALLNET COMMUNICATION SERVICES, INC.
MULTI-LOCATION SUMMARY
APRIL 25,

11:24 WEDNESDAY, MAY 24,

JOHN DOE
ABC COMPANY
1234 MAIN STREET
YORKTOWN, ANYSTATE 99999

LOCATION	ANI	DURATION	CALLS	DOMESTIC USAGE	MAXCESS DISCOUNT	INTL USAGE	FEDERAL TAX	STATE LOCAL TAX	NONUSAGE CHARGE	OTHER CHARGES	TOTAL AMOUNT
STORE=45											
ATLANTA	2125552773	237	17	$37.37	$-0.23	$0.00	$2.47	$1.23	$4.09	$-0.33	$44.59
STORE=47											
BAKERSFIELD	2125552443	755	148	$129.60	$-0.86	$10.52	$9.25	$4.61	$15.33	$-1.25	$167.20
BAKERSFIELD	2125555299	690	156	$136.03	$-0.84	$1.02	$9.04	$4.51	$14.99	$-1.22	$163.54
STORE		1445	304	$265.63	$-1.69	$11.54	$18.29	$9.12	$30.31	$-2.46	$330.74
STORE=58											
BEVERLY HILLS	2125556839	581	52	$114.56	$-0.70	$0.00	$7.56	$3.77	$12.53	$-1.02	$136.70
STORE=62											
FRESNO	2125550077	463	149	$111.31	$-0.68	$0.00	$7.35	$3.66	$12.17	$-0.99	$132.82
FRESNO	2125558010	10	3	$2.32	$-0.01	$0.00	$0.15	$0.08	$0.25	$-0.02	$2.77
STORE		473	152	$113.63	$-0.69	$0.00	$7.50	$3.74	$12.43	$-1.01	$135.59
STORE=78											
STUART	2125550267	572	47	$87.11	$-0.58	$7.67	$6.26	$3.12	$10.37	$-0.84	$113.10

Management reports are becoming increasingly important in choosing a long-distance carrier. The better ones give you improved control over your long-distance costs and in managing your long-distance use. Figure 20-3 shows a sample report from Allnet.

SUMMARY

This chapter acquainted the reader with the basic terminology relating to current telecommunications equipment and services options.

Descriptions and features were given for private branch exchange, key telephone system, centrex, automatic and uniform call distributors, monitoring systems, voice response units, and automatic dial recorded message players.

Major emphasis was given to tips and guidelines on whether to lease or purchase telecommunications equipment and how to choose a long-distance service.

CHAPTER

21

Legal and Ethical Issues

INDUSTRY statistics project that over eight million people in the United States will be employed in some phase of telemarketing in the 1990s. One of the fastest growing segments of American business, telemarketing has a great deal to offer our society, including equal opportunities to a diverse work group, such as the elderly and disabled. Moreover, it creates none of the environmental problems that manufacturing companies and local authorities must face and solve.

It is therefore particularly painful to see the industry's reputation maligned by frauds perpetrated by a greedy few. These abuses have had an impact—not only on the public, but on legitimate telemarketers who have been hurt by the press, stringent laws, and negative public opinion. Telemarketers must observe ethical practices as well as involve themselves in educating legislators about the economic and social importance of their industry.

ADRMP

As explained in Chapter 20, the ADRMP is used to make telephone presentations of prerecorded messages to either preprogrammed or randomly selected lists of clients. These machines are cost-effective for specialized campaigns that need large volumes of calls. For instance, catalog companies sometimes employ them to inform customers of orders that are in.

ADRMPs can be programmed to make calls sequentially, so that they may, for example, reach a hospital or nursing home and dial into every room. The public is rightfully outraged by such an invasive use of marketing technology. One characteristic of older model ADRMPs is that they did not disconnect within thirty seconds after an unwilling prospect had hung up. This feature, in particular, led to certain emergency situations that have inflamed the public (there have been cases of medical emergencies when ADRMPs have seized the line and prohibited the making of outside calls for help). Because of these abuses, many states have passed laws controlling ADRMPs. The prudent telemarketer will check relevant state laws before beginning a program incorporating this technology.

ADVERTISING

Recently, the public has complained of unsolicited calls promising prizes if the consumer signs up for or purchases certain items or a trip. Sometimes a postcard is received giving an 800 number and awarding a bonus if one calls and signs up for a trip. This area is ripe for fraud, and consumers should be wary of this approach.

ASTERISK LAWS

Florida was the first state to pass an ''asterisk law''; it became effective in 1988. Other states are following. The asterisk laws give consumers the right to say they don't want to receive marketing phone calls. Telephone company consumers may choose to have an asterisk next to their name in the telephone book. This would mean ''no phone solicitations.'' In the state of Florida, an offender is fined $10,000 per call to a subscriber with an asterisk.

Clearly, most reputable telemarketers prefer not to disturb people who do not want to receive calls. Basically, it's a waste of time and money. However, the asterisk laws can be very difficult to follow. In the state of Florida, for instance, there are over 100 telephone directories and no central data base. Therefore, anyone calling would have the responsibility of verifying all directories.

FUND-RAISING

There have been some unfortunate abuses in the name of charity. It is widely known that in some campaigns only about 5 percent—or less—of the money raised actually goes to charitable purposes. Most pending legislation affects disclosures required in solicitations and registration with the state.

HOURS

Many states have laws restricting hours of solicitation to between 9 A.M. and 9 P.M. on weekdays, with which most ethical telemarketers agree. Some states are trying to introduce a 4 P.M. limit on weekdays.

MONITORING

Most telemarketing professionals feel that monitoring employees is crucial to training and quality control. However, some workers' rights groups claim that it denies their right to privacy. Today, most states have laws governing monitoring stating that one or both of the parties being monitored must be aware of it. A proposed federal law would preempt such state laws.

In California, Delaware, Florida, Georgia, Illinois, Maryland, Michigan, Pennsylvania, and Washington, it is illegal to monitor without the consent of all parties. In other words, both the agent and the customer have to agree that a supervisor can listen in on the call. This makes constructive monitoring all but impossible. In other states, only one party needs to be informed, and this situation can still prove useful.

The American Telemarketing Association and the Direct Marketing Association, as well as most reputable companies, feel that prohibiting monitoring ultimately hurts the consumer. A telemarketing management team cannot objectively assess agents' performances if they know they are being monitored. When representatives ask the supervisor to listen in and comment on their work, this request is difficult to honor in states where the customer must be interrupted and agree. When clients are asked to accommodate the taping or beep, they often get anxious, and the conversation becomes unnatural. Some companies work within the law on their inbound telemarketing programs by stating on their answer tape that "portions of this call may be recorded."

REGISTRATION

In many states, telemarketing companies must register with the state attorney general's office and pay an annual fee. Generally the laws declare unfair and deceptive telephone solicitations to be an unfair act under the consumer protection act and require telephone solicitors to register with the department of licensing and pay an annual fee to conduct business in the state.

This type of legislation, in itself, is acceptable. But it is often difficult to plow through the red tape of registration. It took someone in California a week to collect all the information requested! A few laws require registration with the secretary of state and a $25,000 bond. In these states, there are sometimes exceptions, such as for newspapers or political campaigns.

TAXES

Over the past few years, many states have become interested in collecting use taxes. They perceive direct marketing to be a threat to the local businesses on whom they rely for tax revenue. The issue to telemarketers is whether direct marketing companies not based in a given state will be required to collect that state's sales and use tax from customers residing in the state.

TELECOM REGULATION

Both the American Telemarketing Association (ATA) and the Direct Marketing Association (DMA) track legislation that affects the telecommunications industry. Laws dealing with telephone rates and taxes, for instance, directly impact the telemarketing business.

Unsolicited Calls

Asterisk and ADRMP regulations are included in this category of legislation and are often piggybacked with other related issues. In some states, there is legislation that requires telephone solicitors, in addition to making specified disclosures, to inquire within thirty seconds of beginning a conversation whether the person being solicited is willing to permit the call.

900 Service

In June 1989, the United States Supreme Court made its first ruling on a 900 service when it declared that a federal ban on ''indecent'' commercial telephone messages violates the constitutional right to free speech. Beyond the ''realm of the senses,'' no other legislation has come up restricting a 900 number. However, with its increasing popularity and promise of enormous profits, some unscrupulous vendor will undoubtedly figure out a way to misuse the technology! It is therefore important to track pending regulations in this exciting new area.

Future Legislation

Suppose, in a few years, you are discussing a classified telemarketing campaign over a video conferencing system and your competitor has succeeded in linking up to your meeting! Title III, the federal wiretap statute, is the primary law protecting the privacy and security of business and personal communications. When it was written in 1917, the statute covered only "aural" communication via a common carrier analog network and face-to-face communication. No one was concerned about electronic mail, cellular telephones, paging devices, computer-to-computer data transmissions, video teleconferencing, etc.

Title III of the Omnibus Crime Control and Safe Streets Act of 1968 was amended in 1986 to protect against any unauthorized interception of "electronic" communication. The law now includes microwave, video, fiber optics, and data communications. What amendments will the year 2010 see?

In May 1989, the *Wall Street Journal* published a piece on the state of "junk FAX." In the last year, several states have passed legislation restricting or banning unsolicited promotional FAXs. One typical bill, which covers both FAXs and ADRMPs, prohibits any person who uses a machine that electronically transmits messages or facsimiles of documents through connection with the telephone network from transmitting unsolicited advertising material for the sale of any realty, goods, or services.

The DMA is tracking new legislation carefully and has taken the position that strict regulation of FAX advertising could eventually hurt direct marketing and telemarketers. Those in favor of legislation say that, besides tying up machines, junk FAX is an invasion of privacy. When it is transmitted, the owner of the machine is forced to pay the bill! "It's like someone took your car on a short drive to make a sales pitch and didn't ask your permission," says Thomas A. Papageorge, a Los Angeles deputy district attorney. "If someone did that, you'd be outraged. But advertisers can FAX you an ad against your will."[1]

Many businesses also fear that the ad bombardment will get heavier as more companies publish FAX number directories. Programs that allow manufacturers to randomly dial FAX numbers already exist. Bill McCue, president of Public FAX, Inc., an Orange, California, publisher of a FAX directory and trade machine, is trying to get advertisers to use some discretion in determining the length of their ads and when they are sent. Although Mr. McCue opposes FAX restrictions, he himself has seen how annoying unwanted transmissions can be. He once received an ad for hours on end when a dialing flaw kept repeating the message every nine minutes! His motto is "FAX unto others as you would have them FAX unto you."[2] What if a marketer gets his hands on the toll-free FAX number you plan to install? Be alert to the issue, and report improper use of toll-free numbers to the DMA and ATA.

[1]"Junk Mail in the Age of Fax," Michele Manges, *Wall Street Journal*, May 3, 1989, p. B1.

[2]*Ibid.*

The ATA and DMA both put out guidelines of ethical standards and practices. Portions of the ATA's *Telemarketing Standards and Guidelines* are reproduced in Appendix 3, and you can write to the DMA Ethics Department, 1120 Avenue of the Americas, New York, New York 10036. The DMA also publishes a *Compendium of Government Issues Affecting Telemarketing* and offers the Telephone Preference Service. Companies subscribing to this service receive quarterly a list of people who do not want to receive calls. The companies can remove these names from their calling lists. The ATA also circulates Consumer Guidelines, endorsed by the National Consumer League and the Federal Trade Commission. It will be mailed free to anyone sending a self-addressed envelope to the American Telemarketing Association, 4605 Lankershim Boulevard, Suite 824, N. Hollywood, California 91602. Or call 818-766-5324.

SUMMARY

This chapter presented a general introduction to some of the legal issues affecting telemarketers including examples of the type of state legislation either passed or being proposed.

The chapter covers such issues as automated dialing recorded message players, advertising, asterisk laws, fundraising, calling hours, and monitoring. Also discussed are telemarketing company registration, taxes, unsolicited calls, 900 services, and future legislation.

Afterword

THE day Napoleon met defeat at Waterloo, another event—perhaps less remarked upon by historians but no less instructive—also occurred. As the smoke of the battle cleared, a small flock of carrier pigeons rose into the uncertain skies and headed for the English Channel. Landing in the waiting hands of the Baron de Rothschild's English agent, they bore advance information—ALLIES VICTORIOUS—that enabled Rothschild to realize a fortune on the London Exchange that very day.

Rothschild had the imagination to look with a fresh eye at the most sophisticated communications technology of the day and the boldness to exploit it with dispatch. As Rothschild used the technology of his day, smart business leaders today will recognize that the phone is their opportunity to maximize profit potential. It is any entrepreneur's key to the integrated, interconnected, "global village."

I hope this book gives entrepreneurial men and women—the Rothschilds of today—the tools they need to use telemarketing effectively. It by no means presents every detail of this growing marketing force. However, it does provide guidelines and a roadmap for avoiding the common pitfalls that can and do occur. I welcome comments and feedback from readers and wish them the best of luck.

APPENDIX

1

Standard Industrial Classification Statistics

The following is reproduced courtesy of Duns Marketing Services, a company of the Dun & Bradstreet Corporation. Please note that all count totals of businesses within each code represent the number of companies which can be obtained through Duns Marketing Services and are not meant to represent all companies that exist within each classification.

The Standard Industrial Classification, commonly referred to as the SIC code, was developed by the U.S. Government in conjunction with U.S. business. It divides virtually all economic activity into 10 major divisions:

Agriculture, Forestry, and Fishing .... 01—09
Mining .... 10—14
Construction .... 15—17
Manufacturing .... 20—39
Transportation, Communications, Utilities .... 40—49
Wholesale Trade .... 50—51
Retail Trade .... 52—59
Finance, Insurance and Real Estate .... 60—67
Services .... 70—89
Public Administration .... 91—97
NonClassifiable Establishments 99

The SIC places each line of business within one of these 10 divisions and assigns it a four-digit code. The first two digits describe the nature of the activity broadly:

15 .... General Building Contractors

The third and fourth digits describe the activity specifically:

1521 .... General House Contractors

The most significant attribute of the SIC system is that it is the one system most frequently used in presenting the basic data about the nation. No other system is as widely used nor does any other describe in detail the entire U.S. economy. Thus, the system provides the enterprising industrial marketer with a key to a wealth of valuable data. The following are examples of some critical questions the SIC system along with other data can help you answer:

- How large is the market for my products and services? (i.e., How many companies are in the same business as those that typically buy my product/service?)
- Where are the greatest concentrations of potential buyers? How is the market dispersed geographically?
- How large are the establishments in those markets, in terms of sales and number of employees?
- Where should I locate my branches, retail outlet and service centers?
- How large is the ''day-time'' working population in a given geographical area?

Major Industry Group Totals

Description		*Count*
01-09	Agriculture, Forestry, and Fishing	293,924
10-14	Mining	50,712
15-17	Construction	782,872
20-39	Manufacturing	549,957
40-49	Transportation, Communications, Utilities	288,078
60-51	Wholesale Trade	656,004
52-59	Retail Trade	1,912,208
60-67	Finance, Insurance and Real Estate	654,503
70-89	Services	2,421,850
90-97	Public Administration	51,786
99	NonClassifiable Establishments	39,467
Grand Total		**7,701,361**

All counts are primary SICs only

Two-digit SIC Totals

SIC	*Description*	*Count*
01-09	**Agriculture, Forestry, and Fishing**	**293,924**
01	Agricultural Production-Crops	147,972
02	Agricultural Production-Livestock	52,174
07	Agricultural Services	88,027
08	Forestry	3,255
09	Fishing, Hunting, and Trapping	2,496
10-14	**Mining**	**50,712**
10	Metal Mining	1,858
12	Coal Mining	4,965
13	Oil and Gas Extraction	38,444
14	Nonmetallic Minerals, except Fuels	5,445
15-17	**Construction**	**782,872**
15	General Building Contractors	283,230
16	Heavy Construction, except Building	42,487
17	Special Trade Contractors	457,155
20-39	**Manufacturing**	**549,957**
20	Food and Kindred Products	31,035
21	Tobacco Products	260
22	Textile Mill Products	12,158
23	Apparel and other Textile Products	30,990
24	Lumber and Wood Products	40,060
25	Furniture and Fixtures	17,428
26	Paper and Allied Products	9,030
27	Printing and Publishing	95,552
28	Chemicals and Allied Products	21,930
29	Petroleum and Coal Products	3,674
30	Rubber and miscellaneous Plastic Products	18,455
31	Leather and Leather Products	4,002
32	Stone, Clay, and Glass Products	22,683
33	Primary Metal Industries	11,061
34	Fabricated Metal Products	48,146
35	Industrial Machinery and Equipment	81,240
36	Electronic and other Electric Equipment	29,231
37	Transportation Equipment	17,261
38	Instruments and Related Products	19,087
39	Miscellaneous Manufacturing Industries	36,674
40-49	**Transportation, Communications, Utilities**	**288,078**
40	Railroad Transportation	2,763
41	Local and Interurban Passenger Transit	20,949

All counts are primary SICs only

SIC	Description	Count
42	Trucking and Warehousing	132,403
43	U.S. Postal Service	742
44	Water Transportation	10,846
45	Transportation by Air	14,301
46	Pipelines, except Natural Gas	822
47	Transportation Services	45,877
48	Communication	30,914
49	Electric, Gas, and Sanitary Services	28,461
50-51	**Wholesale Trade**	**656,004**
50	Wholesale Trade-Durable Goods	418,794
51	Wholesale Trade-Nondurable Goods	237,210
52-59	**Retail Trade**	**1,912,208**
52	Building Materials and Garden Supplies	108,765
53	General Merchandise Stores	51,726
54	Food Stores	223,513
55	Automotive Dealers and Service Stations	245,392
56	Apparel and Accessory Stores	174,680
57	Furniture and Homefurnishings Store	176,769
58	Eating and Drinking Places	383,301
59	Miscellaneous Retail	548,062
60-67	**Finance, Insurance and Real Estate**	**654,503**
60	Depository Institutions	90,339
61	Nondepository Institutions	34,778
62	Security and Commodity Brokers	28,314
63	Insurance Carriers	34,196
64	Insurance Agents, Brokers, and Service	111,022
65	Real Estate	324,670
67	Holding and other Investment Offices	31,184
70-89	**Services**	**2,421,850**
70	Hotels and other Lodging Places	70,679
72	Personal Services	279,046
73	Business Services	395,000
75	Auto Repair, Services, and Parking	221,536
76	Miscellaneous Repair Services	154,559
78	Motion Pictures	35,302
79	Amusement and Recreation Services	85,457
80	Health Services	365,439
81	Legal Services	123,139
82	Educational Services	182,468
83	Social Services	106,531
84	Museums, Botanicals, Zoological Gardens	4,704
86	Membership Organizations	169,894

All counts are primary SICs only

SIC	Description	Count
87	Engineering and Management Services	224,151
88	Private Households	464
89	Services, not elsewhere classified	3,481
90-97	**Public Administration**	**51,786**
91	Executive, Legislative, and General	24,187
92	Justice, Public Order, and Safety	7,068
93	Finance, Taxation, and Monetary Policy	1,119
94	Administration of Human Resources	5,244
95	Environmental Quality and Housing	8,381
96	Administration of Economic Programs	3,823
97	National Security and International Affairs	1,964
99	**NonClassifiable Establishments**	**39,467**
99	**NonClassifiable Establishments**	**39,467**
Grand Total		**7,701,361**

Four-digit SIC Totals

SIC	Description	Count
Agriculture, Forestry, and Fishing		**293,924**
SIC Numbers 0100-0999		
01	**Agricultural Production-Crops**	**147,972**
0111	Wheat Farm	18,418
0112	Rice Farm	2,066
0115	Corn Farm	28,662
0116	Soybean Farm	2,182
0119	Cash Grains, NEC	9,958
0131	Cotton Farm	5,482
0132	Tobacco Farm	640
0133	Sugarcane & Sugar Beet Farm	393
0134	Irish Potato Farm	1,222
0139	Field Crops Exc Cash, NEC	2,084
0161	Vegetable & Melon Farm	3,699
0171	Berry Crop Farm	788
0172	Grape Vineyard	1,175
0173	Tree Nut Grove	644
0174	Citrus Fruit Grove	1,275
0175	Deciduous Tree Fruit Orchard	3,281

SIC	*Description*	*Count*
0179	Fruit & Tree Nut, NEC	441
0181	Grow Flowers/Nursery Products	11,658
0182	Food Crops (Under Cover)	950
0191	General Farms	52,954
02	**Agricultural Production-Livestock**	**52,174**
0211	Beef Cattle Feedlots	2,400
0212	Beef, Cattle, Exc feedlots	14,549
0213	Hogs	3,385
0214	Sheep & Goats	598
0219	Livestock Exc Dairy/Poultry	675
0241	Dairy Farm	10,913
0251	Raising Cooking Chickens	859
0252	Chicken Eggs	1,312
0253	Turkeys & Turkey Eggs	597
0254	Poultry Hatcheries	661
0259	Poultry & Eggs, NEC	358
0271	Fur-Bearing Animal Farms	530
0272	Horses & Other Equines	2,295
0273	Animal Aquaculture	527
0279	Animal Specialties, NEC	2,336
0291	Livestock & Animal Farms	10,179
07	**Agricultural Services**	**88,027**
0711	Soil Preparation Svcs	1,208
0721	Crop Planting & Cultivating	3,768
0722	Crop Machine Harvesting Svcs	1,478
0723	Crops Preparation Exc Cot Gin	2,758
0724	Cotton Ginning	1,443
0741	Livestock Veterinary Svc	2,214
0742	Veterinary Svcs, Animals	15,308
0751	Livestock Svc Exc Veterinary	2,161
0752	Animal Svcs Exc Veterinary	10,253
0761	Farm Labor Contractors	343
0762	Farm Mgt Svcs	940
0781	Landscape Plan/Consult	9,077
0782	Lawn & Garden Svcs	30,964
0783	Ornamental Shrub & Tree Svcs	6,112
08	**Forestry**	**3,255**
0811	Timber Tracts	1,210
0831	Forest Nurseries & Products	282
0851	Forestry Svcs	1,763
09	**Fishing, Hunting, and Trapping**	**2,496**

All counts are primary SICs only

SIC	Description	Count
0912	Finfish	868
0913	Shellfish	896
0919	Misc Marine Products	85
0921	Fish Hatchery & Preserve	444
0971	Hunt/Trap/Propagation	203

Mining 50,712

SIC Numbers 1000-1499

SIC	Description	Count
10	**Metal Mining**	**1,858**
1011	Iron Ores	98
1021	Copper Ores	75
1031	Lead & Zinc Ores	67
1041	Gold Ores	712
1044	Silver Ores	112
1061	Ferroalloy Ores Exc Vanadium	36
1081	Metal Mining Services	480
1094	Uranium-Radium-Vanadium	162
1099	Misc Metal Ores, NEC	116
12	**Coal Mining**	**4,965**
1221	Bit/Lignite Surface Mining	3,115
1222	Bit Coal Underground Mining	806
1231	Anthracite Mining	392
1241	Coal Mining Svcs	652
13	**Oil and Gas Extraction**	**38,444**
1311	Crude Petroleum & Nat Gas	15,275
1321	Produce Natural Gas Liquids	231
1381	Drilling Oil & Gas Wells	4,723
1382	Oil/Gas Field Exploration Svc	5,674
1389	Oil/Gas Field Svcs, NEC	12,541
14	**Nonmetallic Minerals, except Fuels**	**5,445**
1411	Dimension Stone	399
1422	Crushed/Broken Limestone	946
1423	Crushed/Broken Granite	84
1429	Crushed/Broken Stone, NEC	438
1442	Construction Sand & Gravel	2,119
1446	Industrial Sand	187
1455	Kaolin & Ball Clay	56
1459	Clay Refractory Minerals, NEC	162
1474	Potash/Soda/Borate Minerals	31
1475	Phosphate Rock	32

SIC	*Description*	*Count*
1479	Chemical Mineral Mining, NEC	133
1481	Nonmetal Minerals Exc Fuels	209
1499	Misc Nonmetals Exc Fuels	649

Construction **782,872**

SIC Numbers 1500-1799

15	**General Building Contractors**	**283,230**
1521	General House Contractors	188,022
1522	Residential Bldgs exc houses	13,185
1531	Operative Builders	22,315
1541	Industrial Bldg/Warehse	11,357
1542	Nonresidential Bldgs exc ind.	48,351
16	**Heavy Construction, except Building**	**42,487**
1611	Road Construct Exc. El Hways	14,169
1622	Bridge/Tunnel/El Hway Const	1,569
1623	Utility/Pwr Line Construction	12,544
1629	Heavy Construction, NEC	14,205
17	**Special Trade Contractors**	**457,155**
1711	Plumbing, Heating & A/C	112,034
1721	Painting & Paper Hanging	37,138
1731	Electrical Work	72,919
1741	Masonry/Stone Set/Other Work	19,113
1742	Plaster/Wall/Insulation Work	22,146
1743	Tile, Marble, Mosaic Work	6,338
1751	Carpentry Work	21,883
1752	Floor Work, NEC	12,696
1761	Roof/Siding/Sheet Metal Work	34,757
1771	Concrete Work	22,955
1781	Water Well Drilling	6,538
1791	Erect Structural Steel	4,571
1793	Glass & Glazing Work	6,770
1794	Excavation Work	33,766
1795	Wrecking & Demolition Work	1,691
1796	Install/Erect Bldg Equip, NEC	2,580
1799	Special Trade Contractors, NEC	39,259

Manufacturing **549,957**

SIC Numbers 2000-3999

20	**Food and Kindred Products**	**31,035**
2011	Meat Packing Plants	2,630

All counts are primary SICs only

SIC	Description	Count
2013	Sausages/Prepared Products	1,669
2015	Slaughter/Process Poultry	627
2021	Creamery Butter	115
2022	Cheese	786
2023	Processed Dairy Products	204
2024	Ice Cream & Frozen Desserts	867
2026	Fluid Milk	1,108
2032	Canned Specialties	360
2033	Canned Preserves/Jams/Jellies	1,022
2034	Dried Fruit/Veggie/Soup Mixes	227
2035	Fruit/Veggies Seasoning/Sauces	581
2037	Frozen Fruits/Juices/Veggies	312
2038	Frozen Specialties, NEC	604
2041	Flour & Grain Mill Products	566
2043	Cereal Breakfast Foods	85
2044	Rice Milling	93
2045	Prepared Flour Mixes/Doughs	218
2046	Wet Corn Milling	88
2047	Dog & Cat Food	274
2048	Prepared Animal Feeds	2,100
2051	Bread Products Exc Cookie/Crkr	3,513
2052	Cookies & Crackers	666
2053	Frozen Bakery Prods Exc Bread	69
2061	Cane Sugar Exc Refining	61
2062	Cane Sugar Refining	49
2063	Beet Sugar	85
2064	Candy & Other Products	1,300
2066	Chocolate & Cocoa Products	275
2067	Chewing Gum	32
2068	Salt/Roast Nuts/Seeds	90
2074	Cottonseed Oil Mills	71
2075	Soybean Oil Mills	121
2076	Veg Oil Mills Exc Corn/Soy	47
2077	Animal/Marine Fats/Oils	357
2079	Margarine & Other Edible Fats	157
2082	Malt Beverages	224
2083	Malt	45
2084	Wines, Brandy & Brandy Spirits	966
2085	Distilled & Blended Liquors	166
2086	Soft Drinks/Water (Can/Bottle)	2,172
2087	Flavoring Extracts/Syrups, NEC	516
2091	Can/Cure Fish & Seafoods	334

All counts are primary SICs only

SIC	Description	Count
2092	Fresh/Frozen Fish/Seafoods	699
2095	Roasted Coffee	238
2096	Potato/Corn Chips & Snacks	391
2097	Manufactured Ice	877
2098	Macaroni & Noodles	337
2099	Food Preparations, NEC	2,641
21	**Tobacco Products**	**260**
2111	Cigarettes	73
2121	Cigars	66
2131	Chewing/Smoking Tobacco/Snuff	80
2141	Tobacco Stemming/Redrying	41
22	**Textile Mill Products**	**12,158**
211	Cotton Brdwoven Fabric Mills	1,313
2221	Brdwoven Man Fiber/Silk Mills	994
2231	Wool Brdwoven Fabric Mills	316
2241	Narrow Fabric/Smallwares Mills	610
2251	Hosiery Exc Socks, Female	245
2252	Hosiery, NEC	536
2253	Knit Outerwear Mills	1,855
2254	Knit Under/Nightwear Mills	120
2257	Weft Knit Fabric Mills	206
2258	Lace/Warp Knit Fabric Mills	257
2259	Knitting Mills, NEC	211
2261	Finish Cotton Fabrics	1,346
2262	Finish Man Fiber/Silk Fabric	580
2269	Finishers of Textiles, NEC	272
2273	Carpets & Rugs	1,036
2281	Yarn Spinning Mills	478
2282	Yarn Mills	182
2284	Thread Mills	126
2295	Coated Fabrics, Not Rubber	284
2296	Tire Cord & Fabrics	26
2297	Nonwoven Fabrics	94
2298	Cordage & Twine	289
2299	Textile Goods, NEC	782
23	**Apparel and other Textile Products**	**30,990**
2311	Suits/Coats/Overcoats, Male	668
2321	Shirts Exc Work Shirts, Male	966
2322	Underwear/Nightwear, Male	134
2323	Neckwear, Male	283
2325	Separate Trousers/Slacks, Male	585
2326	Work Clothing, Male	334

SIC	Description	Count
2329	Male Clothing, NEC	1,833
2331	Blouses/Shirts, Female	1,672
2335	Dresses, Female	2,929
2337	Suits/Skirts/Coats, Female	1,107
2339	Outerwear, Female, NEC	4,064
2341	Under/Nitewear, Female/Child	781
2342	Bras/Girdle/Garments	170
2353	Hats, Caps & Millinery	546
2361	Dresses/Blouses/Shirts, child	790
2369	Child Outerwear, NEC	640
2371	Fur Goods	549
2381	Gloves no Knit/Leather	145
2384	Robes & Dressing Gowns	157
2385	Waterproof Outerwear	151
2386	Leather/Sheep-Lined Clothing	325
2387	Apparel Belts	484
2389	Apparel & Accessories, NEC	785
2391	Curtains & Draperies	2,171
2392	Housefurnishings	1,551
2393	Textile Bags	425
2394	Canvas & Related Products	1,984
2395	Decorative Stitching (Trade)	1,143
2396	Auto Trim/Apparel Findings	1,697
2397	Schiffli Machine Embroideries	261
2399	Fabric Textile Products, NEC	1,660
24	**Lumber and Wood Products**	**40,060**
2411	Logging	7,633
2421	General Planing/Saw Mills	5,559
2426	Hardwood Dimension/Floor Mills	1,093
2429	Special Product Sawmills, NEC	324
2431	Millwork	5,457
2434	Wood Kitchen Cabinets	7,246
2435	Hardwood Veneer & Plywood	418
2436	Softwood Veneer & Plywood	189
2439	Structural Wood, NEC	1,066
2441	Nail/Lock Corner Boxes/Shook	399
2448	Wood Pallets & Skids	2,005
2449	Wood Containers, NEC	489
2451	Mobile Homes	639
2452	Prefab wood bldgs/components	1,151
2491	Wood Preserving	624
2493	Reconstituted Wood Products	306

All counts are primary SICs only

SIC	*Description*	*Count*
2499	Wood Products, NEC	5,462
25	**Furniture and Fixtures**	**17,428**
2512	Wood Household Furniture	4,427
2512	Upholstered Wood Furniture	2,129
2514	Metal Household Furniture	621
2515	Mattresses/Convertible Beds	1,197
2517	Wood TV/Stereo/Sewing Cabinet	132
2519	Household Furniture, NEC	756
2521	Wood Office Furniture	1,424
2522	Office Furniture Exc Wood	484
2531	Public Bldg/Related Furniture	602
2541	Wood Store Fixtures	2,462
2542	Office Fixtures/Partitions	1,161
2591	Drapery Hardware/Window Shades	1,029
2599	Furniture & Fixtures, NEC	1,184
26	**Paper and Allied Products**	**9,030**
2611	Pulp Mills	204
2621	Paper Mills	1,411
2631	Paperboard Mills	734
2652	Setup Paperboard Boxes	318
2653	Corrugated & Solid Fiber Boxes	2,057
2655	Fiber Cans/Tubes/Drums	375
2656	Sanitary Food Containers	112
2657	Folding Paperboard Boxes	222
2671	Coat/Laminate Paper Packaging	219
2672	Coated & Laminated Paper, NEC	703
2673	Plastic/Foil/Coated Paper Bags	519
2674	Uncoated Paper/Multiwall Bags	154
2675	Die-Cut Paper/Cardboard	345
2676	Sanitary Paper Products	136
2677	Envelopes	250
2678	Stationery/Related Products	234
2679	Converted Paper Products, NEC	1,037
27	**Printing and Publishing**	**95,552**
2711	Publish/Print Newspapers	12,146
2721	Publish/Print Periodicals	7,158
2731	Publish/Print Books	5,555
2732	Print Books	486
2741	Miscellaneous Publishing	6,041
2752	Lithographic Commerce Printing	37,958
2754	Commercial Printing, Gravure	1,000
2759	Commercial Printing, NEC	15,476

All counts are primary SICs only

SIC	Description	Count
2761	Manifold Business Forms	1,059
2771	Greeting Cards	438
2782	Blankbooks/Looseleaf Binders	677
2789	Bookbinding & Related Work	1,299
2791	Typesetting	5,020
2796	Platemaking & Related Svcs	1,239
28	**Chemicals and Allied Products**	**21,930**
2812	Alkalies & Chlorine	133
2813	Industrial Gases	709
2816	Inorganic Pigments	153
2819	Ind Inorganic Chemicals, NEC	1,959
2821	Plastics Materials	1,558
2822	Synthetic Rubber	195
2823	Cellulosic Manmade Fibers	50
2824	Manmade Organic Fibers	148
2833	Medicine/Botanical Chemicals	520
2834	Pharmaceutical Preparations	1,582
2835	In Vitro/Vivo Diagnostics	107
2836	Biological Products	280
2841	Soap/Other Detergents	722
2842	Cleaning Preparations	1,952
2843	Surface Active/Finish Agents	161
2844	Cosmetics/Toilet Preparations	1,818
2851	Paint/Varnish/Other Products	1,989
2861	Gum & Wood Chemicals	140
2865	Cyclic Organic Crudes/Dyes	302
2869	Ind Organic Chemicals, NEC	1,185
2873	Nitrogenous Fertilizers	498
2874	Phosphatic Fertilizers	230
2875	Fertilizers, Mixing Only	482
2879	Pesticides/Farm Chemicals, NEC	693
2891	Adhesives & Sealants	1,070
2892	Explosives	210
2893	Printing Ink	622
2895	Carbon Black	44
2899	Chemicals & Preparations, NEC	2,418
29	**Petroleum and Coal Products**	**3,674**
2911	Petroleum refining	1,534
2951	Asphalt Paving Mixture/Blocks	952
2952	Asphalt Felts & Coatings	393
2992	Lubricating Oils & Greases	683
2999	Petroleum/Coal Products, NEC	112

All counts are primary SICs only

SIC	Description	Count
30	**Rubber and miscellaneous Plastic Products**	**18,455**
3011	Tires & Inner Tubes	403
3021	Rubber & Plastics Footwear	114
3052	Rubber/Plastics Hose/Belting	328
3053	Gasket/Packing/Seal Devices	614
3061	Mechanical Rubber Goods	131
3069	Fabricated Rubber Prdts, NEC	2,723
3081	Plastics Film & Sheet	856
3082	Plastics Profile Shapes	217
3083	Laminated Plastics Shapes	558
3084	Plastics Pipe	283
3085	Plastics Bottles	245
3086	Plastics Foam Products	1,153
3087	Plastic Resins Custom Compnd'g	66
3088	Plastic Plumbing Fixture	308
3089	Plastic Products, NEC	10,456
31	**Leather and Leather Products**	**4,002**
3111	Leather Tanning & Finishing	545
3131	Boot/Shoe Cut Stock/Findings	169
3142	House Slippers	52
3143	Men's Footwear Exc Athletic	320
3144	Women Footwear Exc Athl	182
3149	Footwear Exc Rubber NEC	260
3151	Leather Gloves & Mittens	80
3161	Luggage	459
3171	Women's Handbags/Purses	512
3172	Personal Leather Goods	418
3199	Leather Goods, NEC	1,005
32	**Stone, Clay, and Glass Products**	**22,683**
3211	Flat Glass	523
3221	Glass Containers	181
3229	Pressed/Blown Glassware, NEC	862
3231	Glass Products (Purchased)	2,492
3241	Cement, Hydraulic	371
3251	Brick & Structural Clay Tile	361
3253	Ceramic Wall & Floor Tile	307
3255	Clay Refractories	250
3259	Structural Clay Products, NEC	110
3261	China/Earth Plumb'g Fixtures	130
3262	China Table/Kitchen Goods	55
3263	Whiteware Table/Kitchen Goods	46
3264	Porcelain Electrical Supplies	117

All counts are primary SICs only

SIC	Description	Count
3269	Pottery Products, NEC	1,558
3271	Concrete Block & Brick	1,115
3272	Concrete Products	4,249
3273	Ready-Mixed Concrete	5,423
3274	Lime	120
3275	Gypsum Products	199
3281	Cut Stone & Stone Products	1,700
3291	Abrasive Products	525
3292	Asbestos Products	214
3295	Ground/Treated Minerals/Earths	457
3296	Mineral Wood	366
3297	Nonclay Refractories	194
3299	Nonmetal Mineral Prdts, NEC	758
33	**Primary Metal Industries**	**11,061**
3312	Steel Works & Blast Furnaces	1,943
3313	Electrometallurgical Prdts	101
3315	Steel Wiredrawing/Nails/Spikes	495
3316	Cold-Rolled Steel Products	335
3317	Steel Pipe & Tubes	314
3321	Gray & Ductile Iron Foundries	837
3322	Malleable Iron Foundries	66
3324	Steel Investment Foundries	103
3325	Steel Foundries, NEC	398
3331	Smelt/Refine Copper	36
3334	Primary Production of Aluminum	111
3339	Smelt/Refine Nonferrous Metals	280
3341	Secondary Nonferrous Metals	671
3351	Roll/Draw/Extrude Copper	226
3353	Aluminum Sheet, Plate & Foil	153
3354	Aluminum Extruded Products	291
3355	Aluminum Roll/Drawing, NEC	123
3356	Roll/Draw/extrude Nonfer Metal	289
3357	Draw/Insulate Nonferrous Wire	528
3363	Aluminum Die-Castings	524
3364	Nonferrous Die-Castings	355
3365	Aluminum Foundries	716
3366	Copper Foundries	487
3369	Nonferr Foundry Exc Alum/Cop	473
3398	Metal Heat Treating	742
3399	Primary Metal Products, NEC	464
34	**Fabricated Metal Products**	**48,146**
3411	Metal Cans	508

All counts are primary SICs only

SIC	Description	Count
3412	Metal Ship Barrels/Drums	194
3421	Cutlery	252
3423	Hand/Edge Tools	1,173
3425	Saw Blades & Handsaws	193
3429	Hardware, NEC	2,076
3431	Enameled Iron/Metal Ware	212
3432	Plumbing Fixture Parts	391
3433	Heating Equipment	950
3441	Fabricated Structural Metal	4,048
3442	Metal Doors/Molding/Trim	2,757
3443	Prefab Boiler Shop Plate Work	2,424
3444	Sheet Metalwork	4,950
3446	Ornamental Metalwork	3,613
3448	Prefab Metal Bldgs/Components	1,053
3449	Misc Structural Metalwork	429
3451	Screw Machine Products	1,800
3452	Nuts/Screws/Washers	1,014
3462	Iron & Steel Forgings	650
3463	Nonferrous Forgings	127
3465	Automotive Stampings	677
3466	Crowns & Closures	51
3469	Metal Stampings, NEC	3,625
3471	Electroplate/Polish/Color	4,008
3479	Coat/Engrave/Allied Svcs, NEC	2,566
3482	Small Arms Ammunition	175
3483	Ammo Exc Small Arms	134
3484	Small Arms	325
3489	Ordnance & Accessories, NEC	129
3491	Industrial Valves	356
3492	Fluid Power Valves/Hose	208
3493	Steel Springs, Exc Wire	319
3494	Valves & Pipe Fittings, NEC	1,005
3495	Wire Springs	326
3496	Misc Fabricated Wire Products	1,647
3497	Metal Foil & Leaf	79
3498	Fabricated Pipe/Fittings	789
3499	Fabricated Metal Products, NEC	2,913
35	**Industrial Machinery and Equipment**	**81,240**
3511	Turbines/Generator Sets	322
3519	Int Combustion Engines, NEC	542
3523	Farm Machinery & Equipment	2,674
3524	Lawn/Garden Tractors	300

All counts are primary SICs only

SIC	Description	Count
3531	Construction Machinery	1,667
3532	Mining Machinery & Equip	602
3533	Oil/Gas Machinery & Equipment	1,362
3534	Elevators & Moving Stairways	309
3535	Conveyors/Conveying Equipment	1,040
3536	Overhead Traveling Systems	396
3537	Trucks/Tractors/Trailers	793
3541	Metal Cutting Machine Tools	2,005
3542	Metal Forming Machine Tools	869
3543	Industrial Patterns	845
3544	Special Dies & Tools	8,559
3545	Machine Tools/Accessories	2,864
3546	Power-Driven Handtools	338
3547	Rolling Mill Machinery/Equip	120
3548	Electric/Gas Weld/Solder Equip	335
3549	Metalworking Machinery, NEC	516
3552	Textile Machinery	798
3553	Woodworking Machinery	464
3554	Paper Industries Machinery	405
3555	Print Trade Machinery/Equip	1,056
3556	Food Products Machinery	1,005
3559	Special Industry Mach, NEC	2,813
3561	Pumps & Pumping Equipment	937
3562	Ball & Roller Bearings	279
3563	Air/Gas Compressors	453
3564	Fans/Blowers/Air Purification	900
3565	Packaging Machinery	511
3566	Hi Speed Drive/Gear Changers	286
3567	Indust Process Furnace/Oven	723
3568	Mechanical Transmissions, NEC	288
3569	Indust Machinery/Equip, NEC	2,309
3571	Electronic Computers	1,585
3572	Computer Storage Devices	485
3575	Computer Terminals	399
3577	Computer Peripherals, NEC	2,368
3578	Calculating Mach Exc Computers	354
3579	Office Machines, NEC	609
3581	Automatic Vending Machines	183
3582	Dryclean/Pressing Machines	181
3585	A/C & Heating Equipment	1,638
3586	Measuring & Dispensing Pumps	127
3589	Svc Industry Machinery, NEC	1,790

All counts are primary SICs only

SIC	*Description*	*Count*
3592	Carburetors/Pistons/Valves	267
3593	Fluid Power Cyl/Actuators	171
3594	Fluid Power Pumps & Motors	159
3596	Scales/Balances Exc Lab	193
3599	Industrial Equipment, NEC	31,046
36	**Electronic and other Electric Equipment**	**29,231**
3612	Power & Specialty Transformers	648
3613	Switchgear/board Apparatus	1,116
3621	Motors & Generators	1,044
3624	Carbon & Graphite Products	121
3625	Relays & Industrial Controls	1,502
3629	Electric Ind Apparatus, NEC	505
3631	Househld Cooking Equipment	165
3632	Househld Refrig/Freezers	75
3633	Househld Laundry Equipment	37
3634	Electric Housewares & Fans	459
3635	Househld Vacuum Cleaners	181
3639	Househld Appliances, NEC	277
3641	Electric Lamp Bulbs & Tubes	351
3643	Curren-Carry Wiring Devices	666
3644	Noncurrent-Carry Wiring Dev	277
3645	Res Electric Lighting Fixtures	968
3646	Nonres Electric Lighting	461
3647	Vehicular Lighting Equipment	165
3648	Lighting Equipment, NEC	562
3651	Househld Audio/Video Equipment	1,173
3652	Records/Auto Tapes/Discs	1,358
3661	Telephone/Telegraph Apparatus	1,309
3663	Broadcast/Communications Equip	1,856
3669	Communications Equipment, NEC	1,491
3671	Electron Tubes	162
3672	Printed Circuit Boards	1,648
3674	Semiconductor/Related Devices	1,974
3675	Electronic Capacitors	144
3676	Electronic Resistors	79
3677	Electronic Coils/Transformers	433
3678	Electronic Connectors	182
3679	Electronic Components, NEC	4,637
3691	Storage Batteries	293
3692	Primary Batteries, Dry & Wet	155
3694	Int Combust Eng Electric Equip	702
3695	Mag/Optical Recording Media	206

All counts are primary SICs only

SIC	*Description*	*Count*
3699	Electrical Machinery, NEC	1,849
37	**Transportation Equipment**	**17,261**
3711	Motor Vehicles Bodies	1,288
3713	Truck & Bus Bodies	1,023
3714	Vehicle Parts/Accessories	4,612
3715	Truck Trailers	792
3716	Motor Homes	191
3721	Aircraft	488
3724	Aircraft Engines/Parts	639
3728	Aircraft Parts/Equip, NEC	1,661
3731	Ship Building & Repairing	817
3732	Boat Building & Repairing	3,083
3743	Railroad Equipment	277
3751	Motorcycle, Bicycles & Parts	529
3761	Guided Missiles/Space Vehicles	119
3764	Propulsion Unit Parts	59
3769	Missile/Space Parts/Equip	70
3792	Travel Trailers & Campers	773
3795	Tanks & Tank Components	45
3799	Transportation Equipment, NEC	795
38	**Instruments and Related Products**	**19,087**
3812	Navigation/Guidance Equipment	978
3821	Lab Apparatus & Furniture	526
3822	Automatic Regulating Controls	772
3823	Display/Control Instruments	2,160
3824	Totalizing Fluid Meters	330
3825	Electricity Testers	1,609
3826	Lab Analytical Instruments	427
3827	Optical Instruments & Lenses	748
3829	Measure/Control Devices, NEC	1,650
3841	Surgical/Medical Instruments	2,179
3842	Orthopedic/Prosthetic Appl	2,596
3843	Dental Equipment & Supplies	958
3844	X-ray Apparatus/Tubes	233
3845	Electromed/Therapy Apparatus	325
3851	Ophthalmic Goods	1,627
3861	Photographic Equip/Supplies	1,480
3873	Watches/Clocks Devices/Parts	489
39	**Miscellaneous Manufacturing Industries**	**36,674**
3911	Jewelry, Precious Metal	4,607
3914	Silver/Plated/Stainless Ware	546
3915	Jewelers' Findings/Materials	851

All counts are primary SICs only

SIC	Description	Count
3931	Musical Instruments	805
3942	Dolls & Stuffed Toys	724
3944	Games & Toys	2,067
3949	Sporting & Athletic Goods, NEC	4,329
3951	Pens, Mech Pencils & Parts	176
3952	Lead Pencil/Artists' Mat'ls	328
3953	Marking Devices	1,167
3955	Carbon Paper & Inked Ribbons	196
3961	Costume Jewelry/Novelties	1,678
3965	Fastener/Button/Needle/Pin	542
3991	Brooms & Brushes	455
3993	Signs & Advertising	8,485
3995	Burial Caskets	313
3996	Hard Surface Floor Coverings	57
3999	Mfg Industries, NEC	9,348

Transportation, Communications, Utilities **288,078**

SIC Numbers 4000-4999

SIC	Description	Count
40	**Railroad Transportation**	**2,763**
4011	Railroads, Line-Haul Operating	2,346
4013	RR Switching/Terminals	417
41	**Local and Interurban Passenger Transit**	**20,949**
4111	Local & Suburban Transit	1,520
4119	Local Passenger Transport, NEC	7,747
4121	Taxicabs	5,223
4131	Intercity/Rural Bus Transport	1,488
4141	Local Bus Charter Svc	784
4142	Bus Charter Svc, Exc. Local	1,442
4151	School Buses	2,193
4173	Vehicle Passenger Terminals	552
42	**Trucking and Warehousing**	**132,403**
4212	Local Trucking Without Storage	52,013
4213	Trucking, Exc Local	46,553
4214	Local Trucking With Storage	6,874
4215	Courier Svcs, Exc. by Air	1,386
4221	Farm Prdt Warehse/Storage	2,088
4222	Refrigerated Warehouse/Storage	1,627
4225	General Warehousing & Storage	16,125
4226	Special Warehouse/Storage, NEC	3,248
4231	Motor Terminal Maint Facil	2,489
43	**U.S. Postal Service**	**742**

All counts are primary SICs only

SIC	Description	Count
4311	United States Postal Svc	742
44	**Water Transportation**	**10,846**
4412	Sea Foreign Freight Trans	440
4424	Sea Domestic Freight Trans	303
4432	Great lakes Freight Trans	32
4449	Water Freight Transport, NEC	656
4481	Sea Trans of Passengers	84
4482	Ferries	97
4489	Water Passenger Trans, NEC	527
4491	Marine Cargo Handling	1,077
4492	Towing & Tugboat Svcs	1,029
4493	Marinas	4,400
4499	Water Transport Svc, NEC	2,201
45	**Transportation by Air**	**14,301**
4512	Air Transportation, Scheduled	3,415
4513	Air Courier Svcs	1,072
4522	Air Transport, Nonscheduled	3,247
4581	Airports/Terminal Svcs	6,567
46	**Pipelines, except Natural Gas**	**822**
4612	Crude Petroleum Pipelines	415
4613	Refined Petroleum Pipelines	339
4619	Pipelines, NEC	68
47	**Transportation Services**	**45,877**
4724	Travel Agencies	26,583
4725	Tour Operators	1,799
4729	Arrange Passenger Trans, NEC	1,560
4731	Arrange Trans Freight/Cargo	13,120
4741	Rental of Railroad Cars	189
4783	Packing & Crating	973
4785	Inspect/Weighing Svcs	303
4789	Transportation Svcs, NEC	1,349
48	**Communication**	**30,914**
4812	Radiotelephone Communications	1,659
4813	Phone Communications	7,522
4822	Telegraph/Other Message Comm	915
4832	Radio Broadcasting Stations	8,733
4833	TV Broadcasting Stations	2,421
4841	Cable & Other Pay TV Svcs	6,241
4899	Communications Svcs, NEC	3,423
49	**Electric, Gas, and Sanitary Services**	**28,461**
4911	Electric Svcs	5,975
4922	Natural Gas Transmission	1,139

All counts are primary SICs only

SIC	Description	Count
4923	Nat Gas Transmiss/Distribute	869
4924	Natural Gas Distribution	1,441
4925	Petroleum Gas Products	803
4931	Electric/Other Svcs Combined	853
4932	Gas & Other Svcs Combined	248
4939	Combination Utilities, NEC	311
4941	Water Supply	4,984
4952	Sewerage Systems	892
4953	Refuse Systems	8,693
4959	Sanitary Svcs, NEC	1,435
4961	Steam & A/C Supply	124
4971	Irrigation Systems	694

Wholesale Trade **656,004**

SIC Numbers 5000-5199

SIC	Description	Count
50	**Wholesale Trade-Durable Goods**	**418,794**
5012	Auto & Other Motor Vehicles	8,121
5013	Vehicle Supplies & New Parts	40,293
5014	Tires & Tubes	4,971
5015	Motor Vehicle Parts, Used	4,895
5021	Furniture	10,541
5023	Homefurnishings	12,274
5031	Lumber/Plywood/Millwork	13,857
5032	Brick/Stone/Const Materials	6,996
5033	Roof/Siding/Insulation Mat'ls	2,444
5039	Construction Materials, NEC	8,432
5043	Photo Equipment & Supplies	1,698
5044	Office Equipment	10,029
5045	Computers Equip/Software	15,499
5046	Commercial Equipment, NEC	7,561
5047	Medical/Dental Equip/Supplies	11,415
5048	Ophthalmic Goods	1,316
5049	Pro Equipment & Supplies, NEC	4,390
5051	Metals Svc Centers & Offices	12,041
5052	Coal & Other Minerals & Ores	1,259
5063	Electrical Equip/Wiring	21,029
5064	Electrical Appliances	6,651
5065	Electronic Parts/Equip, NEC	21,376
5072	Hardware	9,206
5074	Plumbing/Heating Equip/Supply	12,201
5075	Heating & A/C Equip/Supplies	5,328

All counts are primary SICs only

SIC	*Description*	*Count*
5078	Refrigeration Equipment	2,949
5082	Construction & Mining Equip	8,039
5083	Farm/Garden Machinery/Equip	15,234
5084	Industrial Machinery/Equip	43,289
5085	Industrial Supplies	18,802
5087	Service Establishment Equip	14,554
5088	Transportation Equip/Supplies	4,856
5091	Sporting/Rec Goods & Supplies	7,730
5092	Toys & Hobby Goods & Supplies	4,054
5093	Scrap & Waste Materials	8,967
5094	Jewelry/Watches/Precious Mtl	12,370
5099	Durable Goods, NEC	24,115
51	**Wholesale Trade-Nondurable Goods**	**237,210**
5111	Printing & Writing Paper	2,012
5112	Stationery & Office Supplies	11,558
5113	Industry/Personal Svc Paper	6,232
5122	Drugs/Druggists' Sundries	7,045
5131	Piece Goods/Other Dry Goods	7,528
5136	Clothing & Furnishings, male	7,851
5137	Female/Child Clothing	10,893
5139	Footwear	2,152
5141	Groceries, General Line	11,749
5142	Packaged Frozen Foods	2,071
5143	Dairy Products	4,097
5144	Poultry & Poultry Products	1,814
5145	Confectionery	5,076
5146	Fish & Seafoods	5,029
5147	Meats & Meat Products	6,434
5148	Fresh Fruits & Vegetables	7,134
5149	Groceries/Related Prdts, NEC	13,025
5153	Grain & Field Beans	7,679
5154	Livestock	3,733
5159	Farm-Prdt Raw Materials, NEC	2,328
5162	Plastics Mat'ls/Basic Forms	2,721
5169	Chemicals/Allied Prdts, NEC	11,164
5171	Petroleum Bulk Terminal	9,077
5172	Petroleum/Prdts Wholesalers	13,061
5181	Beer & Ale	4,360
5182	Wine/Distilled Alcohol Bev	2,548
5191	Farm Supplies	20,924
5192	Book/Periodical/Newspaper	2,684
5193	Flowers/Florists' Supplies	6,897

All counts are primary SICs only

SIC	Description	Count
5194	Tobacco & Tobacco Products	1,692
5198	Paints, Varnishes & Supplies	4,435
5199	Nondurable Goods, NEC	32,207

Retail Trade **1,912,208**

SIC Numbers 5200-5999

SIC	Description	Count
52	**Building Materials and Garden Supplies**	**108,765**
5211	Lumber/Bldg Materials Dealers	35,100
5231	Paint/Glass/Wallpaper Stores	14,713
5251	Hardware Stores	28,772
5261	Lawn & Garden Supply Stores	21,327
5271	Mobile Home Dealers	8,853
53	**General Merchandise Stores**	**51,726**
5311	Department Stores	17,081
5331	Variety Stores	12,500
5399	Misc Gen Merchandise Stores	22,140
54	**Food Stores**	**223,513**
5411	Grocery Stores	161,020
5421	Meat/Seafood Markets	13,826
5431	Fruit & Vegetable Markets	4,618
5441	Candy/Confectionery Stores	6,878
5451	Dairy Products Stores	4,065
5461	Retail Bakeries	20,740
5499	Misc Food Stores	12,366
55	**Automotive Dealers and Service Stations**	**245,392**
5511	Motor Vehicle Dealers	39,133
5521	Used Motor Vehicle Dealers	30,079
5531	Auto & Home Supply Stores	52,664
5541	Gasoline Svc Stations	98,629
5551	Boat Dealers	10,065
5561	RV Dealers	4,990
5571	Motorcycle Dealers	6,760
5599	Automotive Dealers, NEC	3,072
56	**Apparel and Accessory Stores**	**174,680**
5611	Male Clothing/Accessory Stores	20,634
5621	Women's Clothing Stores	61,972
5632	Female Accessory Stores	12,155
5641	Child Wear Stores	9,795
5651	Family Clothing Stores	14,664
5661	Shoe Stores	32,034
5699	Misc Apparel/Accessory Stores	23,426
57	**Furniture and Homefurnishings Stores**	**176,769**

All counts are primary SICs only

SIC	*Description*	*Count*
5712	Furniture Stores	50,420
5713	Floor Covering Stores	25,019
5714	Curtain & Upholstery Stores	7,897
5719	Misc Homefurnishings Stores	19,021
5722	Household Appliance Stores	21,839
5731	Consumer Electronics Stores	27,105
5734	Computer/Software Stores	9,673
5735	Record/Tape Stores	8,543
5736	Musical Instrument Stores	7,500
58	**Eating and Drinking Places**	**383,301**
5812	Eating Places	311,650
5813	Drinking Places (bars)	71,651
59	**Miscellaneous Retail**	**548,062**
5912	Drug Stores	50,560
5921	Liquor Stores	39,057
5932	Used Merchandise Stores	39,795
5941	Sporting Goods/Bike Shops	49,830
5942	Book Stores	15,783
5943	Stationery Stores	11,777
5944	Jewelry Stores	38,125
5945	Hobby, Toy & Game Shops	16,467
5946	Camera/Photo Supply Stores	4,779
5947	Gift, Novelty & Souvenir Shops	64,184
5948	Luggage & Leather Goods Stores	2,593
5949	Sewing & Piece Goods Stores	15,808
5961	Catalog & Mail-Order Houses	12,245
5962	Vending Machine Operators	9,069
5963	Direct Selling Establishments	7,871
5983	Fuel Oil Dealers	8,066
5984	Bottled Gas Dealers	5,840
5989	Fuel Dealers, NEC	1,154
5992	Florists	38,366
5993	Tobacco Stores & Stands	2,457
5994	News Dealers & Newstands	2,425
5995	Optical Goods Stores	8,110
5999	Misc Retail Stores, NEC	103,700

Finance, Insurance and Real Estate 654,503

SIC Numbers 6000-6799

60	**Depository Institutions**	**90,339**
6011	Federal Reserve Banks	111
6019	Cent'l Reserve Depository, NEC	34

All counts are primary SICs only

SIC	Description	Count
6021	National Commercial Banks	25,968
6022	State Commercial Banks	26,673
6029	Commercial Banks, NEC	1,770
6035	Fed Chtr Saving Institutions	12,809
6036	Not Fed Savings Institutions	4,531
6061	Credit Unions, Fed Chartered	3,932
6062	Not Fed Credit Unions	11,404
6081	Foreign Bank Branch/Agency	309
6082	Foreign Trade/Int'l Banks	172
6091	Nondeposit Trust Facilities	107
6099	Depository Bank Functions, NEC	2,517
61	**Nondepository Institutions**	**34,778**
6111	Fed/-Sponsored Credit Agencies	1,237
6141	Personal Credit Institutions	11,627
6153	Short-Term Bus Credit Inst	2,008
6159	Misc Bus Credit Institutions	5,395
6162	Mortgage Banker/Loan Officers	9,795
6163	Loan Brokers	4,716
62	**Security and Commodity Brokers**	**28,314**
6211	Security Brokers/Flotation Cos	16,476
6221	Commodity Brokers/Dealers	2,433
6231	Security & Commodity Exchanges	375
6282	Investment Advice	7,122
6289	Sec/Commodity Exchange Svcs	1,908
63	**Insurance Carriers**	**34,196**
6311	Life Insurance	9,986
6321	Accident & Health Insurance	1,642
6324	Hospital & Medical Svc Plans	908
6331	Fire/Marine/Casualty Insurance	6,020
6351	Surety Insurance	10,605
6361	Title Insurance	3,014
6371	Pension/Health/Welfare Funds	1,437
6399	Insurance Carriers, NEC	584
64	**Insurance Agents, Brokers, and Service**	**111,022**
6411	Insurance Agent/Broker/Service	111,022
65	**Real Estate**	**324,670**
6512	Nonresidential Bldgs Operators	69,307
6513	Apartment Bldg Operator	56,638
6514	Dwellings (Not Apts) Operators	7,090
6515	Resid Mobile Homes, Operator	10,553
6517	Lessors of Railroad Property	48
6519	Lessors of Real Property, NEC	5,440

All counts are primary SICs only

SIC	Description	Count
6531	Real Estate Agents & Managers	128,774
6541	Title Abstract Offices	3,145
6552	Land Subdividers/Developers	40,100
6553	Cemetery Subdiv/Developers	3,575
67	**Holding and other Investment Offices**	**31,184**
6712	Bank Holding Cos Offices	1,224
6719	Bank Holding Cos Offices, NEC	8,466
6722	Mgt Invest Offices, Open-End	903
6726	Unit Investment Trusts	625
6732	Educ/Rel/Charitable Trusts	1,101
6733	Trusts Exc Educ/Rel/Charitable	1,418
6792	Oil Royalty Traders	1,839
6794	Patent Owners & Lessors	2,448
6798	Real Estate Investment Trusts	4,019
6799	Investors, NEC	9,141

Services 2,421,850

SIC Numbers 7000-8999

SIC	Description	Count
70	**Hotels and other Lodging Places**	**70,679**
7011	Hotels & Motels	59,535
7021	Rooming & Boarding Houses	1,177
7032	Sporting & Recreational Camps	2,938
7033	RV Parks & Campsites	6,115
7041	Member Hotels/Lodging Houses	914
72	**Personal Services**	**279,046**
7211	Power Laundry, Family/Comm	3,595
7212	Garment Pressing (trade)	8,958
7213	Linen Supply	1,788
7215	Coin-Operated Laundries	16,928
7216	Drycleaning Plant Exc Rug	23,491
7217	Carpet & Upholstery Cleaning	12,767
7218	Industrial Launderers	889
7219	Laundry & Garments Svcs, NEC	5,389
7221	Photographic Studios, Portrait	16,537
7231	Beauty Shops	117,143
7241	Barber Shops	21,312
7251	Shoe Repair/Shine Shops	7,458
7261	Funeral Svc/Crematories	19,949
7291	Tax Return Preparation Svcs	5,968
7299	Misc Personal Svcs, NEC	16,874
73	**Business Services**	**395,000**

All counts are primary SICs only

SIC	Description	Count
7311	Advertising Agencies	23,552
7312	Outdoor Advertising Svcs	1,912
7313	Radio/TV/Publishers' Ad Rep	1,528
7319	Advertising, NEC	2,405
7322	Adjustment/Collection Svcs	5,114
7323	Credit Reporting Svcs	2,134
7331	Direct Mail Ad Svcs	4,525
7334	Photocopy/Duplicating Svcs	6,429
7335	Commercial Photography	9,431
7336	Commercial Art/Graphic Design	18,415
7338	Secretarial/Court Rpting Svc	5,686
7342	Disinfect/Pest Control Svc	12,087
7349	Bldg Cleaning/Maint Svc, NEC	33,365
7352	Medical Equip Rental/Leasing	2,143
7353	Heavy Const Equip Rent/Lease	5,340
7359	Equipment Rental/Leasing, NEC	31,860
7361	Employment Agencies	13,189
7363	Help Supply Svcs	7,897
7371	Computer Programming Svcs	8,879
7372	Prepackaged Software	11,241
7373	Computer Int Systems Design	3,113
7374	Computer Processing/Data Svc	9,373
7375	Information Retrieval Svcs	392
7376	Computer Facilities Mgt Svcs	490
7377	Computer Rental & Leasing	1,418
7378	Computer Maintenance & Repair	2,594
7379	Computer Related Svcs, NEC	12,432
7381	Detective/Guard/Armored Cars	8,814
7382	Security Systems Svcs	1,531
7383	News Syndicates	715
7384	Photofinishing Laboratories	11,788
7389	Business Svcs, NEC	135,208
75	**Auto Repair, Services, and Parking**	**221,536**
7513	Truck Rent/Lease, No Drivers	7,761
7514	Passenger Car Rental	7,953
7515	Passenger Car Leasing	3,476
7519	Utility Trailer & RV Rental	1,560
7521	Automobile Parking	3,002
7532	Top/Body Repair/Paint Shops	46,737
7533	Auto Exhaust Sys Repair Shops	3,747
7534	Tire Retreading & Repair Shops	3,035
7536	Auto Glass Replacement Shops	2,637

All counts are primary SICs only

SIC	Description	Count
7537	Auto Transmission Repair Shops	5,032
7538	General Auto Repair Shops	86,961
7539	Automotive Repair Shops, NEC	26,799
7542	Carwashes	10,895
7549	Auto Svcs Exc Repair/Carwash	11,941
76	**Miscellaneous Repair Services**	**154,559**
7622	Radio & TV Repair Shops	22,405
7623	Refrigeration & A/C Svc	9,951
7629	Elect/Electronic Repair, NEC	19,292
7631	Watch, Clock & Jewelry Repair	3,678
7641	Reupholstery/Furniture Repair	15,754
7692	Welding Repair	12,327
7694	Armature Rewinding Shops	3,099
7699	Repair Shops/Related Svcs, NEC	68,053
78	**Motion Pictures**	**35,302**
7812	Movie & Video Tape Production	11,929
7819	Movie Production Svcs	2,550
7822	Movie/Video Tape Distribution	1,697
7829	Svcs Allied to Movie Dist.	254
7832	Movie Theaters, Exc Drive-In	4,538
7833	Drive-In Movie Theaters	713
7841	Video Tape Rental	13,621
79	**Amusement and Recreation Services**	**85,457**
7911	Dance Studios, Schools & Halls	5,334
7922	Movie Theatrical Producers	5,647
7929	Actors/Musicians/Entertainers	3,694
7933	Bowling Centers	7,266
7941	Pro Sports Clubs & Promoters	1,397
7948	Racing, Inc Track Operation	2,094
7991	Physical Fitness Facilities	8,890
7992	Public Golf Courses	3,932
7993	Coin Amusement Devices	4,601
7996	Amusement Parks	1,474
7997	Membership Sports/Rec Clubs	14,775
7999	Amusement/Rec Svcs, NEC	26,353
80	**Health Services**	**365,439**
8011	Offices of Doctors of Medicine	166,732
8021	Offices & Clinics of Dentists	88,473
8031	Offices, Doctors Osteopathy	5,587
8041	Offices, Chiropractors	20,497
8042	Offices, Optometrists	12,039
8043	Offices, Podiatrists	2,564

All counts are primary SICs only

SIC	Description	Count
8049	Offices, Health Pract'ers, NEC	9,829
8051	Skilled Nursing Care Facility	9,679
8052	Intermediate Care Facilities	1,662
8059	Nursing/Care Facilities, NEC	7,476
8062	Gen Medical/Surgical Hospitals	8,724
8063	Psychiatric Hospitals	1,233
8069	Specialty Hospitals	1,279
8071	Medical Laboratories	6,224
8072	Dental Laboratories	8,327
8082	Home Health Care Svcs	3,152
8092	Kidney Dialysis Centers	462
8093	Spec Outpatient Facility, NEC	7,457
8099	Health & Allied Svcs, NEC	4,043
81	**Legal Services**	**123,139**
8111	Legal Services	123,139
82	**Educational Services**	**182,468**
8211	Elementary & Secondary Schools	141,557
8221	Colleges/Univ/Pro Schools	5,017
8222	Jr Colleges/Tech Institutes	1,782
8231	Libraries	15,326
8243	Data Processing Schools	721
8244	Business & Secretarial Schools	1,133
8249	Vocational Schools, NEC	4,576
8299	Schools/Educational Svc, NEC	12,356
83	**Social Services**	**106,531**
8322	Individual/Family Social Svcs	27,704
8331	Job Train/Vocational Rehab	3,944
8351	Child Day Care Svcs	55,957
8361	Residential Care	8,324
8399	Social Svcs, NEC	10,602
84	**Museums, Botanicals, Zoological Gardens**	**4,704**
8412	Museums & Art Galleries	4,429
8422	Arboreta/Bot Gardens/Zoos	275
86	**Membership Organizations**	**169,894**
8611	Business Assocs	12,808
8621	Professional Organizations	4,363
8631	Labor Union/Similar Labor Org	10,533
8641	Civic/Social/Fraternal Assoc	31,104
8651	Political Organizations	888
8661	Religious Organizations	101,853
8699	Membership Organizations, NEC	7,985
87	**Engineering and Management Services**	**224,151**

All counts are primary SICs only

SIC	Description	Count
8711	Engineering Svcs	42,338
8712	Architectural Svcs	15,416
8713	Surveying Svcs	3,490
8721	Account/Audit/Bookkeeping Svc	60,888
8731	Comm Phys./Biological Research	6,467
8732	Comm/Econ/Socio/Educ Research	9,229
8733	Noncommercial Research Orgs	3,733
8734	Testing Laboratories	3,522
8741	Management Services	17,866
8742	Mgt Consulting Svcs	35,329
8743	Public Relations Svcs	7,815
8744	Facilities Support Mgt Svcs	175
8748	Business Consulting Svcs, NEC	17,880
88	**Private Households**	**464**
8811	Private Households	464
89	**Services, not elsewhere classified**	**3,481**
8999	Services, NEC	3,481

Public Administration **51,786**

SIC Numbers 9000-9721

SIC	Description	Count
91	**Executive, Legislative, and General**	**24,187**
9111	Executive Offices	17,649
9121	Legislative Bodies	3,122
9131	Exec/Leg Offices Combined	384
9199	General NEC	3,032
92	**Justice, Public Order, and Safety**	**7,068**
9211	Courts	566
9221	Police Protection	1,049
9222	Legal Counsel & Prosecution	291
9223	Correctional Institutions	1,210
9224	Fire Protection	3,716
9229	Public Order & Safety, NEC	236
93	**Finance, Taxation, and Monetary Policy**	**1,119**
9311	Finance/Tax/Monetary Policy	1,119
94	**Administration of Human Resources**	**5,244**
9411	Admin of Educational Programs	3,006
9431	Admin, Public Health Programs	1,188
9441	Social/Human Res/Income Admin	952
9451	Vet' Affairs Exc Health/Insur	98
95	**Environmental Quality and Housing**	**8,381**
9511	Air, Water & Solid Waste Mgt	3,249

SIC	Description	Count
9512	Land & Wildlife Conservation	1,674
9531	Admin of Housing Programs	2,537
9532	Admin, Urban Plan'g/Rural Dev	921
96	**Administration of Economic Programs**	**3,823**
9611	Admin, Gen Economic Programs	844
9621	Reg/Admin Transport Programs	1,192
9631	Gov't Regulation of Utilities	354
9641	Reg Agric Mkt'g/Commodities	877
9651	Reg Misc Commercial Sectors	504
9661	Space Research & Technology	52
97	**National Security and International Affairs**	**1,964**
9711	National Security	1,310
9721	Int'l Affairs	654

Nonclassifiable Establishments **39,467**

SIC	Description	Count
99	**Nonclassifiable Establishments**	**39,467**
9999	Nonclassifiable Establishments	19,802

All counts are primary SICs only

APPENDIX

2

Resource Guide

The following material is reproduced courtesy of *Inbound-Outbound* Magazine, which publishes an annual survey of telemarketing suppliers. This is not a recommendation of any supplier or firm listed. Telemarketers can obtain a free subscription to *Inbound/Outbound* by writing to: Telecom Magazines, 12 West 21 Street, New York, N.Y. 10010. In addition the magazine has a service called Telcom Library, which makes available books on telecommunications and services. Telcom Library can be reached at the following toll-free number: 1-800-LIBRARY.

MARKET RESOURCES

From 800 service to workstations: A list of technologies and services—and who supplies them—to help you sell, serve, and keep customers.

800 LONG DISTANCE SERVICE PROVIDER

AT&T
Automated Call Processing
LO-AD Communications
MCI Telecommunications
Pacific Bell
Service 800 SA
US Sprint Communications Co.

900 EQUIPMENT AND PROGRAM SUPPLIERS

900 Services
Apex Voice Communications
Automated Call Processing
Conversational Voice Technology
Dalcomp
Dial Info
First Data Resources
Interactive Telemedia
LO-AD Communications
Network Services Plus
Phone Programs
Phoneworks
Semper Barris
Telephone Entertainment Network
Televation
Tempest Advertising
Touchtone Access
US Audiotest
US Takachiho Corporation

900 LONG DISTANCE SERVICE PROVIDER

AT&T
MCI Telecommunications
Pacific Bell
US Sprint

976 EQUIPMENT

Apex Voice Communications
Audiocom
Eltrex International
Telephonic Equipment
TEL Electronics
US Takachiho

976 PROVIDER

Ameritech
Bell Atlantic
BellSouth
Nynex
Pacific Bell
Southwestern Bell
US West

ANNOUNCEMENT SYSTEMS, TELEPHONE

Audichron
Audiocom
Automation Electronics
BBL

Dacon Electronics
Eltrex International
Interalia
Nel-Tech Labs
MetroTel
Racom
Stok Software
Telephone Announcement Systems
Televation
US Takachiho

ASSOCIATIONS

American Telemarketing Association
Customer Service Institute
Direct Marketing Association
International Customer Service Association
National Association of Telemarketers
National Center for Database Marketing

AUDIOTEX SYSTEMS

ACS Communications
Apex Voice Communications
Audiocom
Automated Call Processing
Card Tel
CommSEL
Compass Marketing
Dialogic
Eltrex International
IOCS
Infoswitch
Interactive Voice Services
Linker Systems
MPSI
Micrologic
Microvoice
Omnivoice
Perception Technologies
Periphonics
Renegade C Software
Soft-Com
Speech Plus
Speech Soft
Speech Systems
Symantec
Syntellect
Talking Technology
Teknekron Infoswitch
Telcom Technologies
Telecorp Systems
Telephonic Equipment
Televation
Tigon
UniVoice
VMX
VSSI
Valor Telecom
Voice Com
Voice Control Systems
Voice Exchange Technologies
Voice Pak
Voice Response
Voice Systems & Services
Voice Technology
Votan
Votrax
Voysys
Wang Information Services
Xedon

AUTO DIALERS, MULTI-LINE

Audiocom
Calling Center Technology
Capital Teleservices
Davox
Digital Systems International
Electronic Information Systems
International Telesystems
MAMS Corporation
Melita Labs
MetroTel
Micrologic
Source Data Systems
Teknekron Infoswitch
Telecom USA Teleconnect Division
Telesystems Source
Televation
TeleVector
Trans World

AUTO DIALERS, SINGLE LINE

ACS Communications
Audiocom
Hummingbird Communications
Ideatech
Me-Di-Co
MetroTel
Micrologic
New Generation Technology
Source Data Systems
Telecom USA Teleconnect Division
Televation
VOAD System

AUTO DIAL RECORDED MESSAGE PLAYERS

Audiocom
Capital Teleservices
Cogata
Comtel Broadcasting
Dadco Data
Eltrex International
MetroTel
Telecorp Systems
Televation

AUTOMATIC ATTENDANTS

Audiocom
Compass Marketing
Dytel
Eltrex International
Enhanced Systems
Genesis
Innovative Technology
Lanier Voice Products
Miami Voice
Micrologic
Microvoice
Newcastle Communications
Northern Telecom
Perception Technologies
Soft-Com
Teknekron Infoswitch
Telcom Technologies
Telecom USA Teleconnect Division
Telecorp Systems
Telephonic Equipment
Televation
Viking Electronics
VMX
Xiox

AUTOMATIC CALL DISTRIBUTOR

Active Voice
AIM Telephone
AT&T
AT&T—Business Markets Group
AT&T—General Business Systems
Amtelco
Aspect Telecommunications
ATM Systems
Audiocom
British Telecom
Cad Com
Cybernetics
DataPlus
Digital Transmission
Executone Information Systems
First Contact Communications
Fujitsu Business Communication
Harris Digital Telephone Systems
Harbinger Group
IBM/Rolm
InteCom
Memorex Telex
Mitel
NEC America
Northern Telecom
Panasonic
Redcom Laboratories
Resale Systems
SRX
Siemens Information Systems
Solid State Systems
Source Data Systems
Startel
Summa Four
TIE/communications
Tadiran
Teknekron Infoswitch
Telcom Technologies
Telecom Equipment
Tele-Line Systems
Telephone Support Systems
Telephonic Equipment

AUTOMATIC CALL DISTRIBUTOR SOFTWARE

Affinitec
Cybernetics
MTC Systems
Newcastle Communications
Nova Systems
PaceCom
Source Data Systems

TCS Management Group
Teknekron Infoswitch
Telecom Technologies
TeleCalc
Telecom USA Teleconnect Division

AUTOMATIC CALL DISTRIBUTOR WORKSTATIONS

Aspect Telecommunications
Digital Transmission
Eltrex International
Teknekron Infoswitch
Source Data Systems
Telcom Technologies

AUTOMATIC CALL SEQUENCERS

ACS
American Telesys
Audiocom
Cobotyx
Executive Systems
First Contact Communications
Integrated Communications Systems
Integrated Data Concepts
Lanier Voice Products
Lincoln Telephone
Lynx
MetroTel
Newscastle Communications
Palco Telecom
Telecom Equipment
Telecom Technologies
Telecom USA Teleconnect Division
Telematrix Industries
Telephonic Equipment
US Takachiho

AUTOMATIC CUSTOMER IDENTIFICATION SYSTEM

Eltrex International
Televation
The Omegas Group

AUTOMATIC NUMBER IDENTIFICATION

Telephonic Equipment
Televation
The Omegas Group

BOOKS/PUBLICATIONS

Actel Marketing
American Communications & Data Research
Audiotex Directory and Buyers Guide
Entrepreneur Magazine
FGI & Affiliated Publishing
General Information
GTE Directories
Harris Publishing
HG Professional Forms
InfoText Magazine
Lakewood Publications
Media Dimensions
Personal Selling Power
Probus Publishing
Publishers Clearing House
Telecom Library
TELECONNECT Magazine
TeleCross
Telemarketing Magazine
Teleprofessional
TKC Consulting
US Telemarketing

CALL-ACCOUNTING SOFTWARE

Abacus Group
Account-A-Call
ATM Systems
Cin-Tech Telemanagement
Complementary Solutions
Enhanced Systems
Harris-Lanier
Instor
Monitech
Nynex
Newscastle Communications
Omnitronics
Perimeter Technology
PaceCom Technologies
RTP Group
Soft-Com
Stryker Systems
Summa Four
Sykes Datatronics
Xiox
XTEND Communications

CALL CENTER SOFTWARE

Affinitec
American Business Systems
Automated Call Processing
Cybernetics
Haven
HTL
Monitec
MTC Systems
Nova Systems
Pacecom
Source Data Systems
TC Telemanagement
TCS Management
Teknekron Infoswitch
Telcom Technologies
TeleCalc
The Omegas Group
XTEND Communications

CALL DIVERTERS

American Telecorp
Telecom USA Teleconnect Division

CALL MONITORING EQUIPMENT

AT&T
American Telesys
Augat/Melco
British Telecom
Capitol Teleservices
Eltrex International
Ideatech
NPRI
Perception Technology
Reproduction Technologies
Solid State Systems
The Omegas Group
TEL Electronics

CELLULAR CARRIER

Aurora Telemarketing
Nynex

CELLULAR PHONES

Aurora Telemarketing
Celluland
Cellutel
Contel Cellular
NEC America BSSD
Oki Telecom

CENTRAL OFFICE ADJUNCT PROCESSORS

AT&T—Network Systems
Compass Marketing
Northern Telecom

CENTRAL OFFICE ENHANCED SERVICES SOFTWARE

Rockwell Communications Sys
Stromberg-Carlson
VMX

CENTRAL OFFICE SWITCHES

AT&T—Network Systems
Northern Telecom
Redcom Laboratories

CHANNEL BANKS

ATI Supply
AT&T
Bell Atlantic
Telecom Equipment

CHANNEL SERVICE UNITS

AT&T
Bell Atlantic
Telecom Equipment

COMMUNICATIONS PC SOFTWARE

Compass Marketing
Complementary Solutions
MTC Systems
Soft-Com
Technology Development
The Omegas Group
XTEND Communications

CONSULTING

Actel Marketing
AIM Telephones
Alpha Con
American Teleshare
Atlantic Software House
Auroa Telemarketing
CTCI
Canova Saunders International
Capitol Teleservices
Carlyle Marketing
Chilton Ellett
Communication Analysis
Connex International
Consultel
David James Group
Engel Associates
Expertel
FGI & Affiliated Publishing
Fifth Medium Marketing
Forum Corporation
Free World Marketing
George R. Walther
High Impact Communication & Training
ISDN Technologies
Impression Mechanix
Incoming Calls Management Institute
Isaac Frydman
Joel Linchitz Consulting Services
Marcon Multivision
Mark IV Resources
Market Intelligence Research
Modem Media
Oetting & Company
Otis Group
Pacific Bell
R M Dudley
RAK Associates
RTP Group
Richard L. Bencin & Associates
Rosell Group Consulting
SNET Telemarketing Consulting
Schlenker Research Services
Scott Ashby Telemarketing Consulting
Select Marketing Information Systems
Silorski-Tuerpe & Associates
Softel Systems
Southwest Performance Group
Stenrich Group
TKC Consulting
Tech/Knowledge
Teknekron Infoswitch
Tel/Mar & Associates
Tele-Consultants International
Tele-Techniques
Telemarketing Design
Telemarketing Consulting Services
Telespectrum
Thinkbank Publishers
US Telemarketing
Vanguard Communications
Vision Skills
Wolfe & Associates
XTEND Communications

CONTACT MANAGEMENT SOFTWARE

Atlantic Software House
Campbell Services
Contact Software International
DayFlo Software
Hugh Carver Group
Omegas Group
Select Marketing Information Systems
Technology Development
Teknekron Infoswitch

CREDIT AND COLLECTIONS SERVICES

Card Tel
Capitol Teleservices
Collection Connection
Davox
Digital Systems
GC Services
ITC
Melita Labs
Source Data Systems
Teknekron Infoswitch
Telecomputer Collection Center
Telesystems Source
Transworld Telephone

CUSTOMER SERVICE AND SUPPORT SOFTWARE

Coffman Systems
Magic Solutions
Omegas Group
Service Magic
Source Data Systems
SysPro

DATABASE ENHANCEMENT SERVICES

American Business Information
Executive Marketing Services
M/A/R/C

DATABASE OPTIMIZATION SERVICES

Executive Marketing Services
Group 1 Software
InfoMedia
M/A/R/C

DATABASE SOFTWARE —LAN COMPATIBLE

Borland
Hugh Carver Group
JEB Systems
Microsoft

DATABASE SOFTWARE —MAINFRAME

Geographic Data Technology
Group One Software
JEB Systems
M/A/R/C

DATA TRANSMISSION EQUIPMENT

ACT Communications
DataWay Systems
DSC Communications
Fibronics International
Fujitsu Business Communication
Gandalf Data
Image Data
Siemens Transmission Systems
Star Datacom
Telecom Equipment
Teleconnect Database Marketing

DATABASE SOFTWARE —PC SINGLE USER

ACS Communications
American Business Information
Ashton Tate
Atlantic Software House
Borland
DayFlo Systems
JEB Systems
Hugh Carver Group
Nova Systems
Omegas Group
Professional Resource
Management
Reference Software

DATABASE SYSTEMS FOR TELEMARKETING

Breakthrough Productions
DayFlo Software
Digital Systems
Geographic Data Technology
JEB Systems
Omegas Group
Select Marketing Information Systems
Source Data Systems

DIAL-IT EQUIPMENT

Audiocom
Automated Call Processing
Televation
Eltrex International
New Generation Technology
Source Data Systems
US Takachiho Corporation

DIAL-IT SERVICES

Automated Call Processing
Capitol Teleservices

DIALING SERVICES

Source Data Systems

DIGITAL VOICE ANNOUNCERS

Audiocom
Audio Marketing Systems
Automation Electronics
Compass Marketing
Dacon Electronics
Eltrex International
Interalia
Nel-Tech Labs
Racom
Source Data Systems
Televation

DIRECTORY ASSISTANCE SOFTWARE

Advanced Interactive Systems
APEX Communications
Brooktrout Technology
Capital Teleservices
Com Dev
Digital Speech Systems
Omegas Group
Votan

DIRECTORY SERVICES EQUIPMENT

Eltrex International

DIRECTORY SERVICES SOFTWARE

Omegas Group
Soft-Com
XTEND Corporation

DISASTER PREVENTION AND RECOVERY EQUIPMENT

Aurora Telemarketing
Comdisco Disaster Recovery Services
SunGuard Recovery Services
XTEND Communication

DISPATCH SYSTEMS

Console Systems
Modorola
Positron
Radio Frequency Data Network Systems

EXECUTIVE SEARCH

Lawrence Executive Search
Telemarketing Recruiters
Telemarketing Search

FACSIMILE MACHINES

Bell Atlantic
Brother International Office Equipment
Canon Micrographics
CITIFAX Express
Computer Integration Associations
Fujitsu Imaging Systems
Lanier Voice Products
OMNIFAX/Teleautograph
PocketFax
Ricoh
Sharp Electronics
Sommers
TIE/communications

FACSIMILE PC CARDS AND FAX SOFTWARE

Compass Marketing
Fujitsu Imaging Systems
Gammalink
Hotelcopy
Quadram

FACSIMILE, PERIPHERAL EQUIPMENT

Lantor
Vada Systems

FINANCE/LEASING COMPANY

ATI Supply
Citicorp Credit Services
IBMRolm
Siemens Information Systems
Telecom Equipment

FURNITURE

Acme Office Group
Allsteel
American Seating
Artoplex
Burroughs Manufacturing
CenterCore
Cole Office Environments
Contemporary Products
Conwed Designscape
CorryHiebert
DoMore
Hamilton Sorter
Harter
Herman Miller
JG Furniture Systems
Panel Concepts
Plieon Manufacturing
Shaw-Walker
Steelcase
Teknion
Trendway

HANDSETS

ACS Communications
ATI Supply
Harris Digital Telephone Systems
MetroTel
Telecom Equipment
TIE/communications

HEADSETS

ACS Communications
Ahern Communications
Allied Telecommunications
ATI Supply
Audiosears Corporation
Automation Electronics
Burco Distributors
Communitech
Compass International
DEKA
GN Netcom/Danavox
Headsets Plus
MetroTel
Nady Systems
Plantronics
Racal Acoustics
Starkey Laboratories
Telecom Equipment
Television Equipment Associates
UNEX
Wicom
Ziehl Associates

HIGH CAPACITY KEY SYSTEMS

Allen Tel
British Telecom
Centel Financial
Lanier Voice Products
Positron Industries
Ricoh
SRX
STC
Tadiran
Telecom Equipment
Turret Equipment

IMTS CAR TELEPHONE SYSTEMS

American Laser Systems
California Microwave

INTEGRATED FULFILLMENT SOFTWARE

Capitol Teleservices

INTERACTIVE VOICE RESPONSE

Active Voice
Advanced Interactive Systems
Advanced Voice Technologies
American Communications & Engineering
American Digital Voice Systems
Apex Voice Communications
Applied Telematics
Applied Voice Technology
Aspect Telecommunications
AT&E Systems
AT&T—Business Markets Group
AT&T—General Business Systems
AT&T Conversant Systems
Audio Response Technologies
Automated Call Processing
Berkeley Speech Technologies
Boston Technologies
Brite Voice Systems

Broadcast Resources
Centigram
Cobotyx
Cognitronics
Coherent Communication Systems
Com Dev
CommSEL
Communicator Asystance Systems
Compass Marketing
Computer Integration Associates
Conversational Voice Technology
Data Acquisition Services
Davox
Dialogic
Digital Sound
Digital Speech Systems
Eltrex International
Interface Technology
InterVoice
IOCS Microlog
Newcastle Communications
Perception Technologies
Soft-Com
VMX-Opcom
Votan

INVENTORY SYSTEMS, SOFTWARE

American Business Systems
Atlantic Software House
Newcastle Communications
Omegas Group
Soft-Com
XTEND Communications

KEY SYSTEMS

ACT Communications
Alcatel
AT&T General Business Systems
American Telesys
Ameriplus
Aurora Telemarketing
CMX Communications
Comdial
Crest
CSE Technologies
DBA Communications
Deka
Executone
Extrom
Fujitsu
Galaxy Communications
GST America
IBM
Inter-Tel
ISOETEC
Iwatsu
Kanda
Lanier Voice Products
Nakayo Telecom
NEC America
North Supply
Panasonic
Sanbar
Sanyo
Siemens
Solitaire
Southwestern Bell
Tadiran
Telamon
Telecom Equipment
Telecom USA
Teleconnect Division
Teledial
Telrad
TIE/communications
Trillium
Toshiba

LAPTOP COMPUTERS

ATI Supply
Bell Atlantic
Data General
Datavue
Epson
GRiD Systems
Hugh Carver Group
Laptop Express
Mitsubishi
NEC America
Sharp Electronics
Tandy Corporation
Toshiba
Zenith Data Systems

LIST OPTIMIZATION SERVICES

American Business Information
Anchor Computer
CCX Network
Demographic Systems
Digital Directory Assistance
Direct Marketing Technology
Dirmark Lists
Epsilon Corporation
Executive Marketing Services
Group 1 Software
M/A/R/C
May & Speh Direct
Metromail
R R Donnelley & Sons/Selectronic
Rexnord Data Systems
Selection Sciences
Smartnames Persoft
Trinet
TRW Information Services Group

LISTS, TELEMARKETING AND MAILING

ABC Mailing Group
Accredited Mailing Lists
ACE Mailing & Telemarketing
ACE Mailing Service
Admail
Am-Pro
Americalist
American Business Information
American Business Lists
American List Council
CCX Network
Compilers Plus Inc.
Direct Marketing Technology
Dirmark Lists
Donnelley Marketing
Information Services
Donnelley Communications
Dun's Marketing Services
Eberle DM Group
Ed Burnett Consultants
Elsevier Business Lists
Executive Marketing Services
Fala Direct Marketing
GMC/ListLab
GSI Marketing Services
Hasson Enterprises
InfoMedia
Kleid Company
Lifestyle America
List Services Corporation
List Technology Systems Group
Listworld
Mal Dunn Associates
May & Speh
Meredith List Marketing
Metromail
Pacific Bell—Business Lists
Preferred Lists
Prescott List Management
Qualified Lists
R L Polk and Company
RMI Direct Marketing
Roman Managed Lists
Royal Silk
Select Marketing
Information Services
Seminars List Services
Standard Rate & Data Service
Stevens List Management
Tele America
Telephone Look-Up
The Franklin Mint
Trinet
TRW Information Services Group
US West Direct
US West Marketing Resources
Uni-Mail Corporation
Walter Karl Company
WS Ponton

LISTS, TELEPHONE NUMBER LOOK UP AND APPEND

American Business Information
Capital Teleservices
Direct Marketing Technology
InfoMedia
Pacific Bell
Sheer Communications
Telematch
Telephone Look-up Service

LONG DISTANCE SERVICE

Allnet Communications
Alltel
AT&T
ATC/Microtel
Aurora Telemarketing
British Telecom
Cable & Wireless/TDX
ITT US Transmission Systems
MCI Telecommunications
SouthernNet Communications

Telecom USA Long Distance Division
US Sprint Communications

MANPOWER PLANNING SOFTWARE

Affinitec
Aspect Telecommunications
Campbell Services
Cybernetics Systems
HTL Telemanagement
IBM/M & SG Rolm Systems
Division
Infoswitch
MTC Systems
McDonnell Douglas Info Systems
Memorex Telex
Monitec Systems
PaceCom Technologies
Perimeter Technology
Pyderlon Management
TC Telemanagement
TCS Management Group
Teknekron Infoswitch
Telcom Technologies
TeleCalc

MARKETING RESEARCH SERVICES

American Business Information
Capital Teleservices
Focus Research
Idelman Telemarketing
Market Intelligence Research
Probe Research
Schlenker Research Services
Select Marketing Information Systems
Sophisticated Data Research
Teleos Resources
TKC Consulting
Walker Research

MONITORING EQUIPMENT AND SOFTWARE

Augat Communications
Eltrex International
Melco
Microscience
Newcastle Communications
Racom
TEL Electronics
Witness Systems

MUSIC-ON-HOLD SYSTEMS

Audio Marketing Systems
Audiocom
Call-Hold Marketing
Eltrex International
Hold'Em Communications
Information On Hold
Lanier Voice Products
Marketing Messages
Messages On Hold
On Hold Productions
Phillip Bell Telecommunication
Please Hold Promotions
Telecom Equipment
Telecom On-Hold Productions
Telephone Audio Productions
Telephonetics
Telesis Audio Productions
The Hold Company
US Takachiho

NEWSLETTERS

FGI & Affiliated Publishing
Hammerstone Direct
Incoming Calls Management
Macron-Multivision
Market Intelligence Research
Newsletter Specialists

OPERATOR SERVICES

Telecom USA Long Distance Division

OPERATOR SERVICES TERMINALS

AT&T
Eltrex International
Digital Switch
Northern Telecom

OUTBOUND TELEMARKETING SYSTEMS

AT&T
Cal Center Technologies
Capitol Teleservices
CRC Information Services
Davox
Digital Systems International
Electronic Information Systems
Executone Information Systems
Galaxy Communications
GSI Marketing Services
International Telesystems
ITC
Melita Electronic Labs
NPRI
National Systems
New Generation Technology
RAIL
Rockwell International
Teknekron Infoswitch
Teledirect International
Telesystems Source
TeleVector
Trans World Telephone

PAGING

Airtronics
ATI Supply
Console Systems
Lanier Voice Products
MetroCast
National Satellite Paging

PBX AIR CONDITIONING SYSTEMS

Airtronics
Wang Laboratories

PBXs (Private Branch Exchanges)

Alcatel
AT&T
Augat
Bell Atlantic
Cardinal Data Systems
Centel Business Systems
Comdial
Ericsson
Executone Information Systems
Fujitsu Business Communication
Fujitsu/GTE
Harris-Lanier
Hitachi
IBM/Rolm
InteCom
Memorex Telex
Mitel
NEC America
Northern Telecom
Panasonic
Redcom Labs
Siemens
Solid State Systems
SRX
Siemens Information Systems
Tadiran
Telecom Equipment
Telecom USA Teleconnect Division
Telenova
TeleVector
Telrad
TIE/communications
Toshiba
Wang Labs

PRESENTATION EQUIPMENT AND SOFTWARE

Hugh Carver Group
Targa Systems

PROMOTIONS ON HOLD

American MessageTel
Audiocom
Audio Marketing Systems
Information on Hold
Jingle Phone Productions
Marketing Messages
On Hold Productions
Phillip Bell Telecommunications
Please Hold Promotions
Sonja-Kaplan Productions
Telecom On-Hold Productions
Telephone Audio Productions
Telephonetics International
Telesis Audio Productions
The Hold Company
The Informer

RADIO DISPATCHING EQUIPMENT

Console Systems
Positron
Vada Systems

SALES AUTOMATION SOFTWARE

AT&T—Business Markets Group
AT&T—Data Systems Group
Arlington Software + Systems
Atlantic Software House
Breakthrough Productions
Brock Control Systems
CRC Information Systems
Call Center Technologies
Campbell Services
Capitol Teleservices
Coffman Systems
Commercial Data Systems
Communicator Asystance Systems
Concurrent Marketing Systems
Contact Software International
Contemporary Software Concepts
Coral Group
Database Systems
Datacorp Business Systems
Demographic Systems
Digital Publications
Dilg Publishing
Early Cloud & Company
Eighty/20 Software
EKD Computer Sales & Supplies
EMIS Software
Esprit Software Technology
Excalibur Sources
Experience in Software
Four Sales
Fourgen Software Technologies
GRiD Systems
GSI Transcomm
Galaxy Communications
High Caliber Systems
Hugh Carver Group
IDSC Rental
Information Management Associates
JEB Systems
Lantor
MegaPhone
NPRI
Nynex Information Resources
National Systems
Opus
Profidex
Remote Control
Richmond Software
Ridgewood Macs and Olsen
RYDEX Industries
Sales & Marketing Systems
Sales Technologies
Scientific Marketing/ForSales
Scott Computing Systems
Software of the Future
Spectrum Systems Int'l
Supersell Software
System Vision
TESS
Tarp Information Systems
TeLeVell
Technology Development
Telesell
Tetley Technologies
The Haven
Travis DataTrak
US Business
Van Arsdale Associates

SOFTWARE, FORECASTING

Affinitec
Cybernetics
HTL
Hugh Carver Group
JEB Systems
MTC Systems
Nova Systems
Pacecom
Select Marketing Information Systems
TCS
Technology Development

T-1 TRANSMISSION EQUIPMENT

ATI Supply
AT&T
MetroTel
Telecom USA Long Distance Division

TELECOMMUNICATIONS MANAGEMENT SOFTWARE

Abacus Group
Account-A-Call
Automated Call Processing Corporation
Com Dev
Mitel Datacom
Soft-Com
Solid State Systems
Summa Four
Sykes
Xiox
XTEND Communications

TELECOM SYSTEMS INTEGRATOR

AT&T—Systems Integration Division
AlphaCon
Computer Consoles
Digital Support Systems
EDS
GC Services/Systems Division
Gateway Software Systems
Hager Telecommunications
ISDN Technologies Corporation
Information Exchange
Infoswitch
Me-Di-Co
Nynex Complex Systems Integration Group
Nynex Information Resources
PhiTech
Pyramid Technology
Sente
Sequoia Systems
US Takachiho
Wang Information Services
XTEND Communications

TELECONFERENCING DEVICES

Confertech International
Darome
PictureTel
Shure Teleconferencing Systems
Telephonic Equipment

TELECONFERENCING SERVICE BUREAU

AT&T
Confertech
Darome
MCI Telecommunications
Telecom USA Long Distance
TeleRx
US Sprint Communications

TELEMARKETING SERVICE BUREAU

800 Experts Telemarketing
800 Speed Order Systems
ABC Phone Power
Advanced Telemarketing
Aggrey Telemarketing Group
Alert Communications
American Telemarketing Specialists
AmeriCall
American Airlines Direct Marketing
American Tele/Response Group
American Telephone Marketing Group
Ameridial
AmeriPhone Telemarketing
Amerispan/Division of Strategic Marketing SystemsAmeritel
Amres Telemarketing
Answerall Technology Northeast
APAC Telemarketing
Applied Telemarketing Services
Ashby Telemarketing Consulting
Astro Marketing
AT&T—American Transtech
Aurora Telemarketing
Automated Call Processing
Automated Phone Exchange
Automated Telemarketing Services
Berkeley Marketing
Boston Direct
Bottom Line Technologies
Brandywine Marketing Services
Britcom Telemarketing
Budget Marketing
Call Masters
CallCenter Services
Capitol Teleservices
Care Call/Market Call
Carlyle Marketing
CDA Telecenter
CDC Telemarketing

Chicago Telemarketing Connection
Circulation By Phone
Communicall
Communications Center
Computer Assisted Telemarketing
ComTel Marketing
Consolidated Telemarketing
Consumers Marketing Research
Contel-A-Marketing
Contract Marketing Consultants
Cox and Cox Marketing
Custom Telemarketing
CWT/The Calling Company
DR Milford Marketing
Dialamerica Marketing
Dialog Immediate Response
Direct Line Response
Direct Marketing Concepts
Direct Marketing Guaranty
Direct Response Ability
Direct Response Broadcasting
Direct Telemarketing Services
Edge Teleservicing Center
Edward Blank and Associates
Effective Telemarketing
Electronic Direct Marketing
Electronic Marketing Associates
Electronic Specialists
Enertex Marketing
Entertel
Exceptional Telemarketing
Exclusive Marketing Group
ExecuCall
Factor Fox and Associates
Finserv Computer
Fortune 800
Gannett Direct Marketing Services
GLS Telemarketing
Grolier Telemarketing
GSI Marketing Services
GTE Telemarketing
Hancock Information Group
Heritage Telemarketing
Huntsinger and Jeffer
ICT Group
Idelman Telemarketing
IMPACT Telemarketing
IMPCO
Impulse Sales & Marketing
Industrial Telemarketing
Associates
Info/800
InfoCision Management
Inquiry Handling Services
INTEL Telemarketing
Inter-Media Marketing
Interwest Marketing
J & J Haimes
JC Penny Telemarketing
Kapular Telemarketing
The Kleid Company
LCS Industries
Lead Marketing International
Lee Stevens Companies
Lester Telemarketing
Lomas Telemarketing
Magazine
Marketplace Telemarketing
Marathon Telemarketing Systems
Marcom
Marcon-Multivision
Mardex
Mark IV Resources
Market Motivators
MarketTrack
May Telemarketing
MISTIX
NICE/A Cincinnati Bell Company
North American Telemarketing
Nynex Telemarketing Services
Olympia Publishing
Phone Marketing America
Phone Power
Power Line (A PCH Company)
Precision Telemarketing
PrimeNet DataSystems
Pro Direct Response
Pro-Tel Marketing
Professional
Telemarketing Specialists
PSI Telemarketing
Quality Telemarketing
Response Communications
Ring Response
RMH Telemarketing
RMI Direct Marketing
Roadman TeleDirect
Ron Weber and Associates
Roska Direct
RSVP Marketing
Ruppman Marketing Services
Select Marketing
Information Systems
Shalimar Services
Shaw MacLeod Associates
Shepard Poorman Communications
SITEL
Smartline
Somar Marketing Services
Spantel
SRO Personable
Touch Telemarketing
Star Marketing Center
Stephen Dunn & Associates
Syntax Marketing Services
Tacticall Marketing
TCI Telemarketing
Tele America
Tele-K Marketing Services
Tele-Mark Services
TeleCall
TeleCenter
Telecom Center, Division of Reese
Telecon USA DataBase Marketing
TeleCross
Teleforce
Telemark
Telemarketing & Associates
Telemarketing 4U
Telemarketing Concepts
Telemarketing East/West
Telemarketing Enterprises
Telemarketing For Success
Telemarketing
Telemarketing Institute
Telemarketing Management
Telemarketing Resource Center
Telemarketing Service Bureau
Telemarketing Specialists
Telemarketing Systems
Telemarketing USA
TeleMarketing West
The Telephone Marketing Group
Telephone Marketing Resources
Telephone Marketing Services
Telephone Response Technology
TELERx/Division of
BBDO Worldwide
TeleSystems Marketing
TeleTech Telecommunications
The Direct Response
The Service Bureau
The TeleCenter
The Telemarketing Company
Trans-Continental Telemarketing
TransAmerica Telemarketing
US Telemarketing
USA 800
Utell International Telemarketing
WATS Marketing of America
WATS Marketing Outbound
West Telemarketing
Working Phones Iowa
World Book Telemarketing
Young America Direct
Zacson

TELEMARKETING SOFTWARE

ACS Communications
Adelie
Admit Computer Services
Arlington Software + Systems
Brock Control Systems
Broderbund Software
Business Works
CRC Information Systems
Call Center Technologies
Coffman Systems
Commercial Data Systems
Concurrent Marketing Systems
Contact Software International
Database Systems
Datacorp Business Systems
Dilg Publishing
EKD Computer Sales & Supplies
EMIS Software
Early Cloud & Company
Eighty/20 Software
Esprit Software Technology
Excalibur Sources
Experience in Software
IDSC Rental Company
Information Research
Information Resources
Innovation Specialities
Innovative Microsystems
Inquiry Intelligence Systems
Inquiry Plus
Inquiry Systems & Analysis
InstaPlan
Inter-Active Micro
Interactive Systems
People & Contacts
Planning Works
Polaris Software
Popular Programs
Powerhouse Systems
Practical MarketingMSystems
PRO-TEM Software
Prophecy Development
Quandu Computing

Quantime
R & D Software
Resource One Softworks
JEB Systems
Lantor
MegaPhone
NPRI
Nynex Information Resources
National Systems
Opus
Professional Resource Mgmt
Profidex
Remote Control
Richmond Software
SaleMaker
Sales Consultants
Scientific Marketing/ForSales
Software of the Future
Spectrum Systems International
Supersell Software
System Vision
TESS
TeLeVell
Technology Development
Telesell
Tetley Technologies
Travis DataTrak
Van Arsdale Associates

TRAINING AND SEMINARS

ABC TeleTraining
Advanced Educational Techs
Affinitec
American Management Association
AT&T—Training & Education
Atlantic Software House
Capitol Teleservice
Carlyle Marketing
Chilton Ellett
Discus Electronic Training
Double Five
Forum Group
High Impact Comm & Training
Impression Mechanix
Incoming Calls Management Inst
Learning International
Marcon-Miltivision
McGraw-Hill Training Systems
Mission Communications
Monad Trainers Aid

National Center for Database Marketing
Pacific Bell
Phone for Success
Phone Pro
Redwood Training Association
Tele-Marketplace
Tele-Techniques
Telemarketing 4U
Telephone "Doctor"
Telespectrum
Training Consultants

TURRETS

Allen Tel
British Telecom
Centel Financial
Lanier Voice Products
Positron Industries
Rich
SRX
STC
Tadiran
Telecom Equipment
Turret Equipment

USED EQUIPMENT

Bell Atlantic
Communications Equipment Brokers
Consolidated Communications
Intelliserve
Resale Systems
RSI Resource Systems
Single Point of Contact
Southwest Brokers
Teknekron Infoswitch
Tele-Computer Systems

VOICE MAIL/ MESSAGING SYSTEMS

AB Communications
ACS Communications
Advanced Voice Technologies
American Digital Voice
American Telesystems
Aspect Telecommunications
AT&T
Brooktrout Technology
Compass Marketing

Dialogic
Genesis Electronics
Hold 'Em Communications
Innovative Technologies
IOCS
Lanier Voice Products
Miami Voice
Microlog
Newcastle Communications
North Supply
Octel
Perception Technologies
Phone Base Systems
Soft-Com
Teknekron Infoswitch
Telephonic Equipment
VMX
Voice Mail Systems
Voicemail International
Votan
Wang Information Services

VOICE/DATA TERMINALS

Aspect Telecommunications
AT&T
British Telecom
Davox
Harris-Lanier
Memorex Telex
Northern Telecom
Panasonic
Positron
Rich
Siemens
Turret Equipment
Zaisan

VOICE RECOGNITION

AT&T Conversant Systems
Advanced Information Systems
Covax
Dialogic
Microlog
Speech Systems
Voice Connection
Voice Control Systems
Voice Information Systems
Votan

SOURCE LIST

More than 1,300 suppliers to the business of sales, customer support and marketing automation and services.

AA Telephone
516-922-2257

AB Communications
212-714-2770

Abacus Group
617-924-4433

ABC Mailing Systems
404-424-7769

ABC Phone Power
313-534-1700

ABC TeleTraining
312-879-9000

Abend Associates
401-467-3890

Access 800
714-846-1923

Account-A-Call
818-846-3340

Accredited Mailing Lists
212-889-1180

ACE Mailing & Telemarketing
415-863-4223

ACE Mailing Services
404-431-2500

Acme Office Group
718-387-6400

Acquis Communications
714-648-0250

ACS Communications Agency
516-466-7980

ACS Communications
408-438-3883
800-538-0742

ACT Communications
816-471-4945

Actel Marketing
212-674-2540

Active Voice
206-441-4700

Adelie Corporation
617-354-0400

Admail Corporation
800-732-1111
741-0096

Admit Computer Services
516-249-1244

Advanced Educational Techs
619-579-7366

Advanced Interactive Systems
617-899-4700

Advanced Telemarketing
214-830-1800

Advanced Voice Technologies
615-885-4170

AERUS
714-978-2228

Affinitec
314-569-3450

Aggrey Telemarketing Group
202-293-3485

Ahern Communications
617-471-1100

AIM Telephones
201-515-9400

Airtronics
312-333-4055

Alcatel
601-287-3771

Alden Group
212-867-6400

Alert Communications
213-259-8000

Allen Tel
714-546-3522

Allied Electronics
817-336-5401

Allied Resources
707-648-0905

Allied Telecommunications
617-969-3550

Allnet Communications
313-647-6920

Allsteel
312-859-2600

Alltel
216-650-7000

Alltel Texocom
404-448-5210

Alitone Communications
619-693-3761

AlphaCan Corporation
404-587-2626

Am-Pro
508-777-8100
800-626-6500

Am-Pro Mailing List Company
508-777-8100

American Business Lists
402-331-7169

American Communications
& Data Research
805-498-3074
800-248-1937

American Telemarketing Specialists
817-565-9415

American Telephone Marketing
Group
703-790-3636

AmericaList
216-494-9111

AmeriCall Corporation
312-810-0892

American Airlines Direct Mktg
817-355-8213

American Business Images
212-768-0640

American Business Information
402-593-4500

American Business Systems
508-250-9600

American Communications
& Engineering
805-581-3318

American Digital Voice Systems
201-946-9288

American Laser Systems
805-967-0423

American List Council
609-497-1002

American Management Association
518-891-0065

American Management Systems
703-841-6000

American Media
800-262-2557

American Seating
616-454-5280

American Tele/Response Group
215-789-7000

American Telecorp
415-595-7000

American Telemarketing Association
818-995-7338

American Telephone Distributors
816-891-0500

American Teleservice Systems
301-252-4400

American Teleshare
714-553-1500

American Telesys
601-923-8282

American Telesystems
404-266-2500

Ameridial
216-497-5506

AmeriPhone Telemarketing
312-240-7750

Ameriplus
312-495-7700

Amerispan/Strategic
Marketing Systems
305-920-5400

Ameritel Corporation
414-727-3900

Amres Telemarketing
404-873-6308

Amtech Marketing
303-841-6108

Amtelco
608-838-4194

Analytical Computer Software
201-232-2723

Anchor Computer
516-293-6100

Answer America Company
212-832-9170

Answerall Technology Northeast
617-596-1316

APAC Telemarketing
312-671-6100

Apex Voice Communications
415-665-8096

Applied Microsystems
713-240-5555

Applied Telemarketing Services
414-494-7488

Applied Telematics
215-687-3835

Applied Voice Technology
206-641-1760

Arlington Software + Systems
617-641-0290

Artoplex
514-332-4420

Ashby Telemarketing Consulting
813-954-0640

Ashton Tate
203-925-5676

Aspect Telecommunications
408-279-5511
800-541-7799

Astro Marketing
800-247-9999

AT&E Systems
503-620-7787

AT&T
201-221-5846
800-247-1212

AT&T—American Transtech
904-636-2264

AT&T—Business Markets Group
201-221-5990

AT&T—Data Systems Group

AT&T—General Business Systems
201-221-5290

AT&T—International 800
201-658-7319

AT&T—Network Systems
201-631-6000

AT&T—Systems Integration Division
201-658-6400

AT&T—Training & Education
201-658-6738

AT&T Conversant Systems
614-860-5494

ATC/Microtel
404-688-2475

ATD Systems Corporation
818-966-4450

ATE Systems
415-349-8925

ATEX
617-276-7593

ATI Supply
818-889-9236

Atlanta Direct Marketing
404-393-0427

Atlantic Datafurniture
813-874-6989

Atlantic Software House
407-724-4113

Atlantic Telecom
201-377-2111

ATM Systems
214-669-2333

ATSI
703-684-0016

Attune
206-643-5000

Audichron
404-455-7975

Audicost
716-262-6400

Audio Marketing Systems
213-202-8648

Audio Response Technologies
516-742-6565

Audiocom
305-825-4653

Audiosears Corporation
607-652-7305

Audiotex Directory & Buyers Guide
213-479-3533

Augat Communications
206-223-1110

Aurora Marketing Management
609-520-8863

Aurora Telemarketing
402-694-4343

Autolab
713-493-7263

Automated Business Design
312-827-6644

Automated Call Processing
415-989-2200

Automated Communications
612-939-0070

Automated Fulfillment Systems
404-349-7134

Automated Phone Exchange
801-265-2000

Automated Telemarketing Services
612-349-6609

Automation Electronics
415-825-2880

Bach Electronics
203-265-6554

Bartel Software
801-566-5544

BBL
404-441-6464

Bell Atlantic
612-896-1461

Bell Canada Phone Power
416-581-5100

Bell of Pennsylvania
215-578-5335

Benzie Group
404-248-2181

Berkeley Marketing
716-827-5750

Berkeley Speech Technologies
415-841-5083

Berkshire Computer
413-637-0600

Best Power Technology
608-565-7200

Beta Research Corporation
516-935-3800

Borroughs Manufacturing
616-342-0161

Boston Direct
617-247-2424

Boston Tech
617-225-0500

Bottom Line Technologies
213-322-9215

Brandywine Marketing Services
302-999-6900

Breakthrough Productions
619-281-6174

Breakthrough/Systems
609-452-0130

Brewster
203-388-4441

Britcom Telemarketing
312-932-7300

Brite Voice Systems
316-687-4444

British Telecom
212-797-9500

Broadcast Resources
213-831-1145

Brock Control Systems
404-431-1200

Broderbund Software
415-492-3200

Brooktrout Technology
617-235-3026

Brother International Office Equipment Division
201-981-0300

Budget Marketing
800-247-5000

Burco Distributors
804-222-1481

Business By Design
818-841-1300

Business Forecast Systems
617-484-5050

Business Marketing Resources (D&B)
215-391-1600

Business Works
619-455-6094

C & P Telephone
301-595-2317

C&D Charter Power Systems
215-828-9000

Cable & Wireless/TDX
703-790-5300

CACI
212-370-0440

Cad Com
714-494-4723

Caldwell List
404-458-1399

California Microwave
408-732-4000

Call Management Products
303-465-0651

Call Masters
213-457-5601

Call-Hold Marketing
214-855-0664

CallCenter Services
201-567-9314

Calling Center Technologies
214-490-5400

CAM Systems
508-359-4017

Cambar Software
803-747-4539

Camp Corporation
203-271-1977

Campbell Services
313-559-5955

Canon Micrographics
516-488-6700

Canova Saunders International
208-882-1640

Capitol Teleservices
703-478-0220
800-828-4284

CARD-TEL
305-491-7800

Cardinal Data Systems
201-567-1821

Care Call/Market Call
404-469-1922

Carlyle Marketing
312-545-5450

Catalog Media
203-438-2318

CCX Network
501-329-6836

CDA Telecenter
800-542-1277

CDC Telemarketing
309-686-1900

Celluland
213-479-8700

Cellutel
408-734-5000

Centel Financial Systems
212-514-7800

CenterCore Group
800-220-5235

Centigram
408-942-3509

Centrac
201-385-8300

Chelsea Software
916-789-3185

Chicago Telemarketing Connection
312-337-5900

Chilton Ellett
803-345-2929

Chronos Software
415-626-4244

Cincinnati Bell
513-397-6824

Cincom/Target Marketing
513-662-2300

Cintech Tele-Management Systems
503-861-2000

Circulation By Phone
212-557-2777

CIS Corporation
315-437-1900

Citel America
305-558-1133

Citicorp Credit Services
516-391-3529

CITIFAX Express
312-949-5560

CMX
703-982-7057
800-345-2670

Cobotyx
203-748-0095

Code-a-Phone
503-655-8940

Coffman Systems
213-926-6653

Cogata
619-660-0102

Cognitronics
203-327-5307

Coherent Communication Systems
516-231-1550

Cole Office Environments
717-854-1545

Collection Connection
804-463-7360

Com Dev
813-753-6411

Comdial
804-978-2200
800-526-5627

Comdisco Disaster Recovery Service
312-518-5240

Command Communications
303-750-6434

Commercial Data Systems
404-799-1000

Commercial Microsystems
404-992-2701

CommSEL
714-646-2440

Communicall
312-764-4200

Communication Analysis
617-244-3636

Communication Systems
800-222-5570

Communications Center
215-576-5000

Communications Data Services
515-246-6849

Communications Equipment Brokers
312-829-8810

Communications for Business
412-487-6415

Communicator Asystance Systems
617-884-3510

Communitech
312-439-4333

Compass International
619-454-9844

Compass Marketing
813-924-1020

Compilers Plus
914-633-5240

Complementary Solutions
404-454-8033

Complete Business Systems
714-841-5868

Complete PC
408-434-0145

Compumark
215-353-7400

Computer Assisted Telemarketing
516-277-7000

Computer Consoles
617-890-0708

Computer for Marketing
415-777-0470

Computer Integration Associates
201-679-9500

Computer Power
201-638-8000

Computer Publishers
312-390-7000

Computer Solutions
716-235-1407

Computoll
212-725-2000

Comsystems
818-988-3010

Comtel Broadcasting
317-877-6050
800-248-5353

ComTel Marketing
215-647-8781

Comverse Technology
516-921-0470

Concurrent Marketing Systems
609-683-7702

Confertech International
303-237-5151

Connex International
203-797-9060

Console Systems
213-670-0610

Consolidated Communications
914-835-5000
800-354-1234

Consolidated Telemarketing
217-348-7050

Consultel
617-647-7777

Consumers Marketing Research
201-440-8900

Contact Software International
214-929-4749
800-627-3958

Contel Cellular
404-698-6179

Contel
212-758-6161

Contel IPC
203-326-7000

Contel-A-Marketing
717-534-9417

Contemporary Products
516-231-4370

Contemporary Software Concepts
215-687-6000

Contract Marketing Consultants
901-366-7567

Control Key/Moscom
716-385-6440

Conversational Voice Technology
312-266-6633

Conwed Designscape
612-331-2540

Coral Group
303-292-6354

Corporate Communicators
203-854-0860

Corry Hiebert
214-506-9500

Covox
503-342-1271

Cox and Cox Marketing
404-421-1412

CRC Information Systems
212-620-5678

Creative Automation Company
312-449-2800

Creative Fulfillment Services
201-374-6077

Creative Insight
416-781-6657

Crescent Communications
404-698-8650

Crest Group
303-691-0661

Crest Industries
206-927-6922

CSS Direct
402-493-7781

CTCI
201-593-0339

CTI
601-287-8081

Custom Telemarketing
919-870-1107

Customer Service Institute
301-585-0730

CWT/The Calling Company
206-684-9600

Cybernaut Software
415-657-0940

Cybernetics Systems International
305-443-1651

Dacon Electronics
201-825-9401

Dadco Data
916-265-3400

Dadelus Tech
713-447-7000

Dale
313-288-9540

Darome
312-399-1610

Data Acquisition Services
619-471-0342

Data Display
303-494-9400

Data Management Services
803-796-1292

Data Options
312-827-7700

DataPlus
703-550-7914

Data Research
612-452-8267

Database Publishing
714-646-1623

Database Systems
602-265-5968

Datacorp Business Systems
216-731-8000

Dataman Information Services
404-252-4799

DATAMAP
612-941-0900

Datamatics Management Services
201-738-9600

DataPlus
703-451-7440
800-368-3747

Datasave
619-724-4448

Dataserv
800-328-6729

DataWay Systems
313-477-6330

David James Group
312-222-0842

Davox
508-667-4455

DayFlo Software
714-474-2901

DBA Communications
604-985-9521

Deka
408-263-1333

Demographic Systems
212-255-8707

Dial Info
415-989-2200

Dial-A-Fax Directories
305-421-2101

Dialamerica Marketing
201-327-0200

Dialog Immediate Response
312-296-7010

Dialogic
201-334-8450

Dialogue
617-848-5555

Digisoft Computers
212-289-0991

Digital Directory Assistance
301-657-8548

Digital Equipment
508-486-5243

Digital Mircowave
408-943-0777

Digital Publications
404-448-6881

Digital Recorders
919-361-2155

Digital Sound
805-569-0700

Digital Speech Systems
214-235-2999

Digital Support Systems
212-777-3333

Digital Systems International
206-881-7544

Digital Transmission
901-423-0655

Digitron Telecommunications
516-334-0130

Dilg Publishing
817-860-0155

Direct Line Response
714-970-6990

Direct Marketing Association
202-347-1222

Direct Marketing Concepts
608-273-5555

Direct Marketing Guaranty
603-882-9500

Direct Marketing Technology
312-517-5600

Direct Response
312-827-7170

Direct Response Ability
804-285-0107

Direct Response Broadcasting
215-925-8585

Direct Telemarketing Services
216-650-4700

Dirmark Lists
404-477-7797

Discus Electronic Training
716-781-1064

Dispatch Consumer Services
614-548-5555

Domore
312-246-4567

Donnelley Marketing
Information Services
312-495-1279

Donnelley Communications
414-872-6178

Doremus
212-964-0700

Double Five
407-668-4058

Doyle & Partners
714-951-6330

DR Milford Marketing
313-540-1707

Dragon Systems
508-965-5200

Drothler & Smith Assoc.
313-540-7900

DSC Communications Business
Network Systems
408-727-3101

DSC Communications
214-519-3000

DSP Technology
214-245-8831

Dunhill International List
305-974-7800

Duns Marketing Services
201-605-6000

Dynamics
404-395-1800

DynaMark
612-482-8593

DynaMedia
716-334-2860

Dynamic Data Systems
303-426-6048

Dynamic Software
803-877-1122

Dytel
312-519-9850

EC Hunter Associates
315-476-3811

Early, Cloud & Company
401-849-0500

Eberle DM Group
703-821-1550

Econocom Telecommunications
901-766-7885

Ed Burnet Consultants
800-223-7777

Edge Teleservicing Center
213-258-4800

Edward Blank and Associates
212-741-8133

Effective Telemarketing
914-328-8868

800 Experts Telemarketing
214-722-1161

800 Speed Order Systems
602-957-4923

Eighty/20 Software
612-448-8849

EKD Computer Sales & Supplies
516-736-0500

Electronic Direct Marketing
416-491-8276

Electronic Information Systems
203-358-0764

Electronic Mail Corporation/America
203-637-8800

Electronic Marketing Associates
516-741-9000

Electronic Specialists
506-655-1532

Electronic Telecommunications
414-452-5600

Elsevier Business Lists
201-361-9060

Eltrex International
603-886-3500

EMIS Software
512-822-8499

Enertex Marketing
212-473-1433

Engel Associates
201-635-9680

Enhanced Systems
404-662-1503

Entertel
913-841-1200

Entrepreneur Magazine
714-555-1212

Envoy Systems
617-890-1444

Epsilon
617-273-0250

Ericsson
214-997-0491

Esprit Software Technology
603-465-3378

Estech
214-985-1250

Evergreen Ventures
215-364-7828

Evets Corporation
714-830-9831

Excalibur Sources
404-956-8373

Exceptional Telemarketing
402-339-5555

Exclusive Marketing Group
404-859-0681

ExecuCall
513-563-8666

Execucom Systems
512-346-4980

Executech Solutions
203-869-2169

Executive Marketing Services
312-355-3003

Executive Systems
804-288-0041

Executone Information Systems
203-655-6500

Experience in Software
415-644-0694

Expertel
215-641-1616

Express Fulfillment Services
615-867-9081

Extrema Systems International
703-648-3181

Factor Fox and Associates
213-473-7777

Fairfield Management Resources
312-706-9141

Fala Direct Marketing
516-694-1919

Far Systems
414-563-2221

Federal Information Systems
202-265-4255

Federal Mailers
305-561-9101

FGI & Affiliated Publishing
201-780-7020

Fibronics International
617-778-0700

Fifth Medium Marketing
312-675-1626

Finserv Computer Corporation
518-374-4430

First Contact Communications
813-965-1827

First Desk Systems
508-533-2203

First Field Information
Retrieval Systems
203-332-7007

First Impressions
402-334-7789

Firstmark
617-965-7989

Fishel Company
614-274-8100

Fleet Specialties
818-340-8181

Focus Forecasting
812-522-7128

Focus Research
203-561-1047

Fortune 800
916-677-7171

Forum Corporation
617-523-7300

Four Sales
714-963-6705

Fourgen Software Technologies
206-542-7481

Franklin Centennial
207-775-2260

The Franklin Mint
215-459-6317

Free World Marketing
714-722-6414

Freeman Associates
617-239-8119

Fujitsu Business Communication
602-921-5900

Fujitsu Imaging Systems
203-796-5794

Fulfillment Associates of Venice
813-497-1148

FutureCall Telemarketing
703-934-0350

Galaxy Communications
212-967-7111

Gandalf
613-226-1717

Gannett Direct Marketing Services
502-454-6660

Gateway Software Systems
214-385-4028

GC Services
201-902-0500

GC Services/Systems Division
713-777-4441

General Services
206-828-4777

Generation Systems
817-540-2269

Genesis Electronics
916-985-4050

Gentner Electronics
801-268-1117

Geographic Data Technology
603-795-2183

George R. Walther
206-340-1200

Geosoft
203-875-7782

Giardini/Russell Advertising
617-926-5030

Glenayre Electronics
206-676-1980

GLS Telemarketing
313-827-4700

GMC/List Lab
617-729-4813

GN Netcom/Danavox
612-941-0171

GoldData Computer Services
215-525-1036

Gordon Kapes
312-676-1750

GPS
512-590-0743

Graham Direct
303-861-9760

Granada Systems Design
212-686-6945

Granite Telecom
603-644-5500

Graph Bridge Software
406-728-0122

Graphicenter
205-871-4942

Great Lakes Communications
312-858-0333

GRiD Systems Corporation
415-656-4700

Grolier TeleMarketing
203-797-3500

Group One Software
301-982-2000

Growth Design
414-224-0586

GSI Marketing Services
817-540-2269

GSI Transcom
412-963-6770

GTE Directories
214-453-6171

GTE Telemarketing
214-929-1900

Hager Telecommunications
508-435-9551

Hamilton Microelectronics
818-907-1572

Hamilton Sorter
513-870-4400

Hammerstone Direct
513-866-4014

Hancock Information Group
407-682-1556

Harbinger Group
203-849-5000

Harris
800-442-7747

Harris Digital Telephone Systems
415-382-5000

Harris Publishing
800-888-5900

Harris-Lanier
404-329-8000

Harris/3M
404-621-1141

Harter
616-651-3201

Hart Graphics
512-454-4761

Hartman Communications
918-592-5200

Hasson Enterprises
602-273-6000

Hastings and Humble
Public Relations
503-297-6762

Haven Corporation
312-869-3434

HB Distributors
818-701-5100

Headsets Plus
312-528-9494

HeartBeat Computer Workspace
916-755-0610

Heartland Communications Group
515-955-1600

Hedges Communications
417-885-3939

Hedman
312-871-6500

Hello Direct
408-435-1990

Henry Russell Bruce
319-393-2656

Heritage Telemarketing
800-438-5967

Herman Miller
616-772-3300

Hershey Business Products
213-725-0035

Hewlett-Packard
408-720-2465

HG Professional Forms
402-422-1168

Hibbert West
303-297-1601

High Caliber Systems
212-684-5553

High Impact Communication & Training
616-949-5013

Hinda Distributors
312-890-5900

Hitachi America
404-446-8820

Hogan & Associates
913-677-4580

Hold Company
215-643-0700

Hold 'Em Communications
512-249-2140

Holmes
913-232-8222

Homeowners Marketing Services
818-506-1507

Homisco
617-286-1220

Hotelcopy
305-651-5176

HTL Telemanagement
301-236-0782

Hub Mail Advertising-Fulfillment Division
617-542-6290

Hugh Carver Group
201-274-3400

Hummingbird Communications
416-470-1203

Hunter Business Direct
414-332-8050

Huntsinger and Jeffer
804-266-2499

Hyperception
214-826-3508

IBM Corporation
914-642-4000

IBM/Rolm
408-986-5399

ICSA
312-644-6610

ICT Group
215-757-0200

ICT Telephone Marketing Solutions
609-667-8090

IDA Corporation
701-280-1122

Ideamatics
202-667-9495

Ideatech
202-667-4559
800-247-IDEA

Idelman Telemarketing
402-393-8000

IDSC Rental Company
603-645-6677

Illinois Bell
312-727-4693

Image Data
512-641-8340

IMPACT Telemarketing
609-854-1500

IMPCO
716-473-1432

Impression Mechanix
303-925-9126

Impulse Sales & Marketing
502-368-1984

Incoming Calls Management Institute
301-266-9298

Industrial Telemarketing Associates
201-245-3822

Info-Line
617-933-4100

Info/800
203-536-4996

Infobase Services
212-682-2889

InfoCision Management
216-668-1400

InfoMedia
703-847-0077
800-888-4188

Information Exchange
214-612-2600

Information Line
212-355-6980

Information Management Association
203-261-4777

Information On Hold
408-980-8282

Information Research
804-979-8191

Information Resources
617-494-1400

Information Resources
617-890-1100

Infotext Systems
312-490-1155

Infoswitch Corporation
817-354-0661

InfoText Magazine
714-551-9179

INMAC
408-727-1970

Innerlink Systems
314-567-0565

Innings Telecom
416-757-3251

Innovation Specialties
800-222-8228

Innovative Microsystems
412-922-4999

Innovative Technology
404-998-9970

Inmar Group
512-733-8999

Inquiry Handling Services
818-362-5373

Inquiry Intelligence Systems
312-984-1045

Inquiry Plus
312-595-5059

Inquiry Systems and Analysis
617-542-6290

Institute of Marketing Specialists
617-272-1438

InstaPlan
415-389-1414

INSTOR
415-329-7500

InteCom
214-727-9141

Integrated Data Concepts
213-469-3380

Integrated Marketing Solutions
201-469-0600

Integrated Systems Planning
301-835-1670

Integrated Communications Systems
612-888-3033

Intel Corporation
408-765-1789

INTEL Telemarketing
401-726-1050

Intelligent Technology Group
412-931-7600

Intelliserve
214-929-1414

Intelmed
202-265-4255

Inteltech
703-522-6700

Inter Active Micro
603-938-2127

Interactive Systems
713-789-3866

Interactive Voice Services
215-544-8787

Interalia
612-934-7766

Inter-Direct
312-236-0350

Interface Group
617-449-6600

Interface Technology
314-434-0046

Inter-Media Marketing
215-696-4646

International Customer Service Association
312-644-6610

International Development Marketing
202-546-4770

International List Company
305-974-7800

International Pathfinders
404-659-6007

International Telesystems
703-478-9808

Interport Financial
914-736-2312

Interstate Telemarketing
402-333-1900

Intersystems Corporation
616-344-0220

Inter-Tel
602-961-9000

Intertel Communications
213-476-0638

Intertel Group
206-747-7665

InterVoice
214-669-3988

Interwest Marketing
602-893-0665

Intrastate Telecommunications
516-242-2255

Intratec Systems
214-406-9800

Investors Marketing Source
214-553-9958

IOCS
617-890-2299

IOCS Voice Systems Division
617-890-2299

ISA
415-255-1871

Isaac Frydman
212-316-6169

ISDN Technologies Corporation
425-857-0511

ITS Communications
616-979-2600

ITT US Transmission Systems
201-330-5456

Iwatsu America
201-935-8580

J & J Haimes
717-569-5549

James Squires Consultants
516-766-7400

Jayeness Associates
716-262-6400

JC Penny Telemarketing
800-323-4343

JEB Systems
800-821-1006
603-883-4662

Jefferson Telephone
515-386-2626

Jenkins & Associates
201-825-7778

Jetson Direct Mail Services
516-471-7171

JG Furniture Systems
215-536-7343

Jingle Phone Productions
312-860-5565

JoCom International
212-586-5544

Joel Linchitz Consulting Services
212-431-6700

Judith Leeds Studio
201-226-3552

Judson Gilmore Assoc.
404-587-1994

K Plan Tel
516-242-0111

KC Blair Associates
215-794-0794

Kable Publishers Aide
815-734-4151

Kapular Telemarketing
312-870-6700

Karen Gillick & Associates
312-337-0345

Kennedy Marketing Services
616-776-7228

Keptel
201-389-8800

Key Systems
502-897-3332

Keye Productivity Center
913-491-2781

Kistler
303-399-0900

Kleid Company
212-819-3400

KLS
603-623-5877

KSK Communications
703-734-1880

Kurzweil Applied Intelligence
617-893-5151

L C & S Direct
914-693-2834

L E S Associates
201-934-7570

L. Delaney & Associates
717-824-5452

LM Berry
513-296-2121

Lakewood Publications
612-333-0471

Lamay Associates
203-637-8440

Landex
813-369-5802

Lanier Voice Products
404-329-8174

Lantel Network Systems
714-581-1635
800-525-2525

Lantor
213-324-7070

Laptop Express
303-595-9800

Lawco
209-239-6006

Lawrence Executive Search
516-627-5361

LCS Industries
201-778-5588

Lead Marketing International
817-387-8551

Lead-Mark Telemarketing
602-844-1600

Leads Unlimited
215-885-7701

Leaght
404-980-0679

Learncom
617-576-3100

Learning International
203-965-8444

Lee Stevens Companies
619-232-0700

Lemons Communications
214-252-7519

Len Kanzer & Partners
617-647-7818

Lester Telemarketing
203-488-5265

Leviton
303-867-4913

Lewis & Associates
515-255-3947

Lifestyle America
201-871-7060

Lincoln Telephone
402-466-8337

Linker Systems
714-552-1904

List Services Corporation
203-438-0327

List Technology Systems Group
212-719-3850

Listworld
205-882-1939

LO-AD Communications
213-626-5329

Loan Depot
617-963-2020

Locate
212-509-5115

Logic Design
414-785-1301

Logical Resources
617-651-7555

Lomas Telemarketing
513-469-6290

Lowell
508-756-5103

LPC
312-932-7000

LYNX
617-965-2000

MC Communications
216-835-6575

M&W Direct
717-688-4940

M/A/R/C
214-506-3400

Magazine Marketplace Telemarketing
309-691-4610

Magic Solutions
201-891-6383

Magnetic Systems
617-237-0420

Mal Dunn Associates
818-768-8500

MAMS Corporation
516-671-8336

Management And Imaging Systems
201-218-0900

Management Support Systems
213-397-3557

Manley Group
203-869-2601

Mar-Tel Communications
201-385-7171

Marathon Telemarketing Systems
404-422-3913

Marcom
508-458-0076

Marcom-Multivision
704-333-5816

Mardex
212-675-1008

Mark IV Resources
215-875-7394

Marketplace International
612-929-6131

Market Contact Systems
617-894-0530

Market Direct America
609-921-7200

Market Insight
814-231-2140

Market Intelligence Research
415-961-9000

Market Motivators
414-783-6800

Market Planning Group
617-542-4417

Market Plus Advertising
408-985-7503

Market Power
916-432-1200

Market Pro Corporation
214-907-8722

Market Square Communications
715-344-1199

Market Support International
201-347-9400

Market Track
404-951-0681

Marketechs Services
703-389-8121

Marketing Communication Arts
213-378-1641

Marketing Communications
516-741-1189

Marketing Communications
913-492-1575

Marketing Connections
415-866-1818

Marketing Data Research
206-588-4149

Marketing Decision Group
716-634-2045

Marketing Information Systems
312-491-3885

Marketing Messages
617-527-3023

Marketing Resources Group
415-433-0878

Marketing Technology
402-493-1266

MarketPlace America
317-848-4441

MarketPro Corporation
321-322-5329

Marketron
505-831-4173

Martel Associates
216-289-5212

Marubeni America
212-599-7146

Masel Industries
215-785-1600

Master Lease
215-668-2510

Mastersoft
800-624-6107

May & Speh Direct
312-964-1501

May Telemarketing
402-895-2323
800-338-2600

McCormick Associates
201-297-8600

McDonnell Douglas Applied Communications
408-922-7588

McDonnell Douglas Information Systems
303-220-6049

McGraw-Hill Training Systems
619-481-8184

MCI Telecommunications
202-887-3272

McNichol & Company
414-258-2863

MCRB Service Bureau
818-407-4300

Me-Di-Co
312-249-1213

Meadowlark Enterprises
508-777-4666

Media Dimensions
212-533-7481

Media Winchester
800-824-7385

Mediamark Research
212-599-0444

MegaPhone
213-850-6575

Melita Electronic Labs
404-446-7800

Memorex Telex
805-388-5014

Memory Masters
702-826-1450

Merchant Network
312-394-5600

Meredith List Marketing
515-284-2891

Meridian Technology
404-390-9152

Merle Systems
617-282-1846

Message Management
612-593-1632

Message On Hold Company
713-622-3555

Message Processing Systems
704-527-8888

Metro Seliger Industries
718-278-2500

Metromail
312-620-3300

Metropolitan
Telemarketing Systems
201-308-0466

MetroTel
516-937-3420

METS
317-573-2200

Meyer Associates
612-259-4000

Miami Voice Corporation
800-877-7556

Micro Logic
800-342-5930

Microbase PC Systems
203-223-8918

Microdyne
904-687-4633

Micrelog
301-428-3227

Microscience Corporation
404-998-6551

Microtel
407-750-2655

Microvoice Corporation
714-859-1091

Midwest Business Products
612-722-2626

Miles Advertising
303-220-9977

Milford Marketing
313-540-1707

Miller Meester
612-854-8944

Minute Men Power Supplies
214-446-7363

Mission Communications
408-370-6560

MISTIX
813-572-8585

Mitel
407-994-8500

MJ Dimensions
414-784-3577

Marketing Consultants
& Strategists
416-963-6111

MMS
312-467-9540

Modern Media
203-853-2600

Modern Business Systems
314-634-1800

Mokrynski and Associates
201-488-5656

Molin/Cutter
Telemarketing Services
206-622-4707

Monad Trainers Aid
718-352-2314

Money's Worth
312-348-0903

Monitec Systems
604-689-1481

Morant Data
703-548-3904

Morgan Seminar Group
408-738-8222

MOSCOM
716-385-6440

Motivational Marketing
201-934-6900

Motorola
312-397-5000

MPH Communications
404-252-5859

MPSI
704-527-8888

Marketing & Control Technology
309-786-2440

MSS Corporation
213-397-3557

MTC Systems
800-387-0264
416-449-7620

MTI Systems
516-621-6200

Mullen Telecommunications
303-779-1010

Multi-Tek Software
703-556-1093

MultiLink
617-595-7577

Multimedia Corporation
415-541-0131

NJ Morse
Professional Communications
203-775-6480

NPRI
703-683-9090

Nacom
415-579-1231

Nady Systems
415-652-2411

National Telemarketing Registry
602-957-1311

National Association of Telemarketers
801-375-9400

National Audiotext Centers
904-398-1375

National Bureau of Standards
301-975-2904

National Bureau of Standards
301-975-2904

National Computer Systems
612-894-9494

National Data Corporation
404-621-5567

National Decision Systems
800-877-5560

National Management Systems
703-827-0797

National Planning Data
607-273-8208

National Publicity Services
609-653-9593

National Systems Corporation
312-855-1000

National Tele-Info
614-222-5050

National Telephone Systems
301-230-4653

National Center for
Database Marketing
916-292-3000

National Demographics Lifestyles
303-292-5000

National Telecommunications Equipment
313-626-1900

National Telephone Information Network
213-641-0648

Natural MicroSystems
508-655-0700

NCRI List Management
201-894-8300

NEC America
516-753-7000
800-626-4952

Nel-Tech Labs
603-434-8234

Nelson Business Systems
813-935-2258

Nelson Communications
617-891-3800

Network Communications
612-944-8559

Neuralytics Systems
415-573-9001

New Boston Group
617-576-6000

New Generation Technology
714-848-0871

New Hampton
804-825-4033

New Horizons Technologies
816-471-2525

New Residence Data Marketing
201-666-2212

New York Telephone
212-395-5341

Newbridge Networks
703-834-3600

Newcastle Communications
212-431-7220

Newmark & Associates
213-487-5910

Newsletter Specialists
818-577-0717

Newstrack
303-778-1692

NGT
714-848-0871

NICE/A Cincinnati Bell Company
801-621-6423

Nokia-Mobira
813-536-5553

Norlite Computer Systems
613-591-0320

Norrell Financial Systems
404-239-9671

Norrell Information Services
404-672-5463

North American Telemarketing
619-743-5611

North Coast Direct
216-991-2161

North Shore Agency
516-466-9300

North Supply
913-791-7000

Northern Telecom
214-437-8589

Northern Telecom International Network System
919-992-7600

Nova Marketing Concepts
216-920-3677

Nova Systems
617-354-4241

Nynex
914-644-7178

Nynex Complex Systems Integration Group
914-993-3810

Nynex Information Resources
617-581-4000

Nynex Information Solutions Group
914-993-3805

Nynex Telemarketing Services
212-513-9605

Octel
408-942-6500

Oetting & Company
212-580-5474

OfficeCom
213-426-8091

Ohio Bell Telephone
614-223-8707

Oki Telecom
404-925-0214

Olympia Publishing
501-376-7600

Omegas Group
502-423-8881

Omnigistics
312-990-0050

Omni Telsort
214-956-8297

Omnifax/Telautograph
213-641-3690

Omnitronix
206-624-4985

Omnivoice
216-393-3246

On Hold Productions
201-444-6488

Ontrack Computer Systems
612-937-1107

Opinion Research
609-924-5900

Opus Corporation
301-948-2040

OSPA
818-786-6772

Otis Group
818-704-6624

Outreach Affiliates
212-307-6868

PaceCom Technologies
206-641-8217

Pacific Bell
415-542-1421

Pacific Bell—Business Lists
415-823-6103

Pagex Systems
201-871-0800

Palco Telecom
205-883-3400

Panafax
518-420-0055

Panamax
415-499-3900

Panasonic
201-392-4571

Panel Concepts
714-979-3680

Pathfinder Systems
702-735-4346

People & Contacts
817-332-5203

Perception Technology
617-821-0320

Perimeter Technology
603-882-2900

Periphonics
516-467-0500

Personal Selling Power
703-752-7000

Personnel Strategy Consultants
617-277-0044

Phillip Bell Telecommunication
512-249-2140

PhiTech
415-788-5455

Phoenix Micro Systems
205-721-1200

Phone Bank Systems
517-332-1500

Phone Base Systems
703-893-8600

Phone for Success
212-431-6700

Phone Marketing America
212-674-2798

Phone Marketing Services
612-778-9169

Phone Power
512-822-7400

Phone Pro
317-253-5001

Phone Programs
212-371-5450

Phoneworks
201-343-0022

PictureTel
508-977-9500

Pioneer TeleTechnologies
712-943-1000

Planning Works
614-436-5300

Plåntronics
408-458-4499

Plieon Manufacturing
714-835-9101

Popular Programs
713-579-0481

Positron Industries
212-797-1300
514-738-2200

Power Battery Company
201-523-8630

Power Line (A PCH Company)
516-883-4300

Powerhouse Systems
919-721-0241

Practical Marketing Software
314-434-5254

Precision Software
813-536-0312

Precision Telemarketing
716-288-9810

Preferred Lists
703-931-8000

Prescott List Management
212-684-7000

Prime Computer
617-655-8000

PrimeNet DataSystems
612-885-8800

Pro Direct Response
215-896-8707

Pro-Tel Marketing
312-418-0600

PRO/TEM Software
800-826-2222

Probe Research
201-285-1500

Probus Publishing
312-346-7985

Product Line
303-799-4900

Profaq Systems
713-440-7710

Professional Educators Group
301-654-7070

Professional Resource Management
312-359-3990

Professional Telemarketing Specialists
714-777-5998

Profidex Corporation
201-420-7700

Profit Technology
212-809-3500

Progressive Distribution Services
616-957-5900

Promotion Fulfillment
319-243-0100

Promotional Services
818-989-0019

Prophecy Development
617-451-3430

Prospeak
716-225-9435

PSI Telemarketing
312-878-0800

Public Interest Communication
703-847-8300

Publishers Clearing House
516-883-5432

Pyderion Management
514-364-4843

Pyramid Technology Corporation
201-750-2626

Quadram Corporation
404-564-5603

Qualified Lists Corporation
914-273-6606

Quality Telemarketing
402-572-8170

Quandu Computing
703-264-8900

Quantime
212-420-0954

Quintrex Data Systems
319-363-5508

R & D Software
904-862-0253

RL Polk and Company
313-292-3200

RM Dufley Corporation
415-991-9567

R R Donnelley & Sons/Selectronic
312-574-3878

RDM Sales
212-851-2786

RL Polk & Co.
313-292-3200

Racal Acoustics
301-698-0300

Racal Recorders
800-847-1226

Racom
216-351-1755

Radio Frequency Data Network Systems
312-325-9300

RAIL
214-386-8920

RAK Associates
216-228-2045

Rates Technology
516-360-0157

RCI—Rotelcom
716-475-8306

Real Time Strategies
516-939-6655

Redcom Laboratories
716-924-6500

Redgate Communications
407-231-6904

Redwood Training Associates
415-364-2527

Reference Software
415-541-0222

Referral Systems Group
916-722-2100

Reliable Label
312-852-5300

Remington Associates
602-992-7444

Remote Control
619-481-8577

Renegade C Software
408-727-7764

Reproduction Technologies
219-848-5233

Resale Systems
215-827-7411

Resource One
404-335-5684

Response Communications
609-486-7200

Response Service Plus
215-492-0103

Revelation Technology
206-643-9898

Rexnord Data Systems
414-643-2001

Rhodes Associates
508-820-2701

Rich
312-678-3100

Richard L. Bencin & Associates
216-526-6726

Richmond Software
604-299-2121

Ricoh
201-882-8824

Ridgewood Macs and Olsen
602-956-1987

Ring Response
312-673-6440

Riverside Marketing
201-842-6640

RMH Telemarketing
215-642-2438

RMI Direct Marketing
914-347-4949

Roadman TeleDirect
215-626-9897

Robert G Wallace
619-226-5237

Rockwell International
312-960-0525
800-722-5959

Roman Managed Lists
914-638-2530

Ron Weber and Associates
203-799-0000

Rosell Group Consulting
714-660-0675

Rosesoft
813-952-9211

Roska Direct
215-643-9100

Roxide International
914-235-5300

Royal Silk
201-478-2200

RSI Resource Systems
404-497-1283

RSVP Marketing
617-837-2804

RTP Group
818-304-9146

Ruppman Marketing Services
309-679-4111

Ryan Corporation
215-638-9682

RYDEX Industries
604-278-6772

SAC Telemarketing
904-761-6711

Sale Extension Services
503-639-3595

SaleMaker
214-264-2626
800-433-5355

Sales & Marketing Systems
707-790-3422

Sales Consultants
303-752-2550

Sales International
602-381-3115

Sales Productivity Group
615-361-3800

Sales Technologies
404-841-4000

Salmon Systems
206-441-8100

Sammamish Data Systems
206-867-1485

Sanyo
213-637-3717

Saratoga Systems
408-371-9330

Sawtooth Software
312-866-0870

SBT Corporation
415-331-9900

SRX
214-934-9111

STC Telecom
305-426-4100

Scherrer Resources
215-242-8581

Schlenker Research Services
210-591-1910

Scientific Marketing/For Sales
714-586-5450

Scientific Systems
203-786-5236

Scoop Systems
201-740-0609
800-243-SCOO

Scott Ashby
Telemarketing Consultants
813-954-0640

Scott Computing Systems
404-432-7000

SDG Decision Systems
415-854-9000

Select Marketing
Information Systems
800-252-3456
512-450-0582

Selection Sciences
415-346-7015

Seminars List Services
608-231-3070

Seneca Marketing
716-886-1991

Senior Citizens Marketing Grp
214-480-0777

Sente Corporation
214-931-1941

Sequoia Systems
617-480-0800

Service Bureau
206-455-3614

Service 800 SA
201-361-3500

Shalimar Services Corporation
213-582-9569

Sharp Electronics Corporation
201-529-8949

Shaw MacLeod Associates
416-480-0000

Shaw Walker
616-755-9575

Sheer Communications
516-484-3381

Shepard Poorman Communications
317-293-1500

Sherman Marketing Associates
516-735-6666

Shure Teleconferencing Systems
312-866-2227

Siemens Information Systems
407-994-7232

Siemens Transmission Systems
602-395-5000

Signal Technology
805-683-3771

Significant Statistics
801-377-4860

Sikorski-Tuerpe & Associates
516-261-3066

Sima Design
612-338-0800

Simplsoft Products
303-444-8771

Single Point of Contact
714-859-7600

Sisk Fulfillment Service
301-754-8141

SITEL Corporation
402-496-0724
800-445-6600

SKOPOS
415-962-8590

Skutch
916-786-6186

Smart Software
617-489-2743

Smart Systems Services
312-699-3499

Smartline Corporation
716-842-2107

Smartnames Persoft
617-890-5705

SMG Research
716-263-2614

Smith Company
202-298-7700

SNAP
603-623-5877

SNET Telemarketing Consulting
800-922-0829

Soft-Com
212-242-9595

Softel Systems
408-926-0885

Softool
805-683-5777

Software Intelligence
305-564-5220

Software Marketing Associates
308-236-8989

Software of the Future
800-433-5355
214-264-2626

Software Products International
619-450-1526

Softworks
301-856-1892

Solid State Systems
404-423-4200

Solitaire
404-971-4811

Somar Marketing Services
704-637-6600

Sommers
201-568-3838

Sophisticated Data Research
404-451-5100

Source
214-699-2300

Source Data Systems
319-339-3343
319-366-7361

SourceMate Information Systems
415-381-1011

South Central Bell
205-321-8910

South Hills Electronics
412-921-9000

Southwestern Bell Telephone
314-725-6025

SoutherNet Communications
404-458-4927

Southwest Brokers
800-422-3288

Southwest Performance Group
602-941-8829

Spantel
305-477-2211

Specialized Management Support
714-549-5700

Spectrum
617-890-3400

Spectrum Communication
& Engineering
516-822-9810

Spectrum Digital
703-478-0560

Spectrum Systems International
512-349-9933

Speech Plus
415-964-7023

Speech Soft
201-461-8117

Speech Systems
818-881-0885

Spinnaker Software
617-494-1200

Spirited Marketing Concept
303-320-3920

SRO Personable Touch Telemarketing
404-992-3924

SRX
214-907-6817

Standard Rate and Data Service
312-441-2226

Star Datacom
617-849-1660

Star Marketing Center
218-732-3304

Star Touch Communications
404-431-0015

Starkey Laboratories
612-828-9257

Startel Corporation
714-863-8700

Statistical Innovations
617-489-4492

STC Telecom
407-241-6200

Stedi-Volt
302-292-8058

Steelcase
616-247-2710

Stenrich Group
804-254-8538

Stephen Dunn & Associates
213-392-8591

Stevens List Management
817-776-9000

Stok Software
718-699-9393

Strat-X International
617-494-8282

Strategic Information
703-847-0077

Strategic Marketing Systems
305-920-5400

Stratum
513-231-4302

Strawberry Software
617-923-8800

Street Electronic
805-884-4593

Street Map Software
312-529-4044

Stromberg-Carlson
305-849-3387

Structural Concepts Corp.
616-846-3300

Stryker Systems
818-248-8797

Successware
919-469-0119

Sudor
602-299-0651

Summa Four
603-625-4050

SunGuard Recovery Services
215-341-8824

Supersell Software
416-862-0017

Supplier Warehouse
205-663-2322

Sutherland Group
716-272-8400

SvC Telemarketing
215-627-3535

Sykes Datatronics
716-647-8075

Symantec Crop
408-253-9600

Syntax Marketing Services
619-586-0955

Syntellect
602-264-5900

Sysmark Information Systems
213-544-1974

SysPro
415-254-9753

System Vision Corporation
415-355-7308

Systems of the Future
201-884-2300

TJ Litle & Company
603-893-9333

Tactical Marketing
215-641-1616

Tadiran
813-535-3506

Talking Technology
415-652-9600

Tandy Corporation
817-390-3424

Targa Systems Corporation
203-275-6585

Target Microsystems
415-967-3990

Target Systems Corporation
508-460-9206

Tarp Information Systems
301-546-2223

TBS Marketing
415-537-4700

TC Telemanagement
813-963-6320

TC Telemanagement
813-963-6320

TCI Telecall
302-731-4700

TCI Telecommunications
317-875-5950

TCI Telemarketing
213-276-6145

TCS Management Group
615-327-0811

Tech/Knowledge
818-342-4243

Techni-Quest
714-632-6924

Technologia Systems
312-938-1919

Technology Associates
305-973-4400

Technology Development
603-893-2422

Technology Marketing
407-892-5400

Teknekron Infoswitch
817-354-0661

Teknion
609-866-1111

Tel Control
205-881-4060

TEL Electronics
801-756-9606

Tel Mar
414-449-8219

Tel Mark Sales
414-749-3400

Tel Tec
414-449-8219

TEL-line Systems
701-280-0023

Tel-One Corporation
215-657-2075

Tel-Sel
203-366-4252

Tel/Mar & Associates
818-369-8056

Telafax
213-936-1900

Telamon
317-298-6440

Tel-a-Promotions
714-474-1277

Telcom Technologies
714-620-7711

Tele America
312-480-1560

Tele Broadcasting System
717-729-7121

TeleCenter
314-394-2855

Tele-Communication
713-780-1157

Tele-Computer Systems
617-455-8000

Tele-Consultants International
415-381-7744

Tele-K Marketing Services
914-833-1102

Tele-Line Systems
701-280-0023

Tele-Mark Services
516-746-4055

Telemarketing Company
312-635-1500

Tele-Marketplace
416-691-6526

Tele-Monitor Company
212-989-2345

Tele-Service
508-692-9000

Tele-Techniques
312-338-2424

Tele-Techniques Services
312-470-3540

Tele-Vision
805-492-0418

TeleCalc
206-643-0300

TeleCall
302-731-4700

TeleCenter
914-591-5991

Telecom Center/Division of Reese
703-247-2500

Telecom Consultants Group
312-454-9396

Telecom Equipment
800-444-4411

Telecom International
407-997-5450

Telecom Library
212-691-8215
800-LIBRARY
800-999-0345

Telecom On-Hold Productions
303-292-3303
800-289-8677

TeleCom Services
212-245-2530

Telecom Systems Management
314-441-6100

Telecom USA DataBase Marketing
800-728-7000

Telecom USA Long Distance Division
800-728-7000

Telecom USA Teleconnect Division
800-728-7000

Telecommunications Marketing Resource
401-736-4929

Telecommunications Industries
703-790-0410

Telecommunications Marketing
214-871-5588

Telecomputer Collection Center
713-777-4441

Teleconnect
319-366-6600

TELECONNECT Magazine
212-691-8215
800-LIBRARY
800-999-0345

Teleconnect-Database Marketing
319-366-6600

Telecorp
313-569-7100

Telecorp Systems
404-449-6991

TeleCross
800-338-8307

TeleCross Corporation
319-235-4469

Teledirect International
319-324-7720

Teleforce
408-377-3800

Teleforce
816-531-7776

Telemanagement
404-881-0800

Telemark
404-778-2201

Telemarketing & Associates
214-254-2229

Telemarketing 4U
214-394-7368

Telemarketing Concepts
914-245-0701

Telemarketing Design
913-262-2626

Telemarketing East/West
800-368-2066

Telemarketing Enterprises
214-263-8120

Telemarketing For Success
214-270-2777

Telemarketing
612-420-8551

Telemarketing Institute
605-335-3970

Telemarketing Magazine
800-243-6002

Telemarketing Management
714-997-7049

Telemarketing Recruiters
212-213-1818

Telemarketing Resource Center
508-832-7170

Telemarketing Search
312-372-3201

Telemarketing Service Bureau
206-448-9600

Telemarketing Services
512-342-2414

Telemarketing Specialists
801-350-8700

Telemarketing Systems
617-479-2500

Telemarketing USA
202-452-0050

TeleMarketing West
714-993-9010

Telematch
703-971-6400

Telematrix Industries
718-482-7799

Telemarketing Consulting Services
415-657-4860

Telenova
408-395-2260

Teleos Resources
201-271-1121

Telephone "Doctor"
800-882-9911

Telephone Access
202-393-8360

Telephone Announcement Systems
609-985-1933

Telephone Associates
027-226-6531

Telephone Audio Productions
214-231-8271

Telephone Concepts Unlimited
215-437-4000

Telephone Information Services
312-517-7020

Telephone Look-Up Service
215-321-0706

Telephone Marketing Group
215-576-7000

Telephone Marketing Resources
212-580-5470

Telephone Marketing Services
513-321-1888

Telephone Response Technologies
916-442-1878

Telephone Support Systems
516-352-6800

Telephonetics
305-432-6288
800-446-5366

Telephonic Concepts
303-778-8049

Telephonic Equipment
714-250-9400
800-854-8269

Telephonics
602-837-1710

Teleplan
203-661-4312

TeleProfessional
800-338-8307

TELERx/Division of
BBDO Worldwide
215-641-1616

Telesell
614-461-5840

Teleshare
303-449-7445

Telesis Audio Productions
714-474-1277

Telespectra
212-757-3638

TeleSpectrum
301-987-7300

TeleSystems
713-784-3439

Telesystems Source
201-709-3400

Teletech Business
Telecommunications
605-335-4142

TeleTech Telecommunications
818-501-5595

Televation
312-852-9695

TeleVector
212-947-7573

TeLeVell
408-748-0111

Television Equipment Association
914-763-8893

Telmark
913-432-1414

Telrad
516-921-8300

Tempest Advertising
617-227-7877

TES Communications
404-593-0412

TESCO Controls
503-682-5779

TESS
408-741-1519

Tetley Technologies
314-635-7300

Thinkbank Publishers
817-640-5495

Thompson Recruitment
816-561-6717

Thor
213-487-0130

3X USA Corporation
201-592-6874

TIE/communications
203-926-2031

Tigon
214-733-2700

TKC Consulting
609-683-0030

Telemarketing Specialists of America
312-372-4747

Tone Commander Systems
206-883-3600

Toptech Systems
407-332-5128

Tori
612-894-5128

Toshiba
714-583-3714

Total Media Concepts
201-692-0018

TotalCom Solutions
714-261-1888

Touchtone Access
201-884-0888

Training Consultants
312-498-4064

Trans World Telephone
216-722-5500

Trans-Continental Telemarketing
612-784-0200

TransAmerica Telemarketing
202-383-8300

Travis DataTrak
617-964-8960

TRD Corporation
814-278-6938

Trendway
616-399-3900

Triad Marketing Resources
919-760-4782

TriDos Software Publishers
508-228-8223

Trinet
201-267-3600

TRT
916-442-1878

TRW Information Services Group
714-385-7507

Tudor Group
215-586-6000

Turk Marketing System
504-928-1114

TurnKey Data Solutions
713-894-9400

Turret Equipment Corporation
212-514-9500

TW Comcorp
516-753-0900

UNEX
617-692-9505

Uni-Mail Corporation
212-362-8500

UniVoice
813-924-6022

UNISYS
215-542-3410

USA 800
816-358-1303

US Audiotext
415-838-7996

US Business Corporation
818-713-1088

US Fulfillment Services
703-349-4270

US Sprint Communications
415-627-3802

US Takachiho
714-761-3844
800-421-1858

US Telemarketing
404-381-0100

US Telemarketing
609-778-0500

US Telemonitoring Service
914-634-1331

US Telesys
216-731-5585

US West
800-233-4421

US West Communications
206-345-6342

US West Direct
303-337-8207

US West Marketing Resources
303-669-7440
303-667-0652

Utell International Telemarketing
402-498-4200

Vada Systems
714-687-2492

Valcom
703-982-3900

Valor Telecom
201-673-2000

Van Arsdale Associates
919-851-6917

Vanguard Communications
415-326-1728

Vertical Marketing
203-967-4959

VF Information Services (ICT)
215-666-0611

Viking Electronics
715-386-8861

Viking Software Services
918-745-6550

Vision Skills
612-881-5451

Visions Marketing Services
717-295-8000

ViTel International
415-332-5134

VITEQ
301-731-0400

VMX
408-943-0878

VOAD Systems
213-450-2929

Voice America
312-835-0462

Voice Com
214-980-9746

Voice Connection
714-261-2368

Voice Connection/CCSA
612-944-1334

Voice Control Systems
214-386-0300

Voice Exchange Technologies
314-298-1751

Voice Information Systems
214-746-4344

Voice Mail Systems
312-649-4620

Voice Pak
408-395-2526

Voice Response
800-331-1510

Voice Systems & Services
918-865-1000

Voice Technology
214-243-6366

Voice-PAK
408-373-1600

VoiceCom
404-428-0588

Voicemail International
408-980-4000

Voicetek
617-964-8820

Volt Info Sciences
215-248-9000

Votan
415-490-7600

Votrax
313-588-2050

Voysys Corporation
408-737-2300

VSSI
918-865-1000

Walker Research
317-843-3939

Walter Karl Company
914-273-6700

Wang Information Services
508-967-2062

Wang Laboratories
617-967-4624

WATS Marketing of America
800-351-1000

WATS Marketing Outbound
402-592-1100

Webcor Electronics
516-932-1850

West Com Communications
509-922-8365

West Telemarketing Corporation
402-571-7700

Wicom
818-715-9096

Witness Systems
215-687-7885

Wolfe & Associates
714-259-1530

Working Computer
619-621-0501

Working Phone Iowa
515-673-9777

World Book Telemarketing
312-790-7980

World Research Systems
312-991-1122

WS Ponton
412-782-2360

Xedon
201-825-2911

Xiox Corporation
415-375-8188

Xpedite Systems
201-389-3373

XTEND Communications
212-725-2010

XYCAD group
216-589-5788

Young America Direct
612-467-3366

Zacson Corporation
216-526-3448

Zalsan
415-471-9717

Zenith Data Systems
312-391-7000

Ziehl Associates
516-437-1300

Zoom Telephonics
617-423-1072

APPENDIX

3

Telemarketing Ethics Guidelines

The American Telemarketing Association endorses these guidelines for professional telemarketing practice.

1. Telemarketing call recipients can expect that there is a reason for the call and the call purpose will be accomplished efficiently, courteously, and professionally.
2. The names of both the company and the communicator who makes or receives calls will be clearly identified when every call begins.
3. The communicator will approach each call courteously, and never use abusive language or rude manner.
4. The communicator will accommodate the business person or consumer's time constraints, and, if necessary, schedule a future recall.
5. All telemarketing offers to the business or consumer public will be legal, legitimate, and have recognized value.
   All offers will be fulfilled according to the offer terms.
6. Repeated calls with the same offer will not be made to the same prospect/customer.
   Exceptions are regularly scheduled fund raisers, and membership or renewal drives.
7. Except in cases of public safety, by. previous agreement, or calls to current customers, the business or consumer public can expect a live communicator to introduce the call. The public's time has as much value as ours—the professionals in this industry.
8. All telemarketing equipment will be carefully monitored to ensure proper operation.
   Equipment use will be supervised to ensure *professional* application to telemarketing programs.

9. Telemarketing organizations will follow all federal and state telemarketing regulations.

HOURS/DAYS OF OPERATION

Outbound Calls

Business calls should occur during normal business hours.

Consumer calls should only occur between 8:00 AM and 9:00 PM, local time, unless further restricted by local or state laws.

Exceptions require prior consumer agreement.

Consumer calls should not occur on major holidays: Christmas, New Year's Day, Thanksgiving.

If calls occur on other national or state holidays, or recognized religious days, sensitivity should be shown for consumer inconvenience.

Inbound Calls

Hours and days of operation should be clearly advertised when inbound calls (toll free or consumer paid) are invited through advertising, catalogs, direct mail, media presentations, or other sales methods, to avoid caller inconvenience.

Index

About Joel Linchitz

Joel Linchitz, president and founder of the **Phone for Success**™ Corporation, has developed and implemented telephone marketing programs for major corporate and industrial clients since 1970. He has used the telephone medium successfully in virtually every kind of business environment to increase sales and customer satisfaction, while at the same time providing motivation and job satisfaction for people who use the phone as a contact tool. He has personally sold a variety of products and services over the phone ranging in price from $50 to $500,000.

Popular Author, Lecturer and Expert on the Telephone Medium

A popular lecturer, keynote speaker and expert on telemarketing and teleselling techniques, Joel is also the author of **THE COMPLETE GUIDE TO TELEMARKETING MANAGEMENT** (originally published by the American Management Association), a book that super-salesman Tom Hopkins says " . . . will tremendously increase your overall productivity, and thus your income level." He has also written articles for numerous magazines and publications, including ***Call Center***, ***Telemarketing***, ***TeleProfessional***, and ***The Selling Advantage.*** Joel is a member of the Direct Marketing Association, the National Speakers Association, and has appeared on **CNN**, and the **Money Radio** and **American Radio** networks.

Originator of Seminars That Get Immediate Results

A trainer and consultant to major Fortune 500 companies, he has trained thousands of people to use the telephone effectively. The Linchitz approach is a direct result of his "front line" experience, and succeeds where traditional programs adapted for phone sales have failed. His philosophy is that results should be immediate and continuous! That philosophy is reflected in his two-day **PHONE FOR SUCCESS** seminars and workshops that give participants the opportunity to learn and practice new skills with coaching and supervision. Participants are monitored while selling their own products, so in addition to new confidence and know-how, participants often leave the seminar with new business!

Creator of Unique Training Programs and Materials

Joel creates interactive and self-instructional seminar and workshop materials that are customized for each organization, targeting specific departmental or company-wide needs and objectives. The courses are designed to give participants much needed every-day on-the-job tools for many different kinds of situations and personnel. His introduction of the **TeleTutor**, a compact classroom-in-a-box call simulation device for role play, and the **TeleCoach**™ performance measurement system, are just a few of the innovations he has brought to the industry.

Developer of Telephone Profit Centers for Satisfied Customers

- ***Dale Carnegie*** increased their sales performance by 50% virtually overnight!
- ***Dreyfus Corporation*** got a 500% increase in their conversion of inquiries to sales!
- ***Holland America Cruises*** increased the profitability of the reservations department immediately!
- ***ADP*** got five new appointments per week for each of 600 sales personnel!
- ***Ericsson-GE*** launched a new Hi-Tech product to a pre-qualified market with minimum costs!
- ***Sharp*** dramatically improved dealership market share with the Phone For Success program!
- ***Aetna*** "re-engineered" its entire company for proactive customer relationship retention!
